K-ON!

3

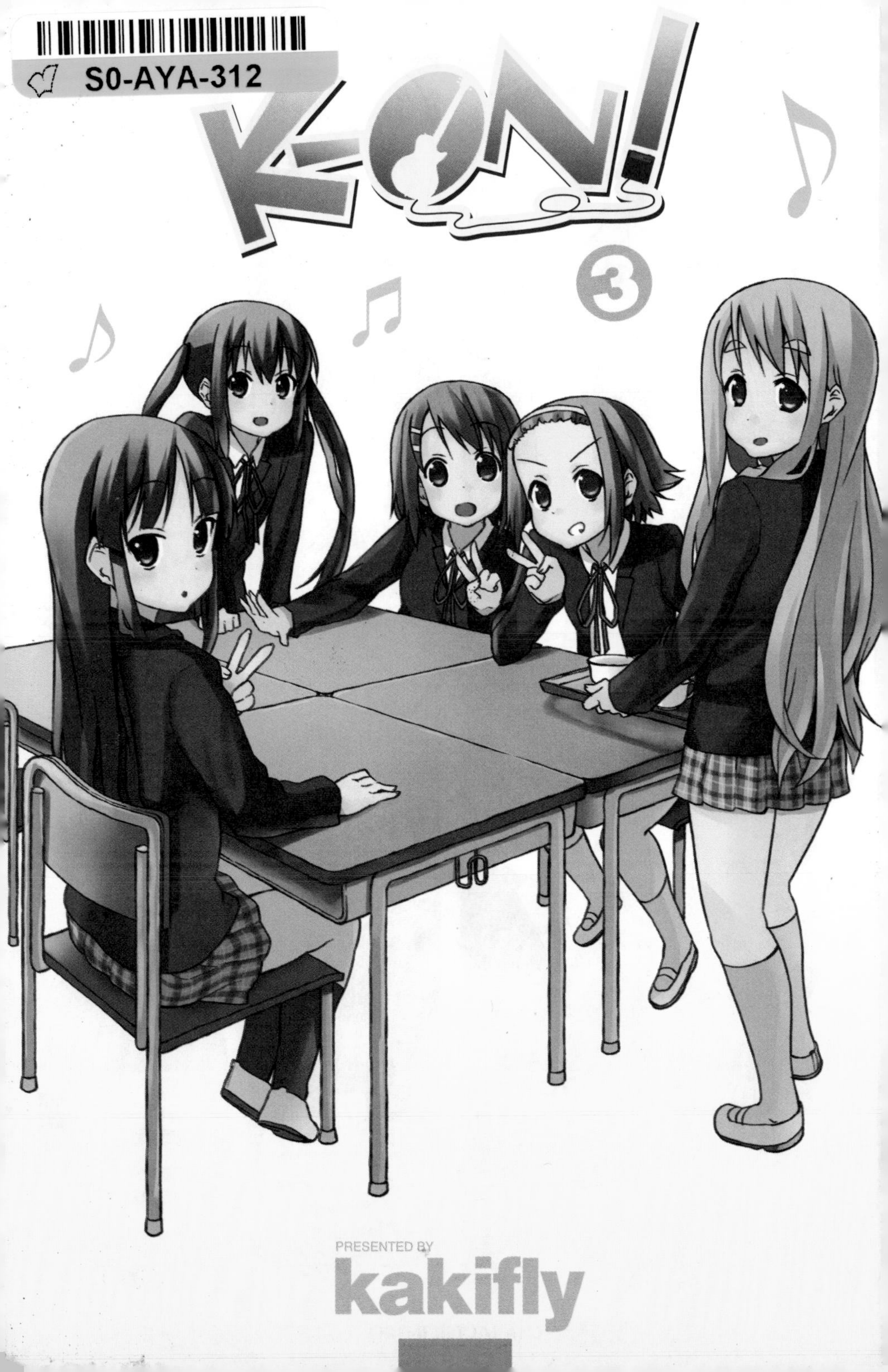

PRESENTED BY

kakifly

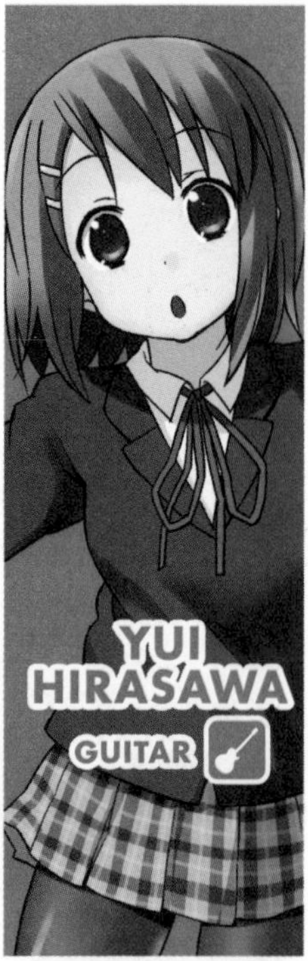
YUI HIRASAWA
GUITAR

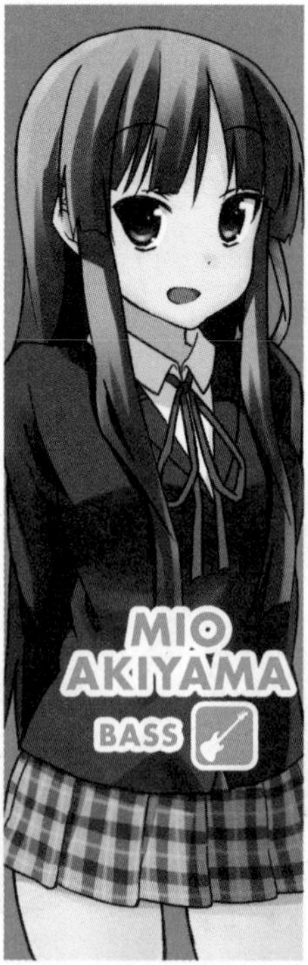
MIO AKIYAMA
BASS

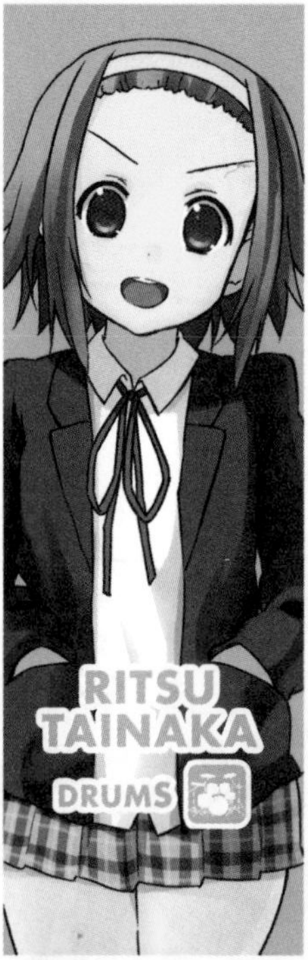
RITSU TAINAKA
DRUMS

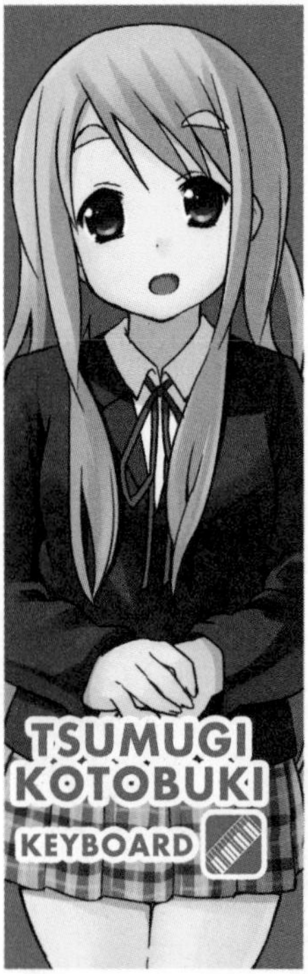
TSUMUGI KOTOBUKI
KEYBOARD

C H A R A C T E R S

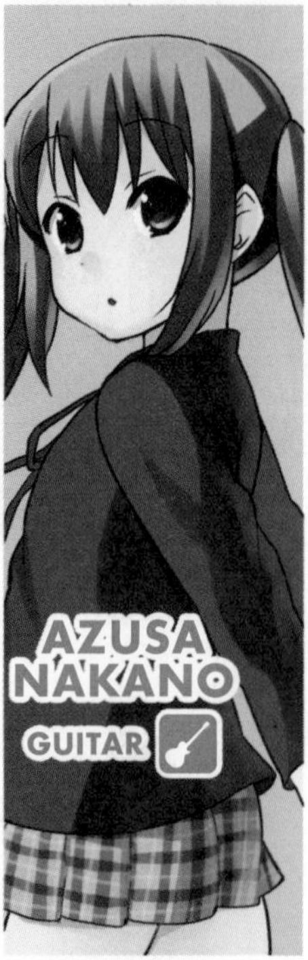
AZUSA NAKANO
GUITAR

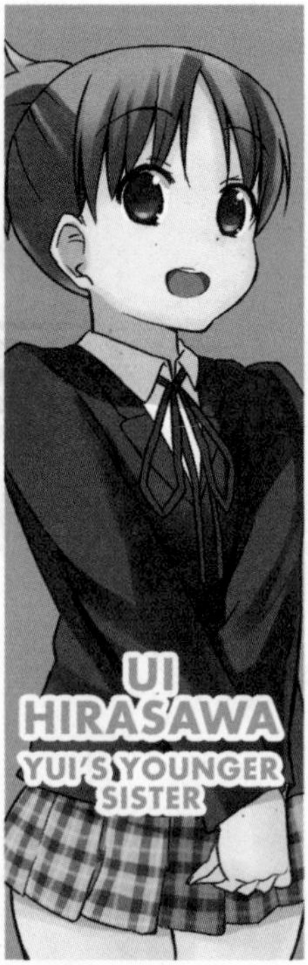
UI HIRASAWA
YUI'S YOUNGER SISTER

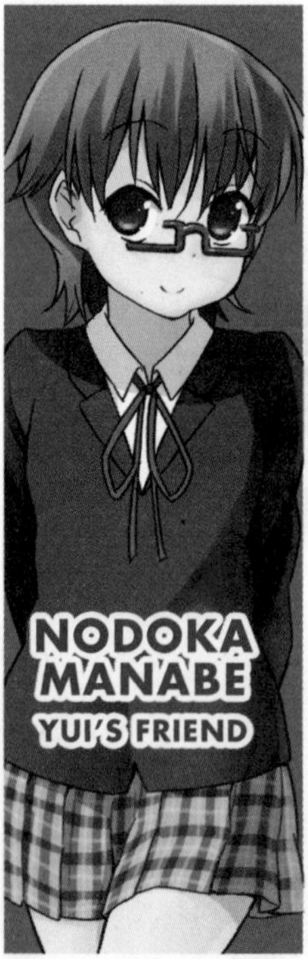
NODOKA MANABE
YUI'S FRIEND

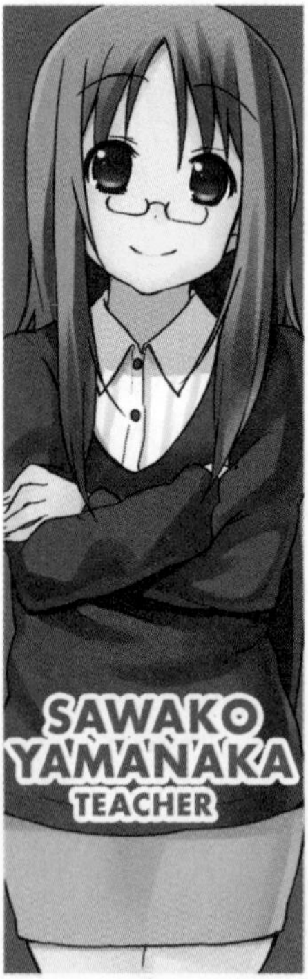
SAWAKO YAMANAKA
TEACHER

K-ON! CHARACTER INTRO kakifly

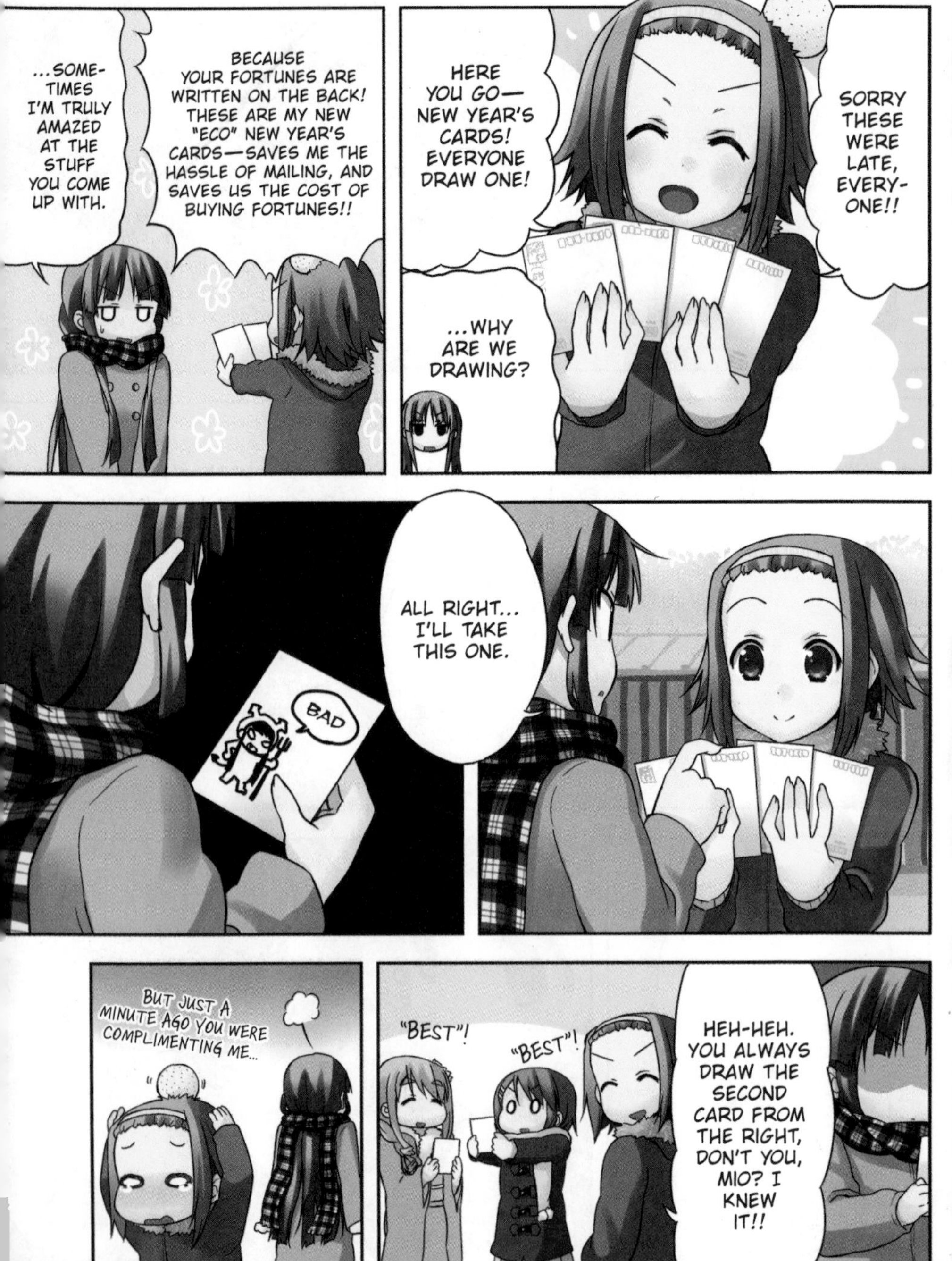
SORRY THESE WERE LATE, EVERY-ONE!!
HERE YOU GO— NEW YEAR'S CARDS! EVERYONE DRAW ONE!
...WHY ARE WE DRAWING?
BECAUSE YOUR FORTUNES ARE WRITTEN ON THE BACK! THESE ARE MY NEW "ECO" NEW YEAR'S CARDS—SAVES ME THE HASSLE OF MAILING, AND SAVES US THE COST OF BUYING FORTUNES!!
...SOME-TIMES I'M TRULY AMAZED AT THE STUFF YOU COME UP WITH.
ALL RIGHT... I'LL TAKE THIS ONE.
BAD
HEH-HEH. YOU ALWAYS DRAW THE SECOND CARD FROM THE RIGHT, DON'T YOU, MIO? I KNEW IT!!
"BEST"!
"BEST"!
BUT JUST A MINUTE AGO YOU WERE COMPLIMENTING ME...

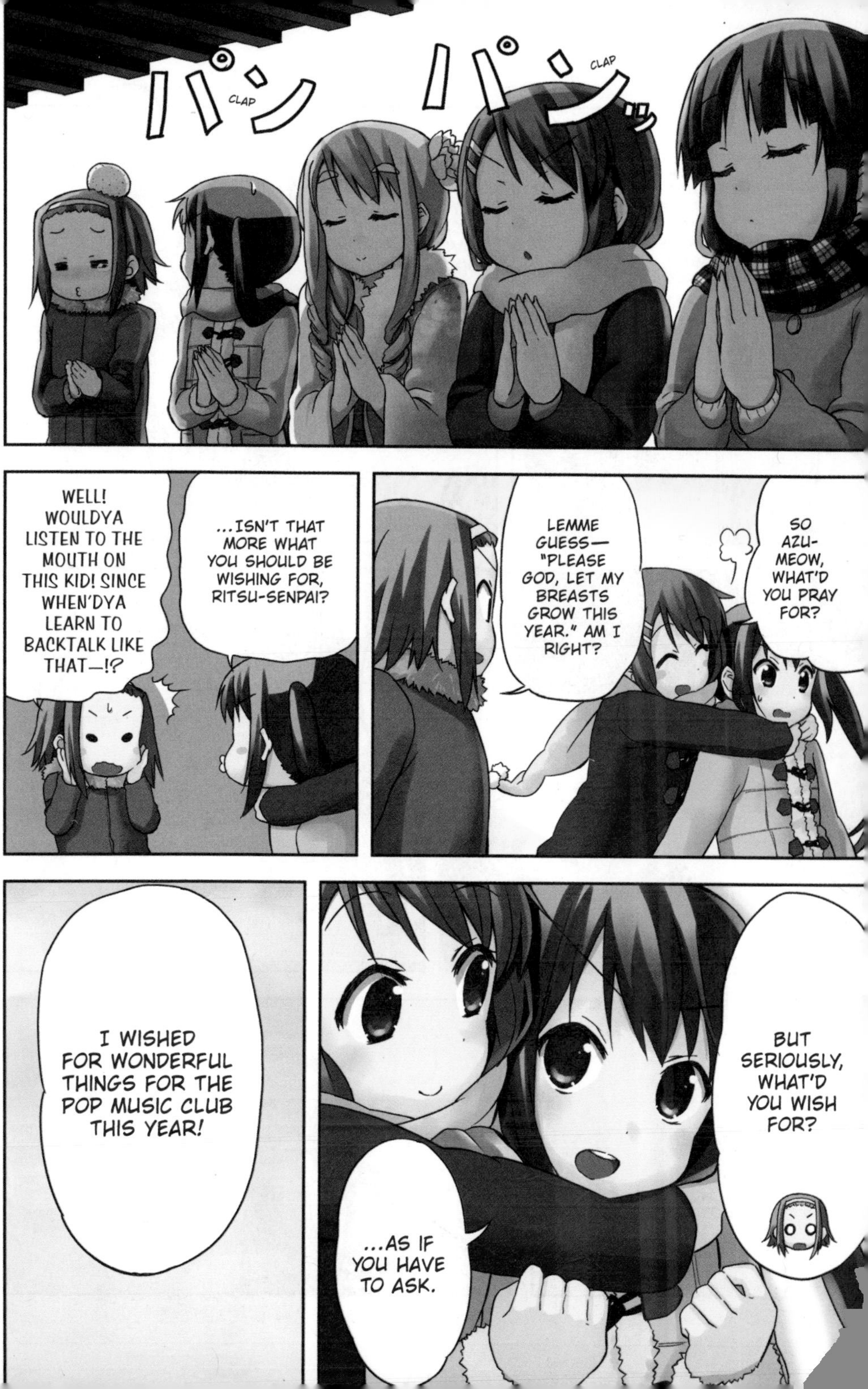
パン
CLAP
パン
CLAP
SO AZU-MEOW, WHAT'D YOU PRAY FOR?
LEMME GUESS— "PLEASE GOD, LET MY BREASTS GROW THIS YEAR." AM I RIGHT?
...ISN'T THAT MORE WHAT YOU SHOULD BE WISHING FOR, RITSU-SENPAI?
WELL! WOULDYA LISTEN TO THE MOUTH ON THIS KID! SINCE WHEN'DYA LEARN TO BACKTALK LIKE THAT—!?
BUT SERIOUSLY, WHAT'D YOU WISH FOR?
...AS IF YOU HAVE TO ASK.
I WISHED FOR WONDERFUL THINGS FOR THE POP MUSIC CLUB THIS YEAR!

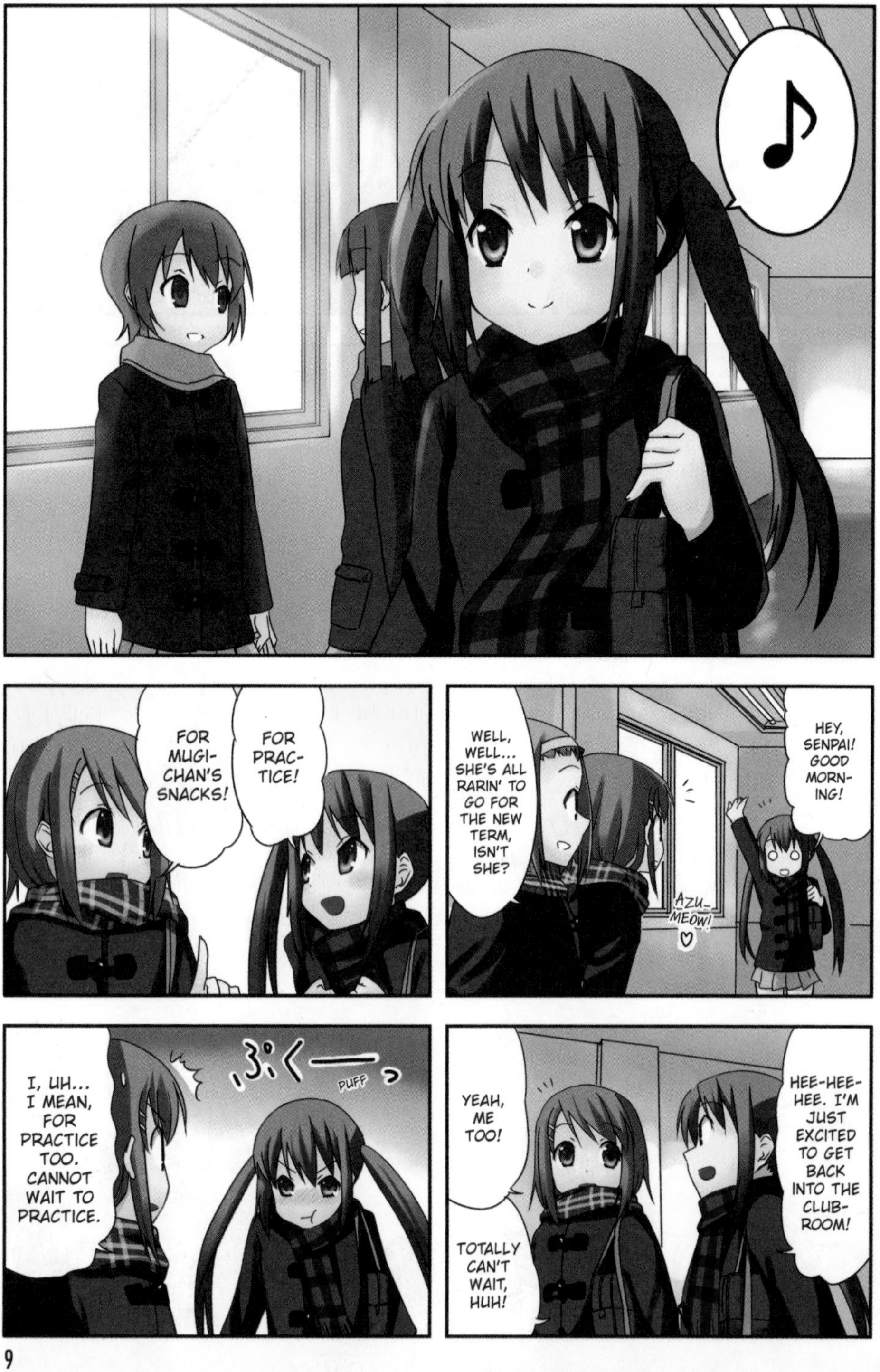
♪
HEY, SENPAI! GOOD MORNING!
AZU-MEOW! ♡
WELL, WELL... SHE'S ALL RARIN' TO GO FOR THE NEW TERM, ISN'T SHE?
FOR PRACTICE!
FOR MUGI-CHAN'S SNACKS!
HEE-HEE-HEE. I'M JUST EXCITED TO GET BACK INTO THE CLUB-ROOM!
YEAH, ME TOO!
TOTALLY CAN'T WAIT, HUH!
ぷくー
PUFF
I, UH... I MEAN, FOR PRACTICE TOO. CANNOT WAIT TO PRACTICE.

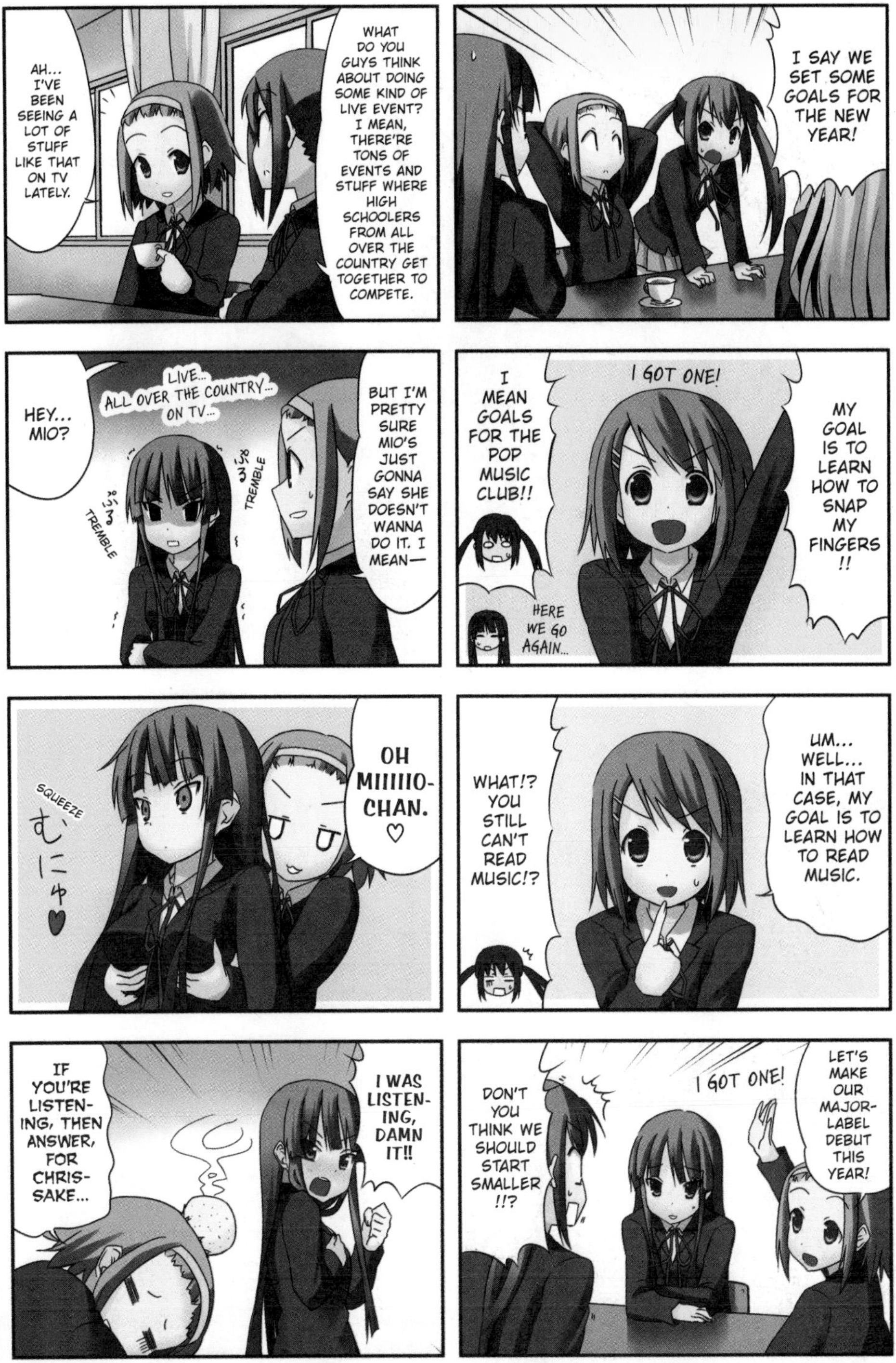
I SAY WE SET SOME GOALS FOR THE NEW YEAR!
I GOT ONE!
MY GOAL IS TO LEARN HOW TO SNAP MY FINGERS!!
I MEAN GOALS FOR THE POP MUSIC CLUB!!
HERE WE GO AGAIN...
UM... WELL... IN THAT CASE, MY GOAL IS TO LEARN HOW TO READ MUSIC.
WHAT!? YOU STILL CAN'T READ MUSIC!?
I GOT ONE!
LET'S MAKE OUR MAJOR-LABEL DEBUT THIS YEAR!
DON'T YOU THINK WE SHOULD START SMALLER!!?
WHAT DO YOU GUYS THINK ABOUT DOING SOME KIND OF LIVE EVENT? I MEAN, THERE'RE TONS OF EVENTS AND STUFF WHERE HIGH SCHOOLERS FROM ALL OVER THE COUNTRY GET TOGETHER TO COMPETE.
AH... I'VE BEEN SEEING A LOT OF STUFF LIKE THAT ON TV LATELY.
BUT I'M PRETTY SURE MIO'S JUST GONNA SAY SHE DOESN'T WANNA DO IT. I MEAN—
LIVE... ALL OVER THE COUNTRY... ON TV...
HEY... MIO?
ぷる TREMBLE
ぷる TREMBLE
OH MIIIIIO-CHAN. ♡
むにゅ♥ SQUEEZE
I WAS LISTENING, DAMN IT!!
IF YOU'RE LISTENING, THEN ANSWER, FOR CHRIS-SAKE...

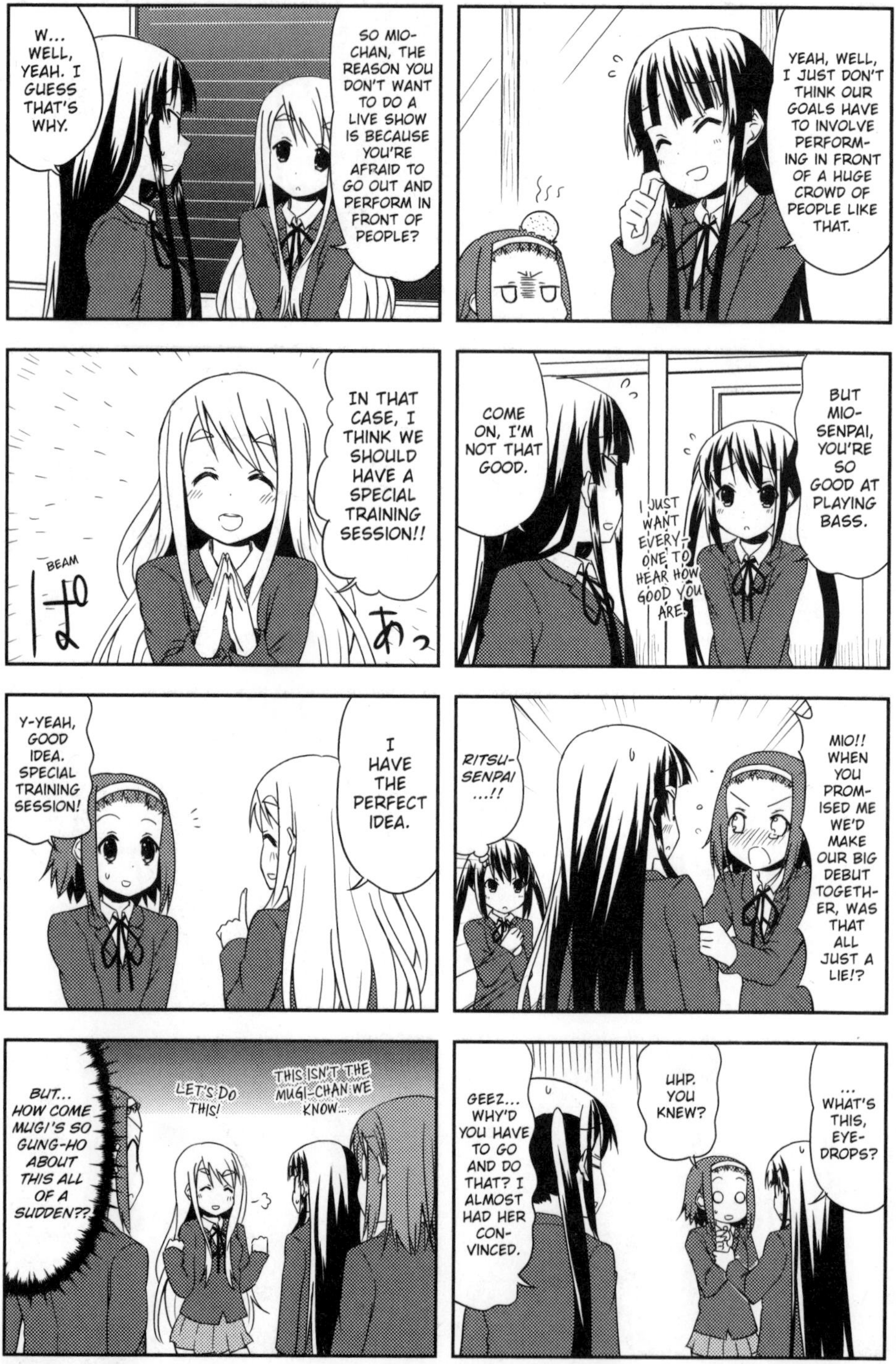
YEAH, WELL, I JUST DON'T THINK OUR GOALS HAVE TO INVOLVE PERFORMING IN FRONT OF A HUGE CROWD OF PEOPLE LIKE THAT.
BUT MIO-SENPAI, YOU'RE SO GOOD AT PLAYING BASS.
I JUST WANT EVERYONE TO HEAR HOW GOOD YOU ARE.
COME ON, I'M NOT THAT GOOD.
MIO!! WHEN YOU PROMISED ME WE'D MAKE OUR BIG DEBUT TOGETHER, WAS THAT ALL JUST A LIE!?
RITSU-SENPAI...!!
...WHAT'S THIS, EYE-DROPS?
UHP. YOU KNEW?
GEEZ... WHY'D YOU HAVE TO GO AND DO THAT? I ALMOST HAD HER CONVINCED.
SO MIO-CHAN, THE REASON YOU DON'T WANT TO DO A LIVE SHOW IS BECAUSE YOU'RE AFRAID TO GO OUT AND PERFORM IN FRONT OF PEOPLE?
W... WELL, YEAH. I GUESS THAT'S WHY.
IN THAT CASE, I THINK WE SHOULD HAVE A SPECIAL TRAINING SESSION!!
あっ
BEAM
ぱ
I HAVE THE PERFECT IDEA.
Y-YEAH, GOOD IDEA. SPECIAL TRAINING SESSION!
THIS ISN'T THE MUGI-CHAN WE KNOW...
LET'S DO THIS!
BUT... HOW COME MUGI'S SO GUNG-HO ABOUT THIS ALL OF A SUDDEN??

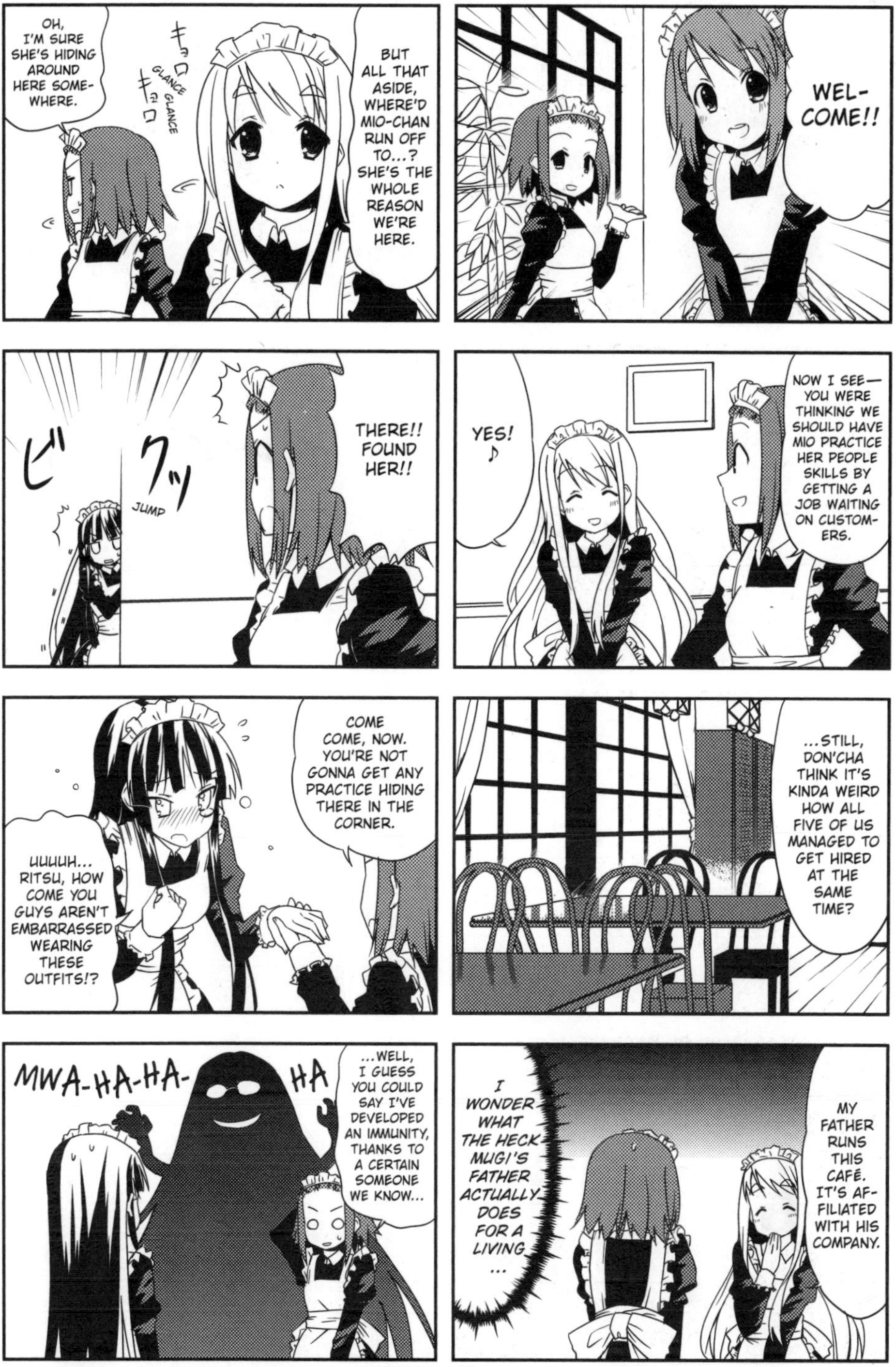
WEL-COME!!
BUT ALL THAT ASIDE, WHERE'D MIO-CHAN RUN OFF TO...? SHE'S THE WHOLE REASON WE'RE HERE.
キョロ キョロ GLANCE GLANCE
OH, I'M SURE SHE'S HIDING AROUND HERE SOME-WHERE.
NOW I SEE— YOU WERE THINKING WE SHOULD HAVE MIO PRACTICE HER PEOPLE SKILLS BY GETTING A JOB WAITING ON CUSTOM-ERS.
YES! ♪
THERE!! FOUND HER!!
ビクッ JUMP
...STILL, DON'CHA THINK IT'S KINDA WEIRD HOW ALL FIVE OF US MANAGED TO GET HIRED AT THE SAME TIME?
COME COME, NOW. YOU'RE NOT GONNA GET ANY PRACTICE HIDING THERE IN THE CORNER.
UUUUH... RITSU, HOW COME YOU GUYS AREN'T EMBARRASSED WEARING THESE OUTFITS!?
MY FATHER RUNS THIS CAFÉ. IT'S AF-FILIATED WITH HIS COMPANY.
I WONDER WHAT THE HECK MUGI'S FATHER ACTUALLY DOES FOR A LIVING...
...WELL, I GUESS YOU COULD SAY I'VE DEVELOPED AN IMMUNITY, THANKS TO A CERTAIN SOMEONE WE KNOW...
MWA-HA-HA-HA

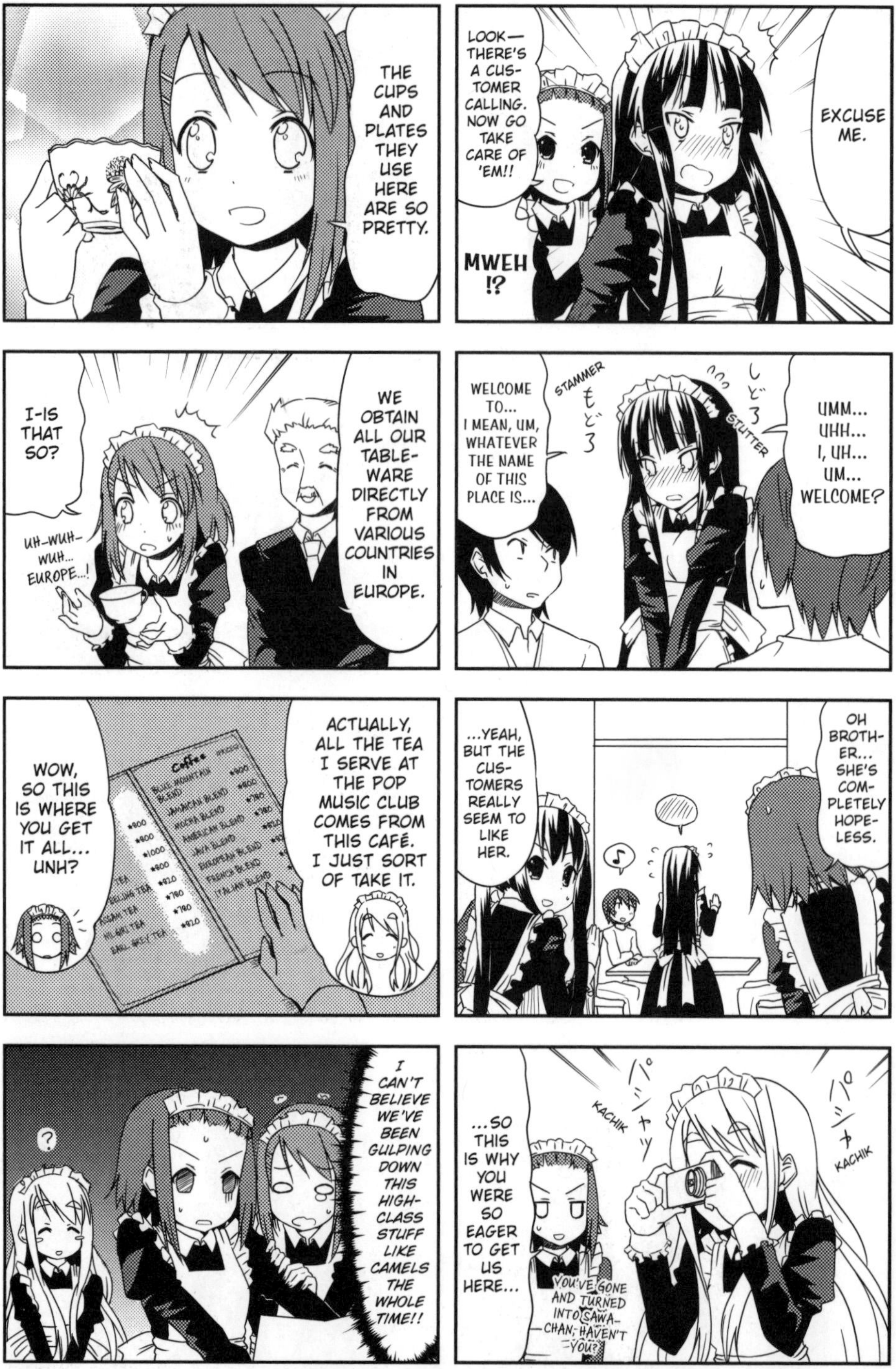
EXCUSE ME.
LOOK— THERE'S A CUS-TOMER CALLING. NOW GO TAKE CARE OF 'EM!!
MWEH !?
UMM... UHH... I, UH... UM... WELCOME?
しどろ STUTTER
もどろ STAMMER
WELCOME TO... I MEAN, UM, WHATEVER THE NAME OF THIS PLACE IS...
OH BROTHER... SHE'S COM-PLETELY HOPE-LESS.
...YEAH, BUT THE CUS-TOMERS REALLY SEEM TO LIKE HER.
パシ KACHIK
パシャッ KACHIK
...SO THIS IS WHY YOU WERE SO EAGER TO GET US HERE...
YOU'VE GONE AND TURNED INTO SAWA-CHAN, HAVEN'T YOU?
THE CUPS AND PLATES THEY USE HERE ARE SO PRETTY.
WE OBTAIN ALL OUR TABLE-WARE DIRECTLY FROM VARIOUS COUNTRIES IN EUROPE.
I-IS THAT SO?
UH-WUH-WUH... EUROPE...!
ACTUALLY, ALL THE TEA I SERVE AT THE POP MUSIC CLUB COMES FROM THIS CAFÉ. I JUST SORT OF TAKE IT.
WOW, SO THIS IS WHERE YOU GET IT ALL... UNH?
I CAN'T BELIEVE WE'VE BEEN GULPING DOWN THIS HIGH-CLASS STUFF LIKE CAMELS THE WHOLE TIME!!
?

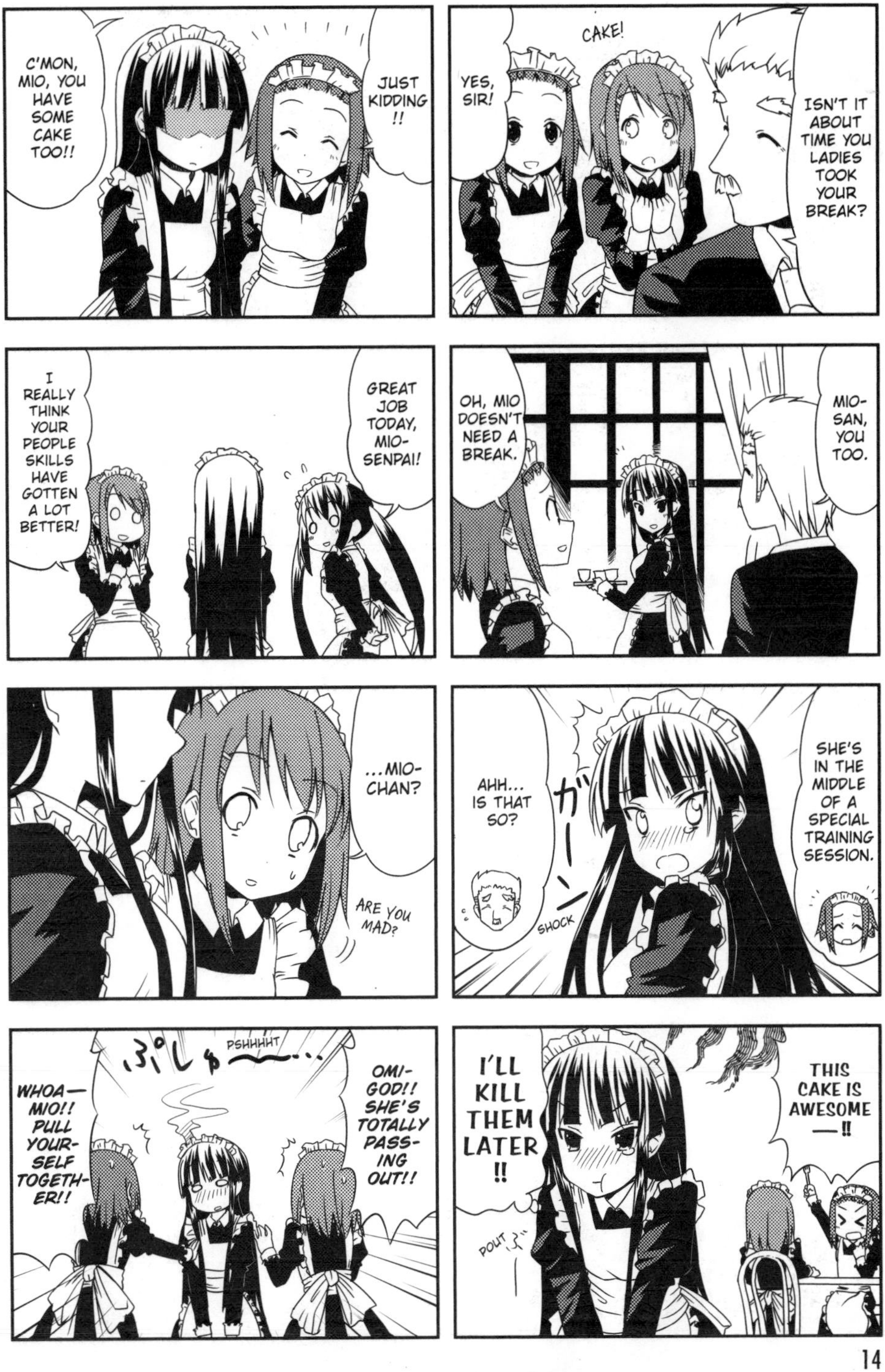
ISN'T IT ABOUT TIME YOU LADIES TOOK YOUR BREAK?
CAKE!
YES, SIR!
JUST KIDDING!!
C'MON, MIO, YOU HAVE SOME CAKE TOO!!
MIO-SAN, YOU TOO.
OH, MIO DOESN'T NEED A BREAK.
GREAT JOB TODAY, MIO-SENPAI!
I REALLY THINK YOUR PEOPLE SKILLS HAVE GOTTEN A LOT BETTER!
SHE'S IN THE MIDDLE OF A SPECIAL TRAINING SESSION.
AHH... IS THAT SO?
ガーン
SHOCK
...MIO-CHAN?
ARE YOU MAD?
THIS CAKE IS AWESOME—!!
I'LL KILL THEM LATER!!
ぷ
POUT
OMI-GOD!! SHE'S TOTALLY PASSING OUT!!
ぷしゅ〜〜…
PSHHHHT
WHOA— MIO!! PULL YOURSELF TOGETHER!!

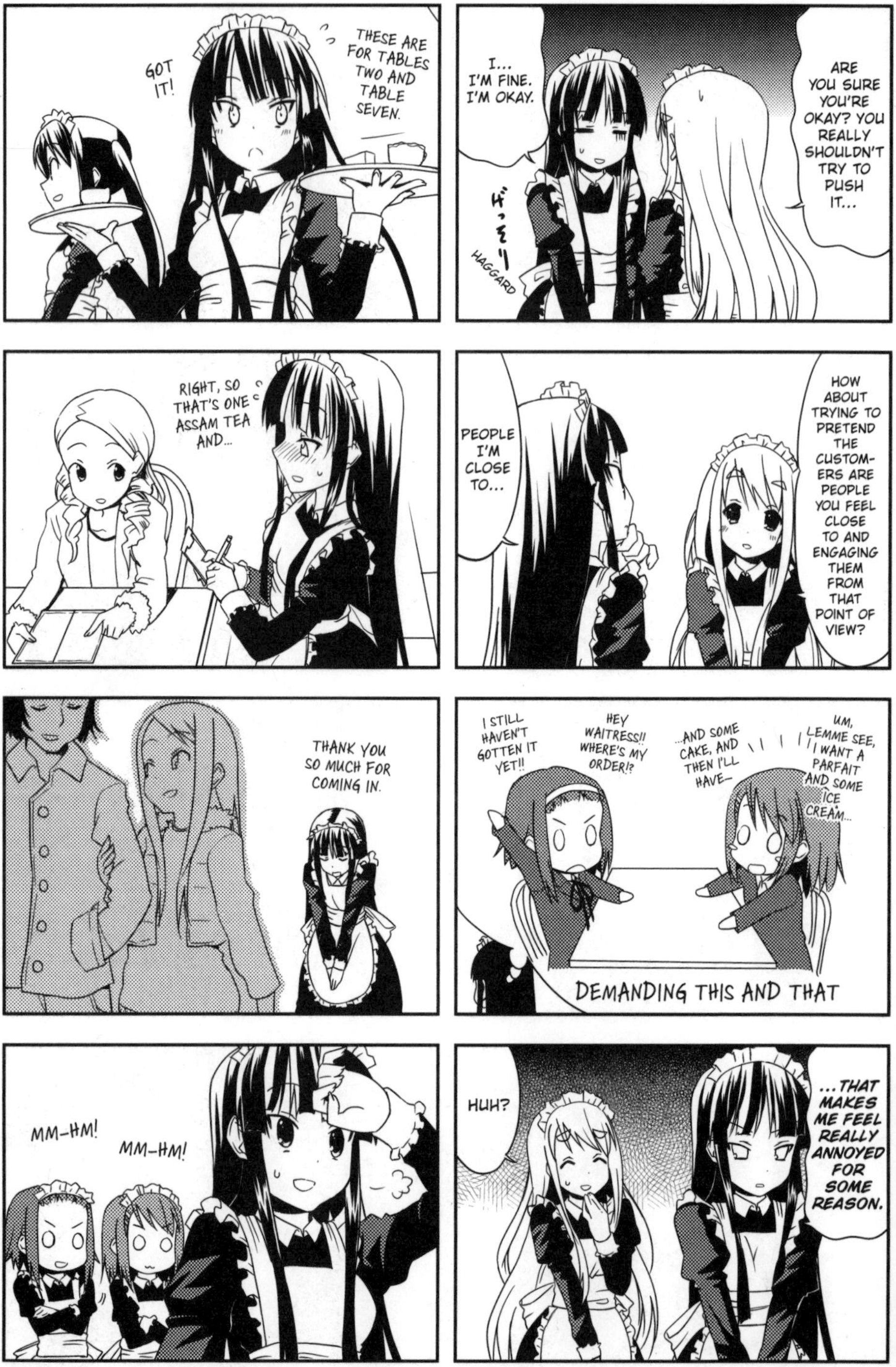
ARE YOU SURE YOU'RE OKAY? YOU REALLY SHOULDN'T TRY TO PUSH IT...
I... I'M FINE. I'M OKAY.
げっそり
HAGGARD
THESE ARE FOR TABLES TWO AND TABLE SEVEN.
GOT IT!
HOW ABOUT TRYING TO PRETEND THE CUSTOMERS ARE PEOPLE YOU FEEL CLOSE TO AND ENGAGING THEM FROM THAT POINT OF VIEW?
PEOPLE I'M CLOSE TO...
RIGHT, SO THAT'S ONE ASSAM TEA AND...
UM, LEMME SEE, I WANT A PARFAIT AND SOME ICE CREAM...
...AND SOME CAKE, AND THEN I'LL HAVE—
HEY WAITRESS!! WHERE'S MY ORDER!?
I STILL HAVEN'T GOTTEN IT YET!!
DEMANDING THIS AND THAT
THANK YOU SO MUCH FOR COMING IN.
...THAT MAKES ME FEEL REALLY ANNOYED FOR SOME REASON.
HUH?
MM-HM!
MM-HM!

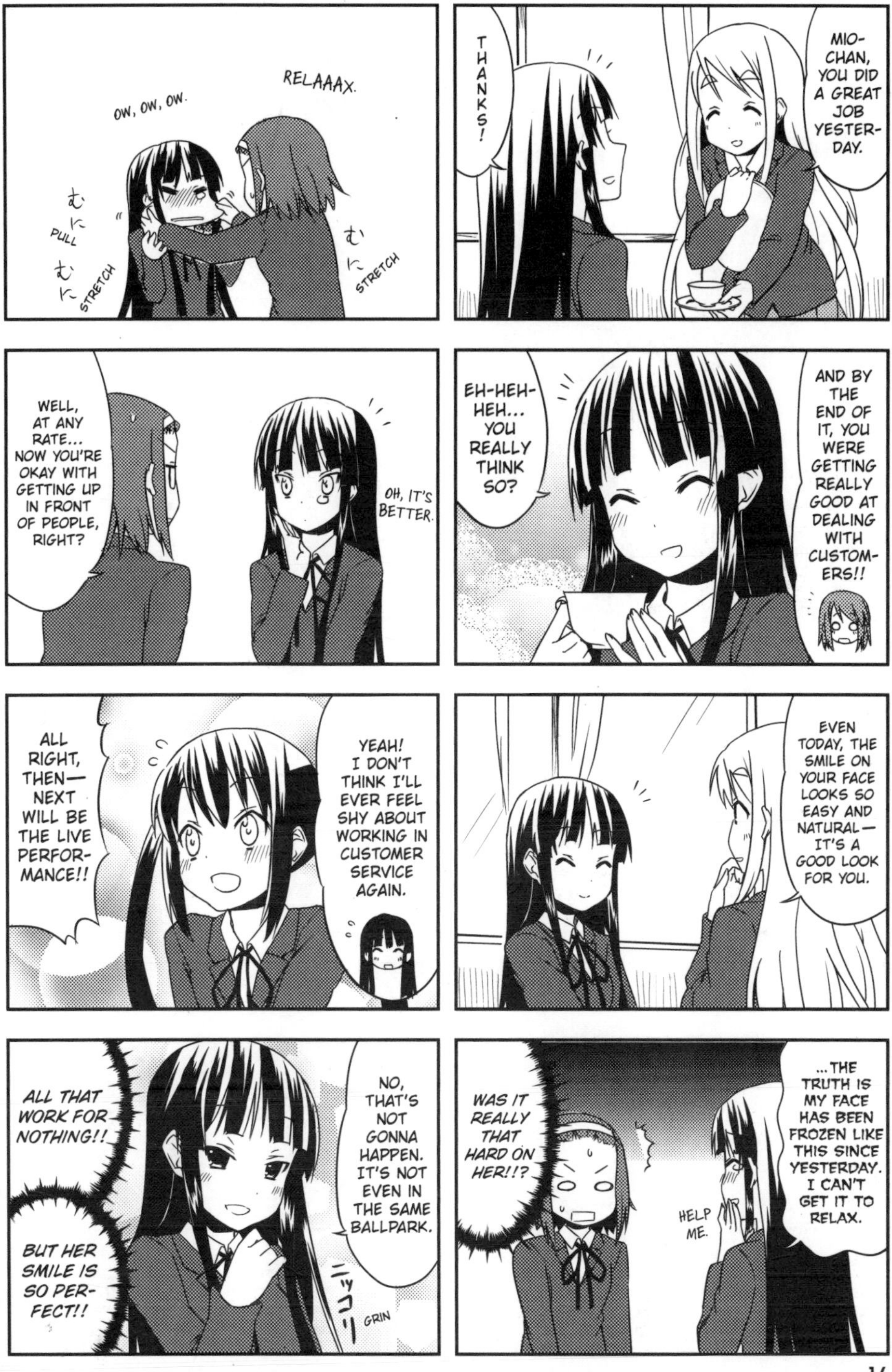
MIO-CHAN, YOU DID A GREAT JOB YESTERDAY.
THANKS!
RELAAAX.
OW, OW, OW.
むにむに
PULL
むに
STRETCH
STRETCH
AND BY THE END OF IT, YOU WERE GETTING REALLY GOOD AT DEALING WITH CUSTOMERS!!
EH-HEH-HEH... YOU REALLY THINK SO?
WELL, AT ANY RATE... NOW YOU'RE OKAY WITH GETTING UP IN FRONT OF PEOPLE, RIGHT?
OH, IT'S BETTER.
EVEN TODAY, THE SMILE ON YOUR FACE LOOKS SO EASY AND NATURAL—IT'S A GOOD LOOK FOR YOU.
YEAH! I DON'T THINK I'LL EVER FEEL SHY ABOUT WORKING IN CUSTOMER SERVICE AGAIN.
ALL RIGHT, THEN—NEXT WILL BE THE LIVE PERFORMANCE!!
...THE TRUTH IS MY FACE HAS BEEN FROZEN LIKE THIS SINCE YESTERDAY. I CAN'T GET IT TO RELAX.
HELP ME.
WAS IT REALLY THAT HARD ON HER!!?
NO, THAT'S NOT GONNA HAPPEN. IT'S NOT EVEN IN THE SAME BALLPARK.
ニッコリ
GRIN
ALL THAT WORK FOR NOTHING!!
BUT HER SMILE IS SO PERFECT!!

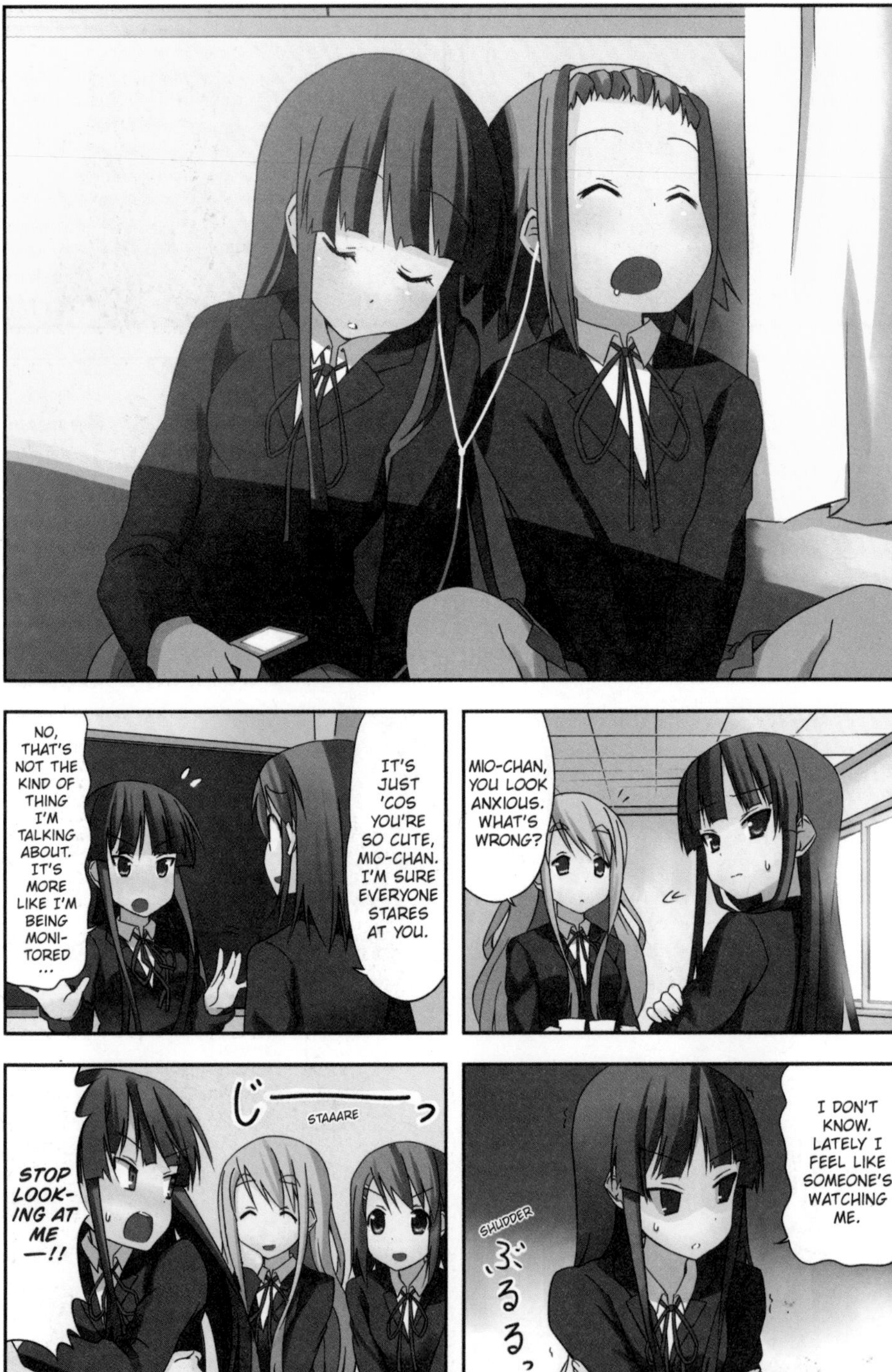
MIO-CHAN, YOU LOOK ANXIOUS. WHAT'S WRONG?
IT'S JUST 'COS YOU'RE SO CUTE, MIO-CHAN. I'M SURE EVERYONE STARES AT YOU.
NO, THAT'S NOT THE KIND OF THING I'M TALKING ABOUT. IT'S MORE LIKE I'M BEING MONI-TORED ...
I DON'T KNOW. LATELY I FEEL LIKE SOMEONE'S WATCHING ME.
SHUDDER
ぶるるっ
じーーーっ
STAAARE
STOP LOOKING AT ME—!!

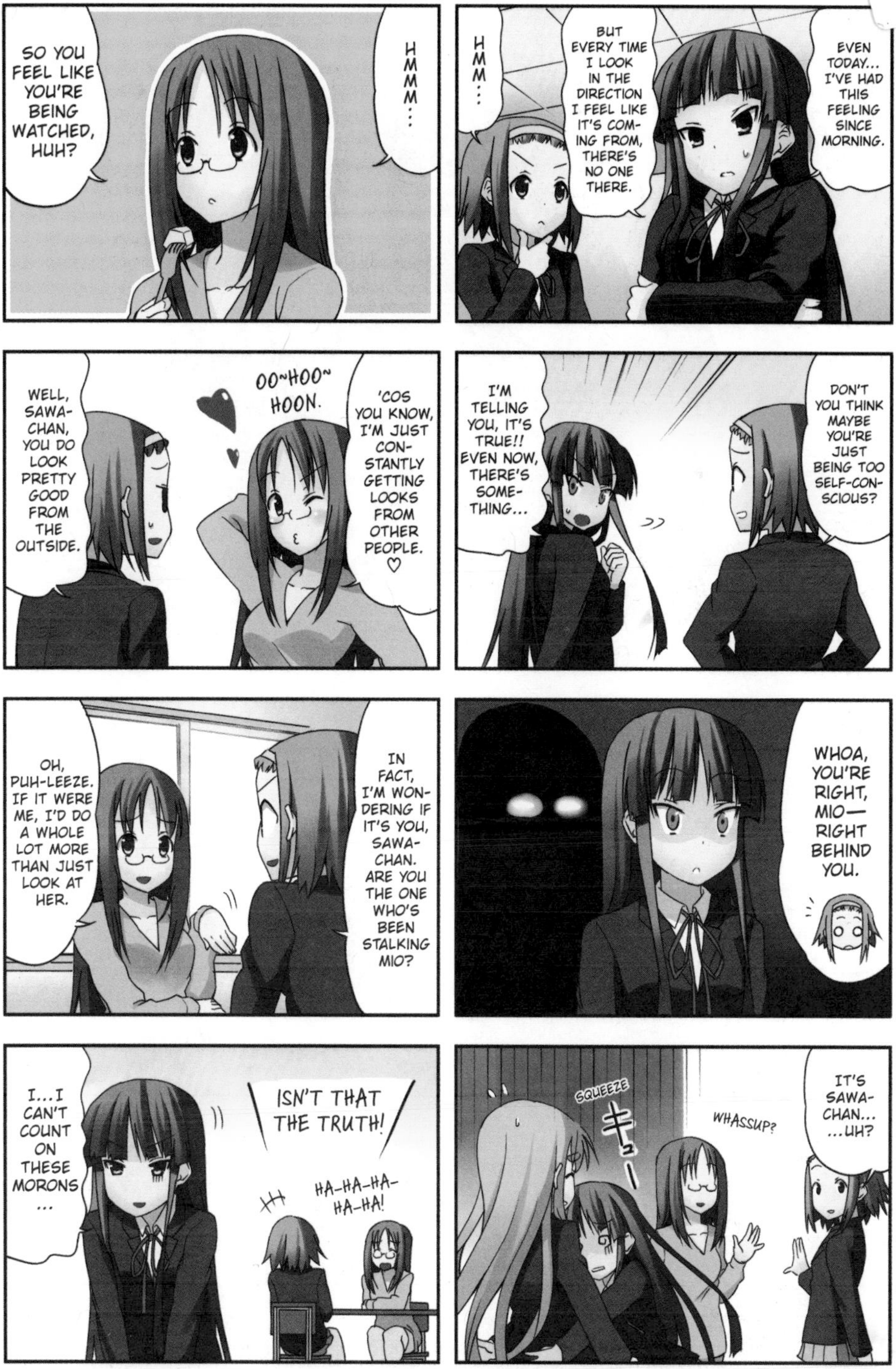
EVEN TODAY... I'VE HAD THIS FEELING SINCE MORNING.
BUT EVERY TIME I LOOK IN THE DIRECTION I FEEL LIKE IT'S COMING FROM, THERE'S NO ONE THERE.
HMM...
HMMM...
SO YOU FEEL LIKE YOU'RE BEING WATCHED, HUH?
DON'T YOU THINK MAYBE YOU'RE JUST BEING TOO SELF-CONSCIOUS?
I'M TELLING YOU, IT'S TRUE!! EVEN NOW, THERE'S SOMETHING...
'COS YOU KNOW, I'M JUST CONSTANTLY GETTING LOOKS FROM OTHER PEOPLE. ♡
OO~HOO~ HOON.
WELL, SAWA-CHAN, YOU DO LOOK PRETTY GOOD FROM THE OUTSIDE.
WHOA, YOU'RE RIGHT, MIO—RIGHT BEHIND YOU.
IN FACT, I'M WONDERING IF IT'S YOU, SAWA-CHAN. ARE YOU THE ONE WHO'S BEEN STALKING MIO?
OH, PUH-LEEZE. IF IT WERE ME, I'D DO A WHOLE LOT MORE THAN JUST LOOK AT HER.
IT'S SAWA-CHAN... ...UH?
WHASSUP?
SQUEEZE
キュー
ISN'T THAT THE TRUTH!
HA-HA-HA-HA-HA!
I...I CAN'T COUNT ON THESE MORONS...

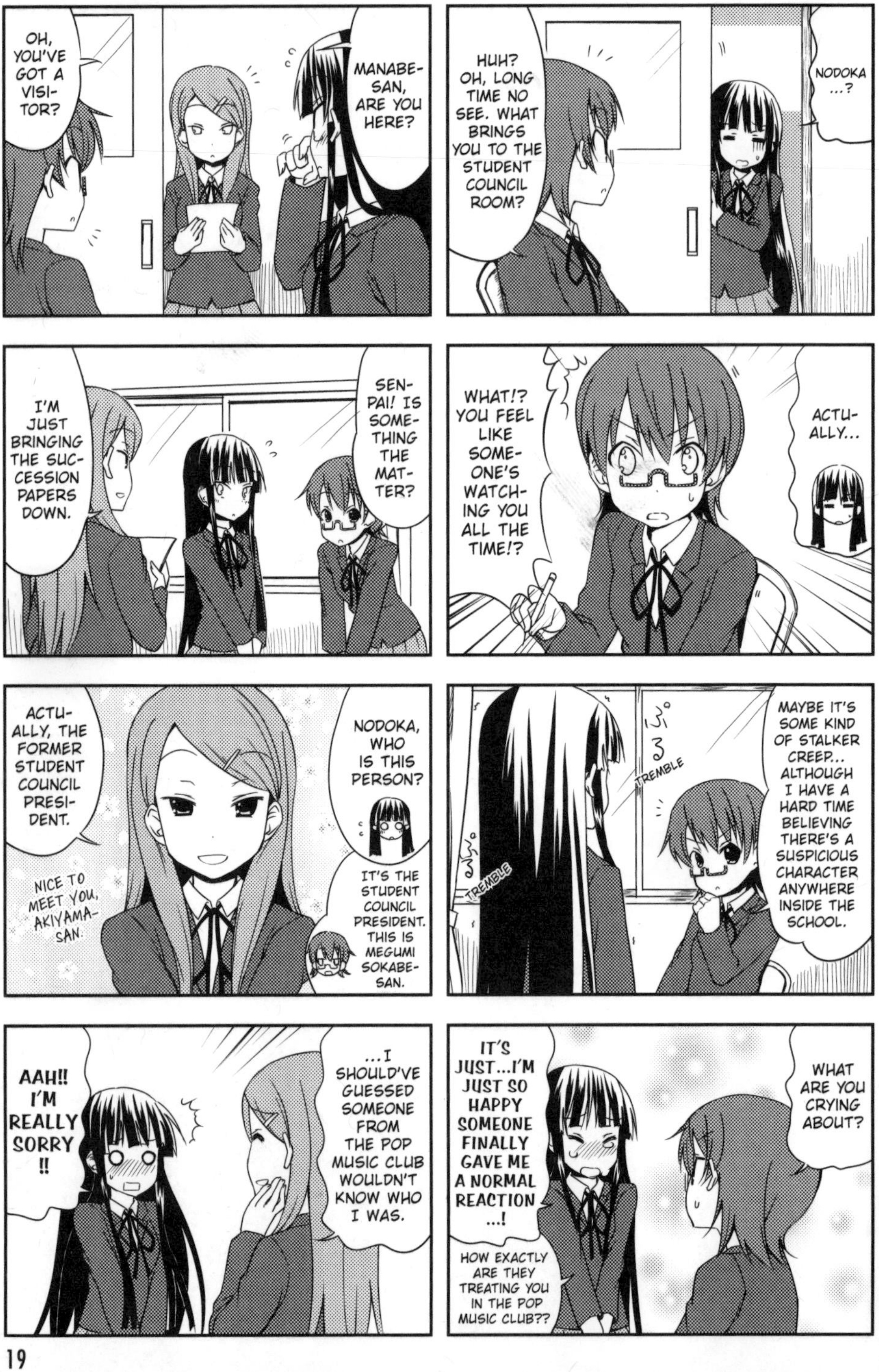
NODOKA ...?
HUH? OH, LONG TIME NO SEE. WHAT BRINGS YOU TO THE STUDENT COUNCIL ROOM?
MANABE-SAN, ARE YOU HERE?
OH, YOU'VE GOT A VISITOR?
ACTUALLY...
WHAT!? YOU FEEL LIKE SOMEONE'S WATCHING YOU ALL THE TIME!?
SENPAI! IS SOMETHING THE MATTER?
I'M JUST BRINGING THE SUCCESSION PAPERS DOWN.
MAYBE IT'S SOME KIND OF STALKER CREEP... ALTHOUGH I HAVE A HARD TIME BELIEVING THERE'S A SUSPICIOUS CHARACTER ANYWHERE INSIDE THE SCHOOL.
TREMBLE
TREMBLE
NODOKA, WHO IS THIS PERSON?
IT'S THE STUDENT COUNCIL PRESIDENT. THIS IS MEGUMI SOKABE-SAN.
ACTUALLY, THE FORMER STUDENT COUNCIL PRESIDENT.
NICE TO MEET YOU, AKIYAMA-SAN.
WHAT ARE YOU CRYING ABOUT?
IT'S JUST...I'M JUST SO HAPPY SOMEONE FINALLY GAVE ME A NORMAL REACTION ...!
HOW EXACTLY ARE THEY TREATING YOU IN THE POP MUSIC CLUB??
...I SHOULD'VE GUESSED SOMEONE FROM THE POP MUSIC CLUB WOULDN'T KNOW WHO I WAS.
AAH!! I'M REALLY SORRY !!

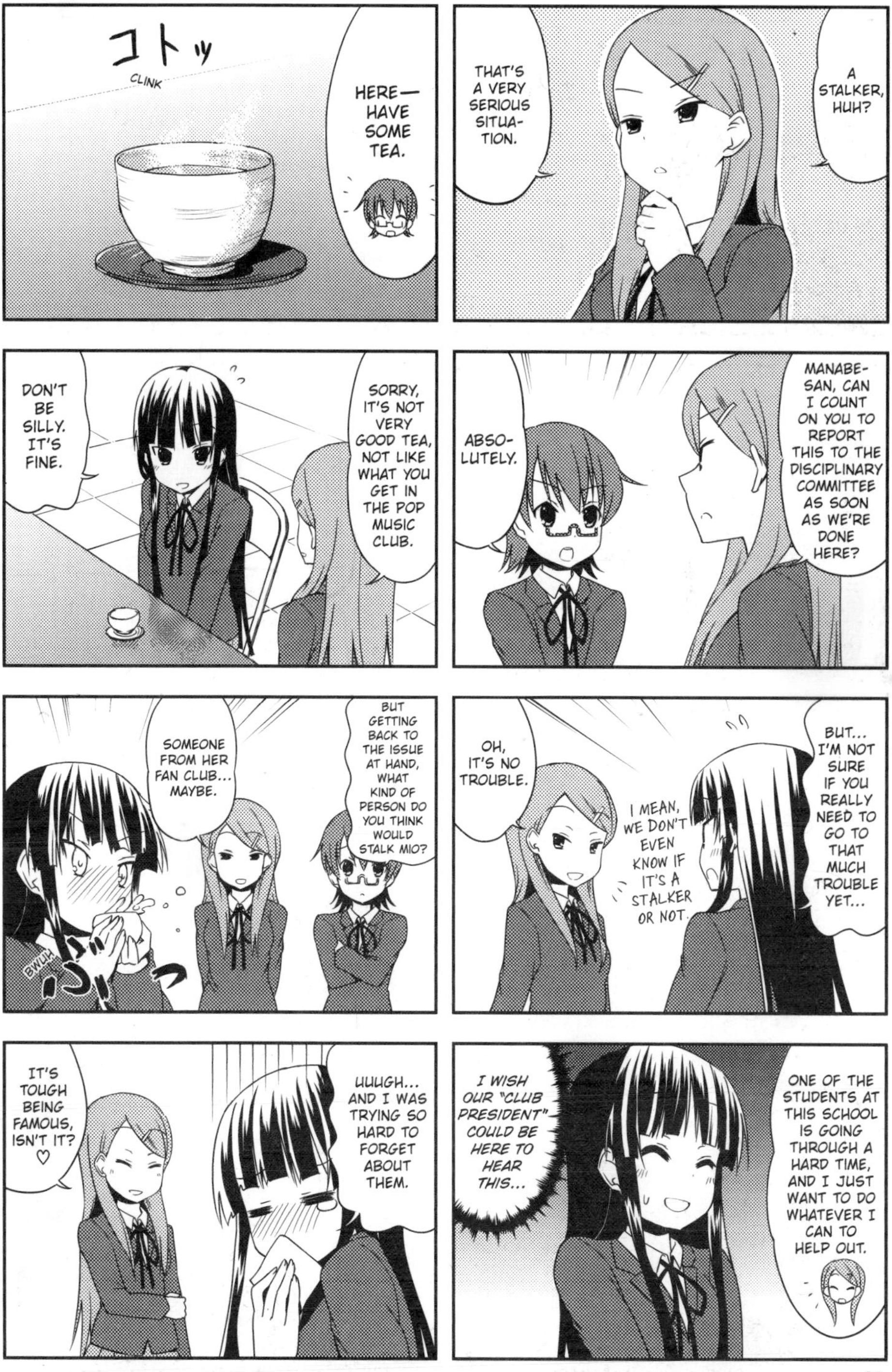
A STALKER, HUH?
THAT'S A VERY SERIOUS SITUA-TION.
HERE— HAVE SOME TEA.
コトッ
CLINK
MANABE-SAN, CAN I COUNT ON YOU TO REPORT THIS TO THE DISCIPLINARY COMMITTEE AS SOON AS WE'RE DONE HERE?
ABSO-LUTELY.
SORRY, IT'S NOT VERY GOOD TEA, NOT LIKE WHAT YOU GET IN THE POP MUSIC CLUB.
DON'T BE SILLY. IT'S FINE.
BUT... I'M NOT SURE IF YOU REALLY NEED TO GO TO THAT MUCH TROUBLE YET...
I MEAN, WE DON'T EVEN KNOW IF IT'S A STALKER OR NOT.
OH, IT'S NO TROUBLE.
BUT GETTING BACK TO THE ISSUE AT HAND, WHAT KIND OF PERSON DO YOU THINK WOULD STALK MIO?
SOMEONE FROM HER FAN CLUB... MAYBE.
BWUH
ONE OF THE STUDENTS AT THIS SCHOOL IS GOING THROUGH A HARD TIME, AND I JUST WANT TO DO WHATEVER I CAN TO HELP OUT.
I WISH OUR "CLUB PRESIDENT" COULD BE HERE TO HEAR THIS...
UUUGH... AND I WAS TRYING SO HARD TO FORGET ABOUT THEM.
IT'S TOUGH BEING FAMOUS, ISN'T IT? ♡

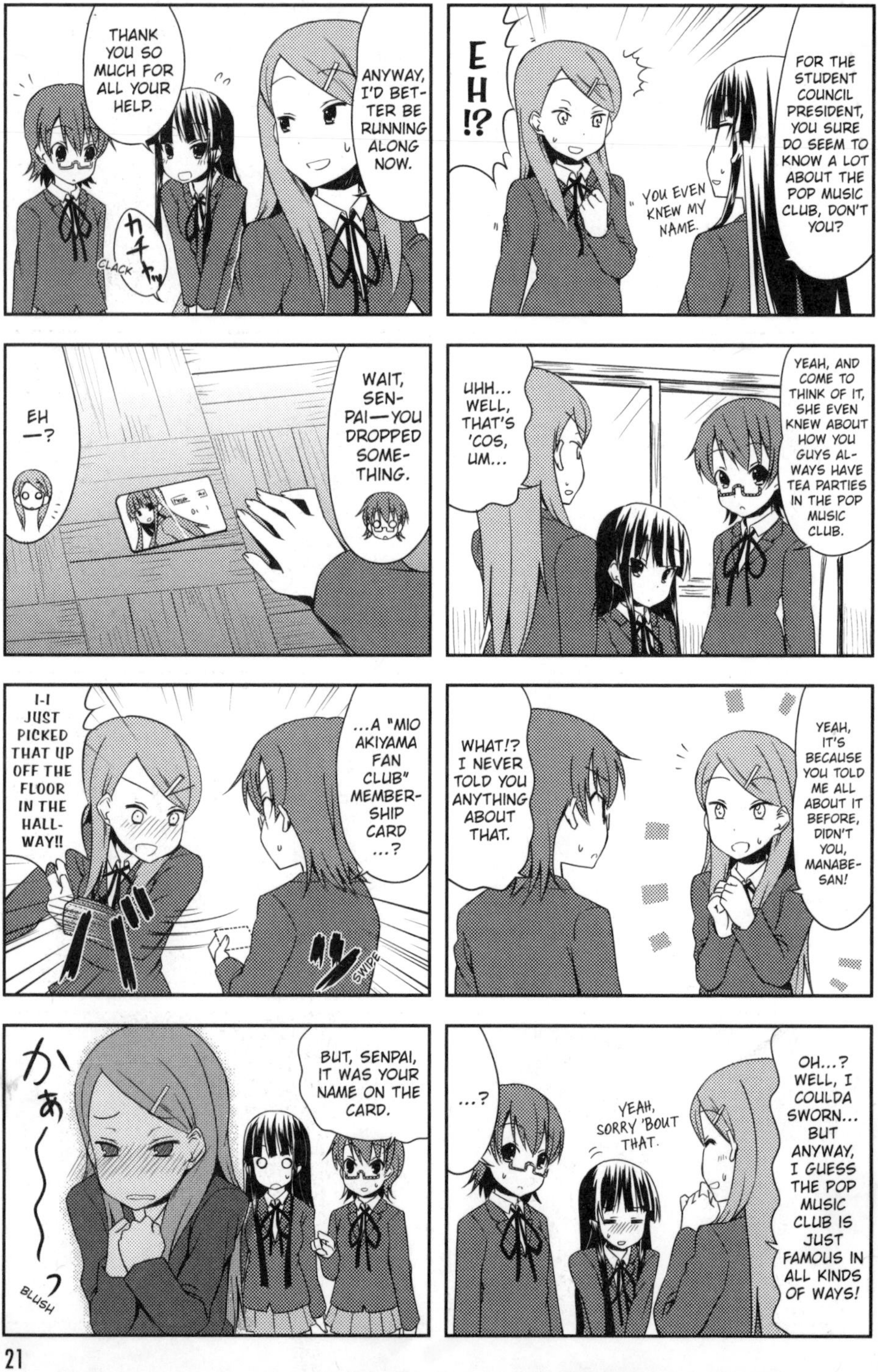

FOR THE STUDENT COUNCIL PRESIDENT, YOU SURE DO SEEM TO KNOW A LOT ABOUT THE POP MUSIC CLUB, DON'T YOU?
YOU EVEN KNEW MY NAME.
EH!?
ANYWAY, I'D BETTER BE RUNNING ALONG NOW.
THANK YOU SO MUCH FOR ALL YOUR HELP.
カチャッ
CLACK
YEAH, AND COME TO THINK OF IT, SHE EVEN KNEW ABOUT HOW YOU GUYS ALWAYS HAVE TEA PARTIES IN THE POP MUSIC CLUB.
UHH... WELL, THAT'S 'COS, UM...
WAIT, SENPAI—YOU DROPPED SOMETHING.
EH—?
YEAH, IT'S BECAUSE YOU TOLD ME ALL ABOUT IT BEFORE, DIDN'T YOU, MANABE-SAN!
WHAT!? I NEVER TOLD YOU ANYTHING ABOUT THAT.
...A "MIO AKIYAMA FAN CLUB" MEMBERSHIP CARD ...?
I-I JUST PICKED THAT UP OFF THE FLOOR IN THE HALLWAY!!
SWIPE
OH...? WELL, I COULDA SWORN... BUT ANYWAY, I GUESS THE POP MUSIC CLUB IS JUST FAMOUS IN ALL KINDS OF WAYS!
YEAH, SORRY 'BOUT THAT.
...?
BUT, SENPAI, IT WAS YOUR NAME ON THE CARD.
かぁ~~っ
BLUSH

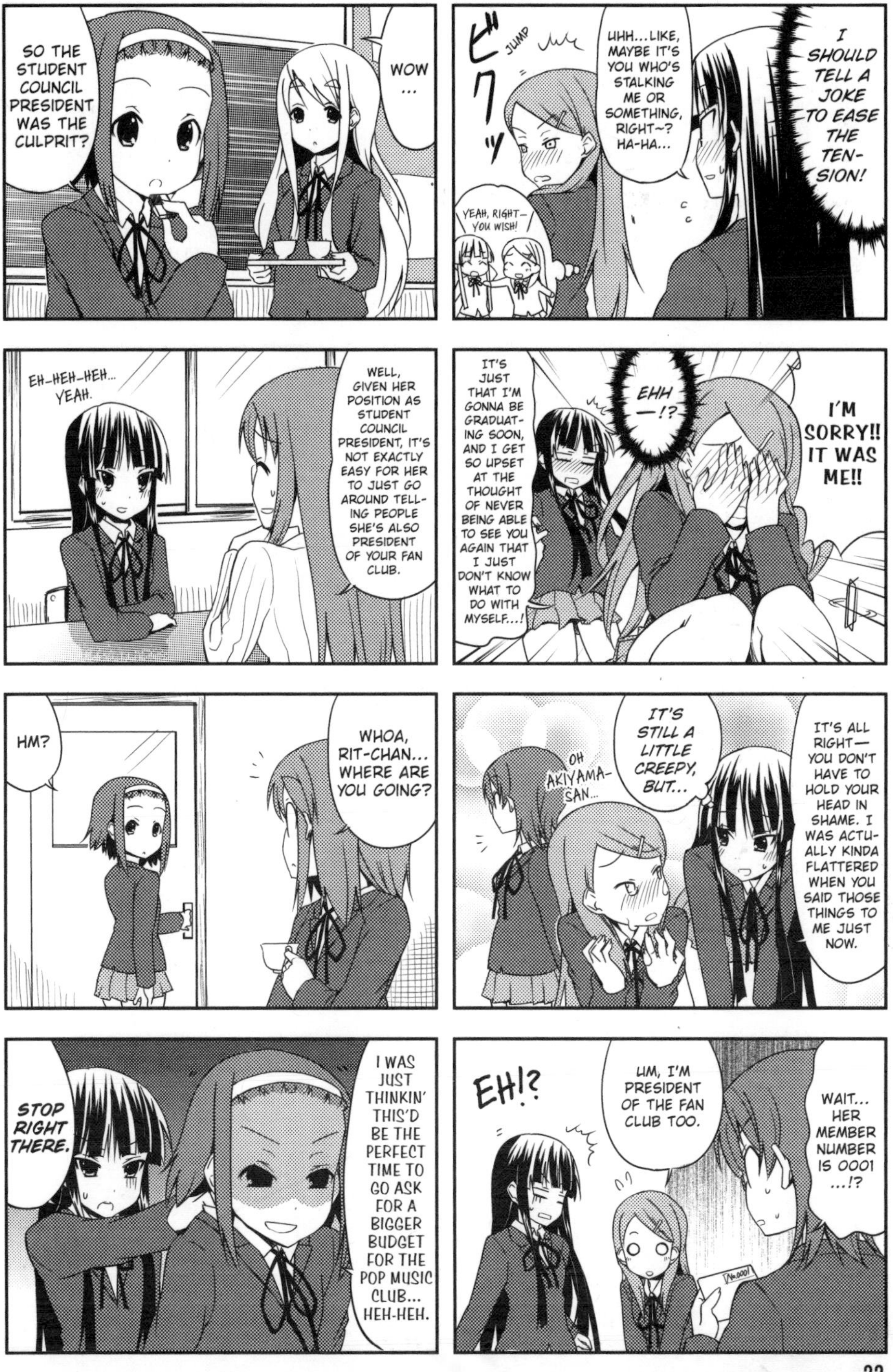
I SHOULD TELL A JOKE TO EASE THE TENSION!
UHH... LIKE, MAYBE IT'S YOU WHO'S STALKING ME OR SOMETHING, RIGHT~? HA-HA...
JUMP
YEAH, RIGHT— YOU WISH!
I'M SORRY!! IT WAS ME!!
EHH—!?
IT'S JUST THAT I'M GONNA BE GRADUATING SOON, AND I GET SO UPSET AT THE THOUGHT OF NEVER BEING ABLE TO SEE YOU AGAIN THAT I JUST DON'T KNOW WHAT TO DO WITH MYSELF...!
IT'S ALL RIGHT— YOU DON'T HAVE TO HOLD YOUR HEAD IN SHAME. I WAS ACTUALLY KINDA FLATTERED WHEN YOU SAID THOSE THINGS TO ME JUST NOW.
IT'S STILL A LITTLE CREEPY, BUT...
OH AKIYAMA-SAN...
WAIT... HER MEMBER NUMBER IS 0001 ...!?
UM, I'M PRESIDENT OF THE FAN CLUB TOO.
EH!?
WOW ...
SO THE STUDENT COUNCIL PRESIDENT WAS THE CULPRIT?
WELL, GIVEN HER POSITION AS STUDENT COUNCIL PRESIDENT, IT'S NOT EXACTLY EASY FOR HER TO JUST GO AROUND TELLING PEOPLE SHE'S ALSO PRESIDENT OF YOUR FAN CLUB.
EH-HEH-HEH... YEAH.
WHOA, RIT-CHAN... WHERE ARE YOU GOING?
HM?
I WAS JUST THINKIN' THIS'D BE THE PERFECT TIME TO GO ASK FOR A BIGGER BUDGET FOR THE POP MUSIC CLUB... HEH-HEH.
STOP RIGHT THERE.

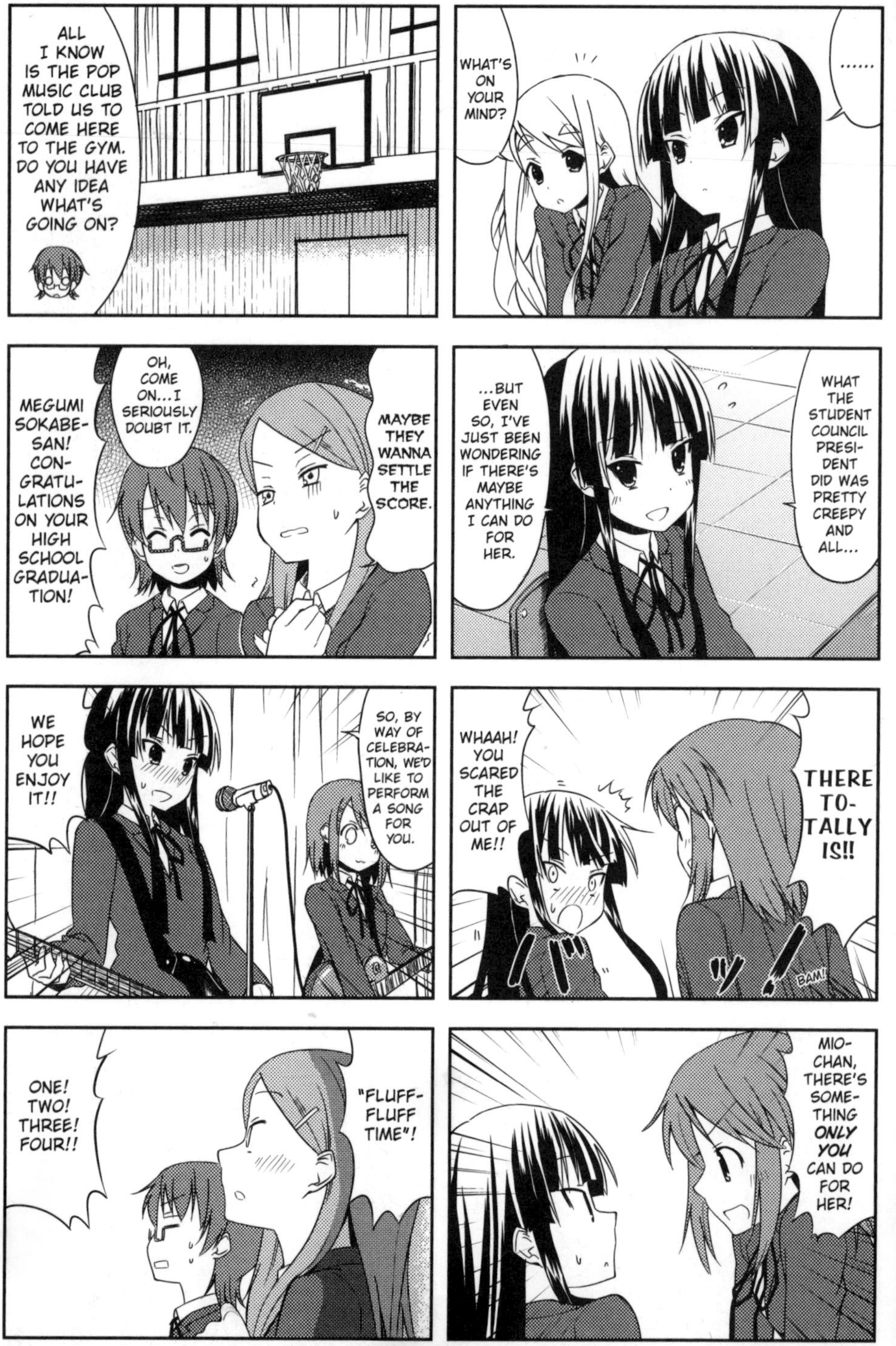
......
WHAT'S ON YOUR MIND?
WHAT THE STUDENT COUNCIL PRESIDENT DID WAS PRETTY CREEPY AND ALL...
...BUT EVEN SO, I'VE JUST BEEN WONDERING IF THERE'S MAYBE ANYTHING I CAN DO FOR HER.
THERE TO-TALLY IS!!
WHAAH! YOU SCARED THE CRAP OUT OF ME!!
BAM!
MIO-CHAN, THERE'S SOME-THING ONLY YOU CAN DO FOR HER!
ALL I KNOW IS THE POP MUSIC CLUB TOLD US TO COME HERE TO THE GYM. DO YOU HAVE ANY IDEA WHAT'S GOING ON?
MAYBE THEY WANNA SETTLE THE SCORE.
OH, COME ON...I SERIOUSLY DOUBT IT.
MEGUMI SOKABE-SAN! CON-GRATU-LATIONS ON YOUR HIGH SCHOOL GRADUA-TION!
SO, BY WAY OF CELEBRA-TION, WE'D LIKE TO PERFORM A SONG FOR YOU.
WE HOPE YOU ENJOY IT!!
"FLUFF-FLUFF TIME"!
ONE! TWO! THREE! FOUR!!

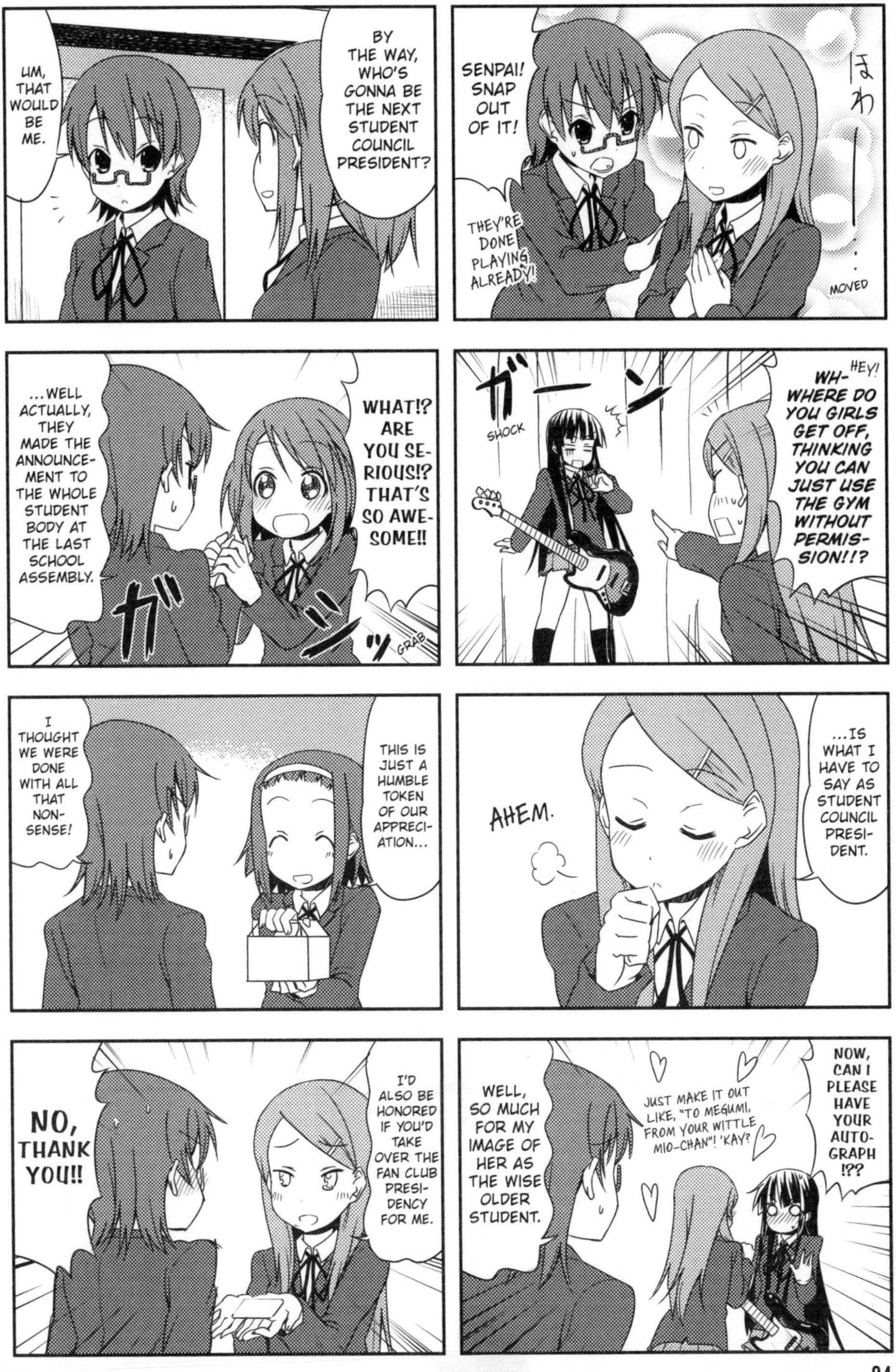

ほわー……
SENPAI! SNAP OUT OF IT!
MOVED
THEY'RE DONE PLAYING ALREADY!
HEY!
WH-WHERE DO YOU GIRLS GET OFF, THINKING YOU CAN JUST USE THE GYM WITHOUT PERMISSION!!?
ガーン
SHOCK
...IS WHAT I HAVE TO SAY AS STUDENT COUNCIL PRESIDENT.
AHEM.
NOW, CAN I PLEASE HAVE YOUR AUTOGRAPH!??
JUST MAKE IT OUT LIKE, "TO MEGUMI, FROM YOUR WITTLE MIO-CHAN"! 'KAY?
WELL, SO MUCH FOR MY IMAGE OF HER AS THE WISE OLDER STUDENT.
BY THE WAY, WHO'S GONNA BE THE NEXT STUDENT COUNCIL PRESIDENT?
UM, THAT WOULD BE ME.
WHAT!? ARE YOU SERIOUS!? THAT'S SO AWESOME!!
...WELL ACTUALLY, THEY MADE THE ANNOUNCEMENT TO THE WHOLE STUDENT BODY AT THE LAST SCHOOL ASSEMBLY.
ガシッ
GRAB
THIS IS JUST A HUMBLE TOKEN OF OUR APPRECIATION...
I THOUGHT WE WERE DONE WITH ALL THAT NONSENSE!
I'D ALSO BE HONORED IF YOU'D TAKE OVER THE FAN CLUB PRESIDENCY FOR ME.
NO, THANK YOU!!

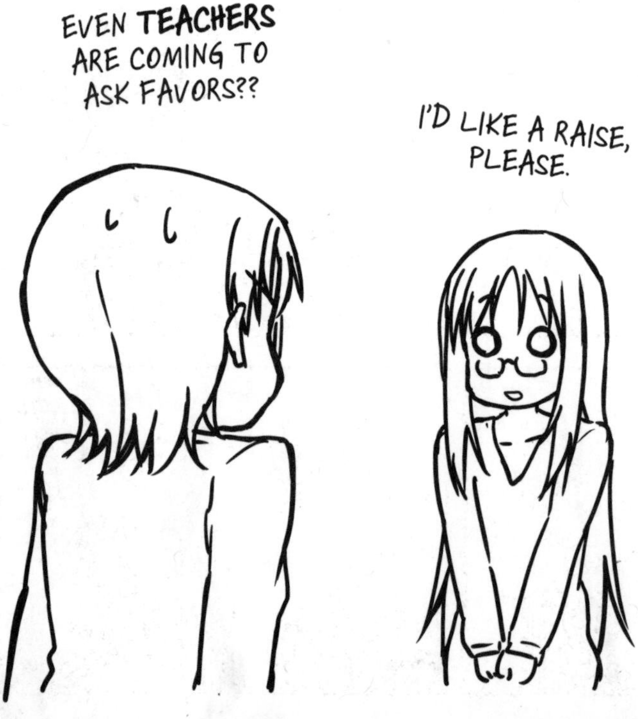

I'D LIKE A RAISE, PLEASE.
EVEN **TEACHERS** ARE COMING TO ASK FAVORS??

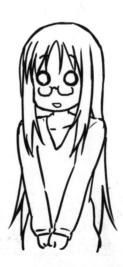

WHO ARE
YOU??

I'D LIKE A PART
IN THE SERIES,
PLEASE.

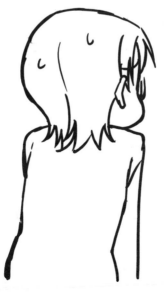
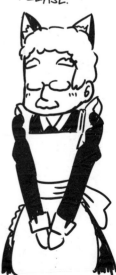

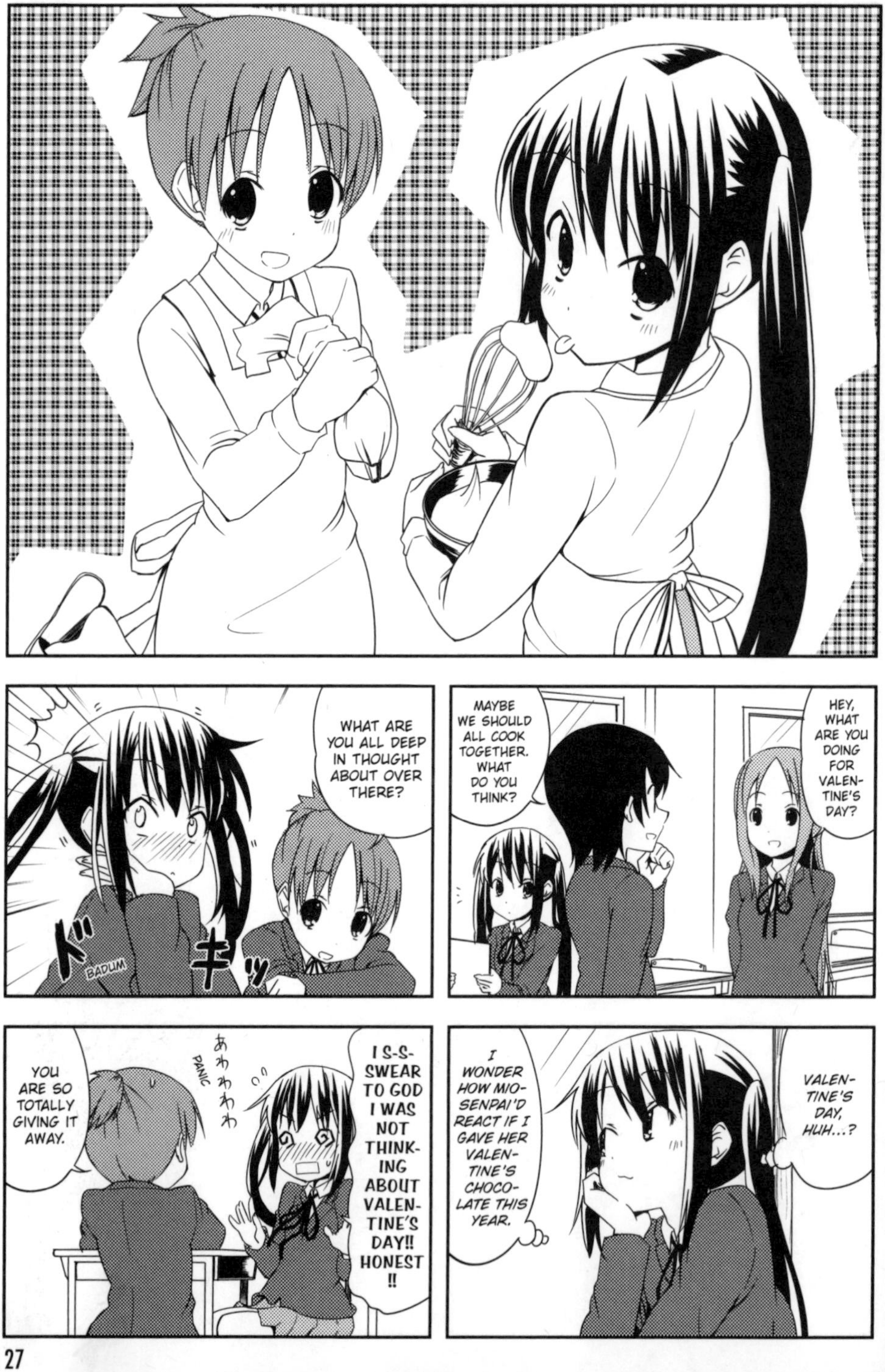
HEY, WHAT ARE YOU DOING FOR VALEN-TINE'S DAY?
MAYBE WE SHOULD ALL COOK TOGETHER. WHAT DO YOU THINK?
WHAT ARE YOU ALL DEEP IN THOUGHT ABOUT OVER THERE?
ドキッ
BADUM
VALEN-TINE'S DAY, HUH...?
I WONDER HOW MIO-SENPAI'D REACT IF I GAVE HER VALEN-TINE'S CHOCO-LATE THIS YEAR.
I S-S-SWEAR TO GOD I WAS NOT THINK-ING ABOUT VALEN-TINE'S DAY!! HONEST !!
あわわわわ
PANIC
YOU ARE SO TOTALLY GIVING IT AWAY.

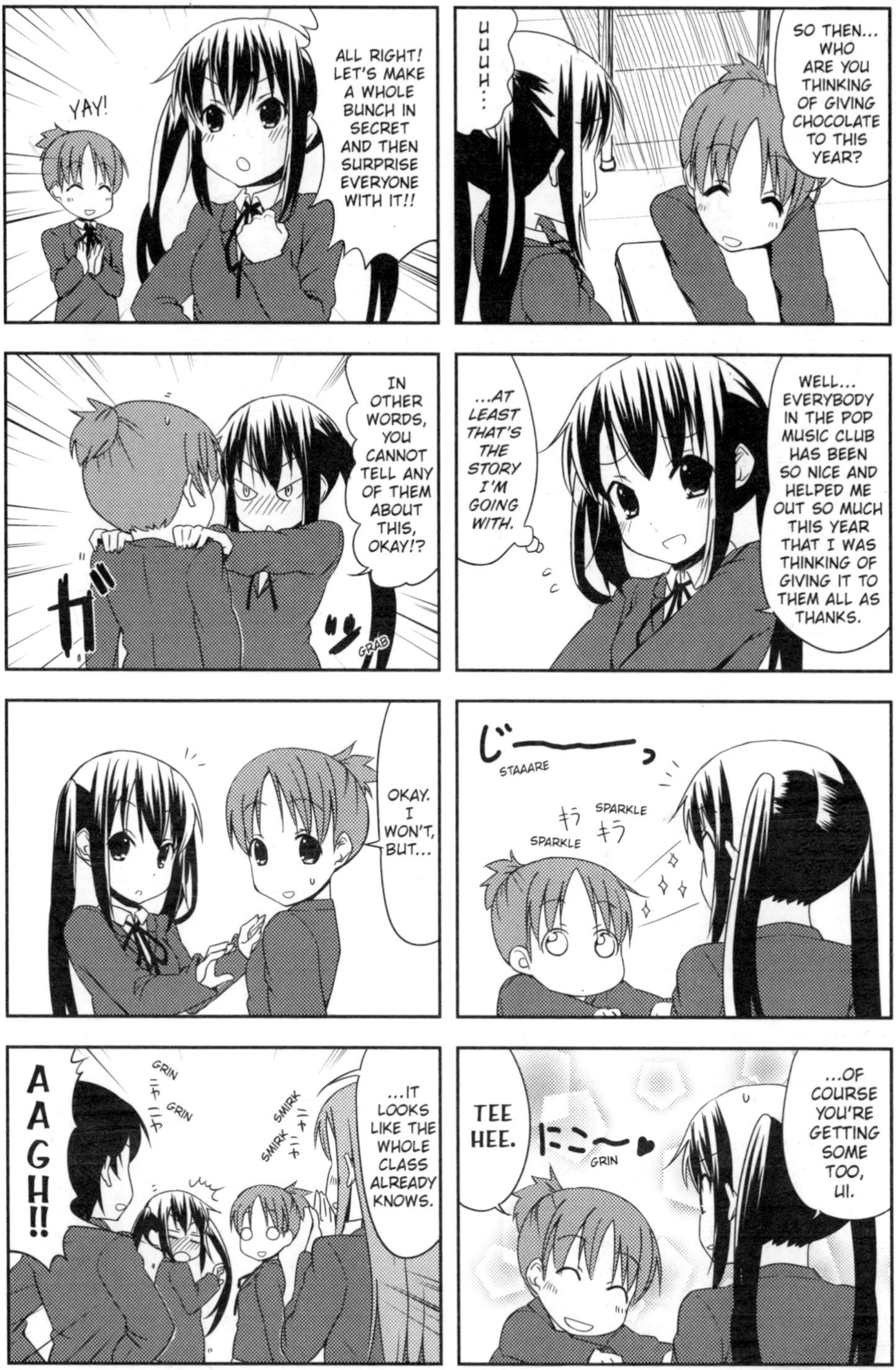
SO THEN... WHO ARE YOU THINKING OF GIVING CHOCOLATE TO THIS YEAR?
UUUH...
WELL... EVERYBODY IN THE POP MUSIC CLUB HAS BEEN SO NICE AND HELPED ME OUT SO MUCH THIS YEAR THAT I WAS THINKING OF GIVING IT TO THEM ALL AS THANKS.
...AT LEAST THAT'S THE STORY I'M GOING WITH.
じーーーっ
STAAARE
キラ
SPARKLE
キラ
SPARKLE
...OF COURSE YOU'RE GETTING SOME TOO, UI.
にこ～♥
GRIN
TEE HEE.
ALL RIGHT! LET'S MAKE A WHOLE BUNCH IN SECRET AND THEN SURPRISE EVERYONE WITH IT!!
YAY!
IN OTHER WORDS, YOU CANNOT TELL ANY OF THEM ABOUT THIS, OKAY!?
ガッ
GRAB
OKAY. I WON'T, BUT...
...IT LOOKS LIKE THE WHOLE CLASS ALREADY KNOWS.
ニヤ
SMIRK
ニヤ
SMIRK
ニヤ
GRIN
ニヤ
GRIN
AAGH!!

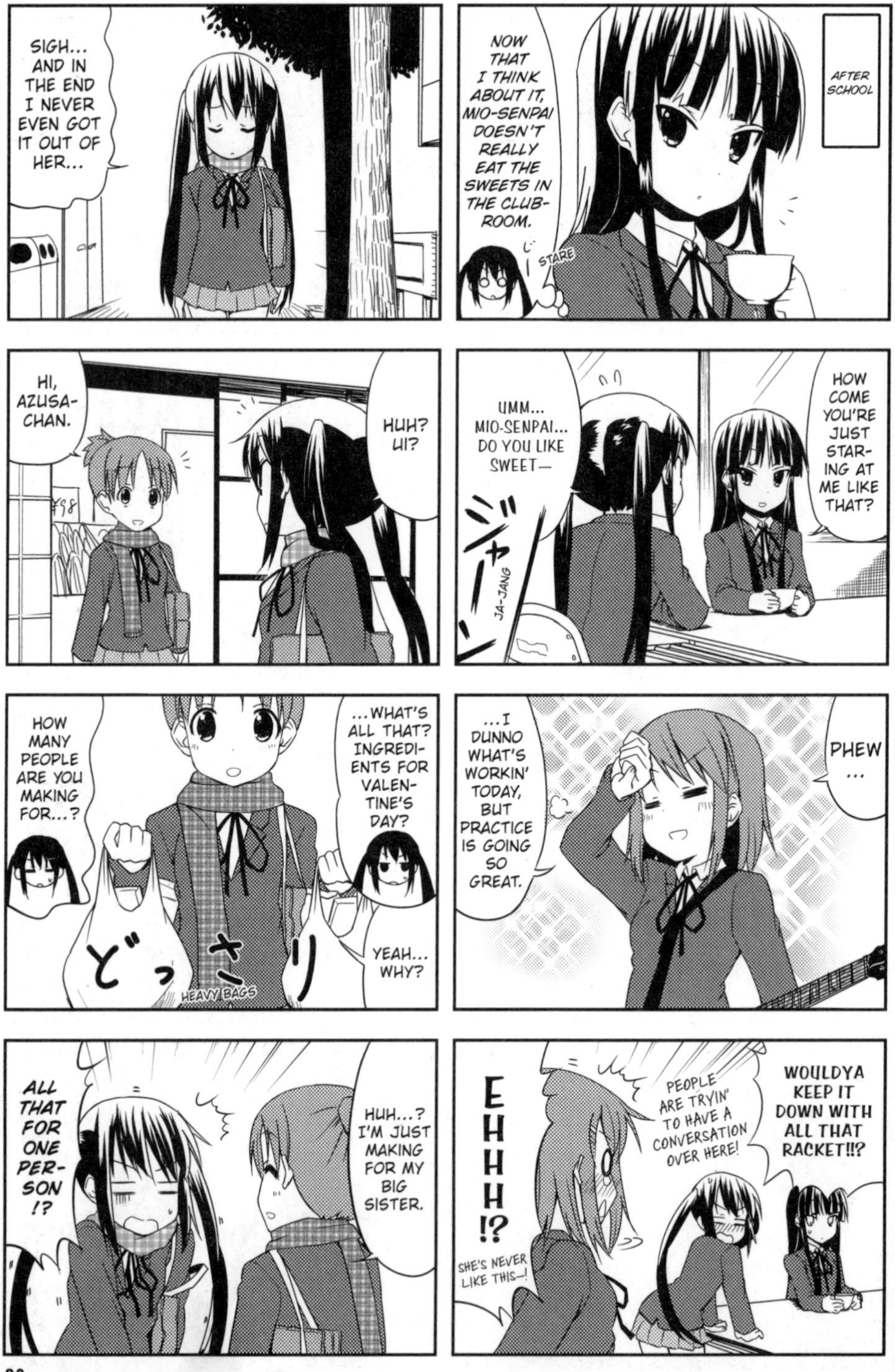
AFTER SCHOOL
NOW THAT I THINK ABOUT IT, MIO-SENPAI DOESN'T REALLY EAT THE SWEETS IN THE CLUB-ROOM.
STARE
HOW COME YOU'RE JUST STARING AT ME LIKE THAT?
UMM... MIO-SENPAI... DO YOU LIKE SWEET—
JA-JANG
PHEW...
...I DUNNO WHAT'S WORKIN' TODAY, BUT PRACTICE IS GOING SO GREAT.
WOULDYA KEEP IT DOWN WITH ALL THAT RACKET!!?
PEOPLE ARE TRYIN' TO HAVE A CONVERSATION OVER HERE!
EHHHH!?
SHE'S NEVER LIKE THIS—!
SIGH... AND IN THE END I NEVER EVEN GOT IT OUT OF HER...
HUH? UI?
HI, AZUSA-CHAN.
...WHAT'S ALL THAT? INGREDIENTS FOR VALENTINE'S DAY?
YEAH... WHY?
HOW MANY PEOPLE ARE YOU MAKING FOR...?
HEAVY BAGS
HUH...? I'M JUST MAKING FOR MY BIG SISTER.
ALL THAT FOR ONE PERSON!?

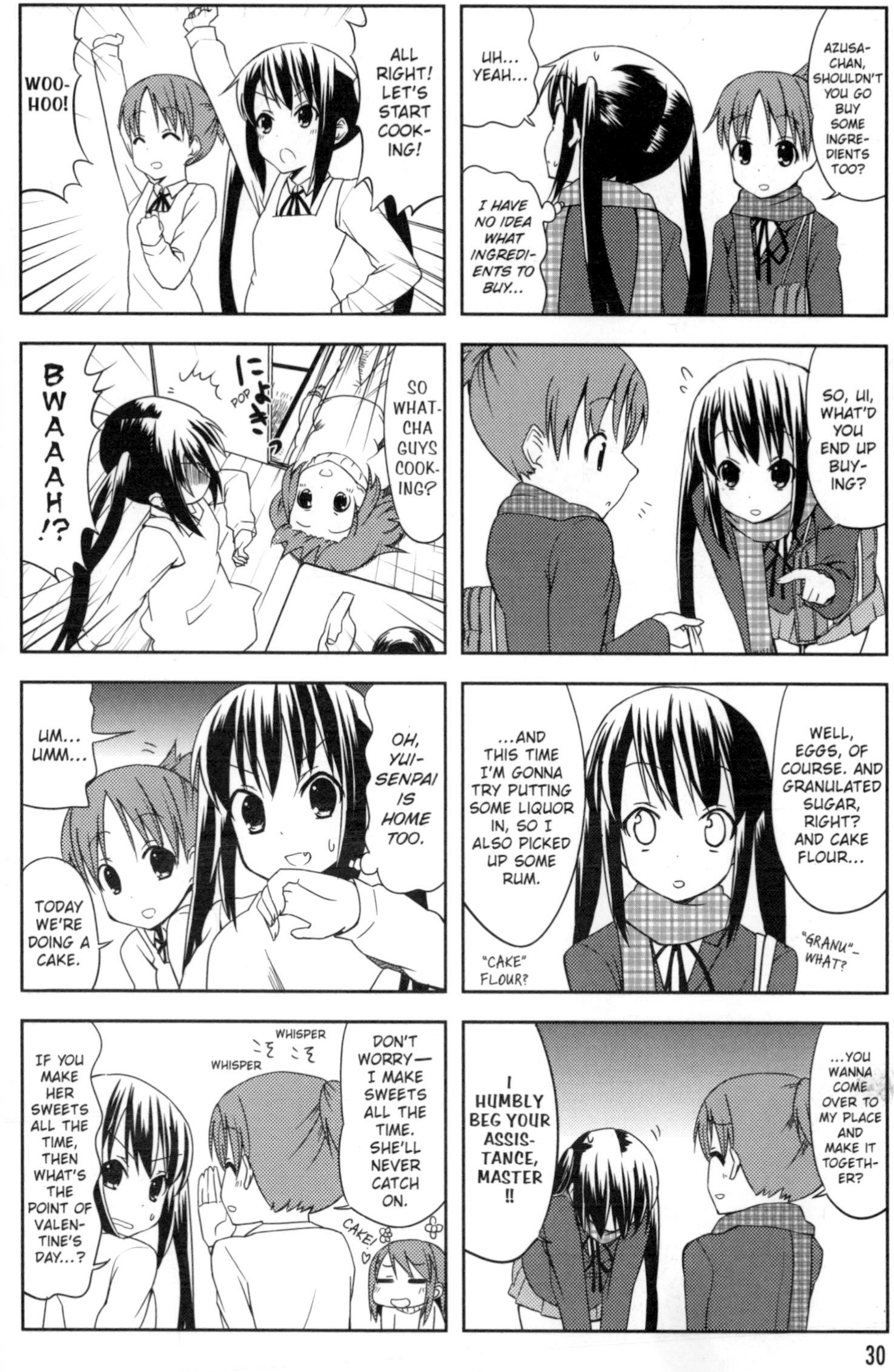
AZUSA-CHAN, SHOULDN'T YOU GO BUY SOME INGREDIENTS TOO?
UH... YEAH...
I HAVE NO IDEA WHAT INGREDIENTS TO BUY...
SO, UI, WHAT'D YOU END UP BUYING?
WELL, EGGS, OF COURSE. AND GRANULATED SUGAR, RIGHT? AND CAKE FLOUR...
...AND THIS TIME I'M GONNA TRY PUTTING SOME LIQUOR IN, SO I ALSO PICKED UP SOME RUM.
"GRANU"-WHAT?
"CAKE" FLOUR?
...YOU WANNA COME OVER TO MY PLACE AND MAKE IT TOGETHER?
I HUMBLY BEG YOUR ASSISTANCE, MASTER!!
ALL RIGHT! LET'S START COOKING!
WOO-HOO!
SO WHATCHA GUYS COOKING?
にょきっ
POP
BWAAAAH!?
OH, YUI-SENPAI IS HOME TOO.
UM... UMM...
TODAY WE'RE DOING A CAKE.
DON'T WORRY—I MAKE SWEETS ALL THE TIME. SHE'LL NEVER CATCH ON.
こそこそ
WHISPER
WHISPER
IF YOU MAKE HER SWEETS ALL THE TIME, THEN WHAT'S THE POINT OF VALENTINE'S DAY...?
CAKE!

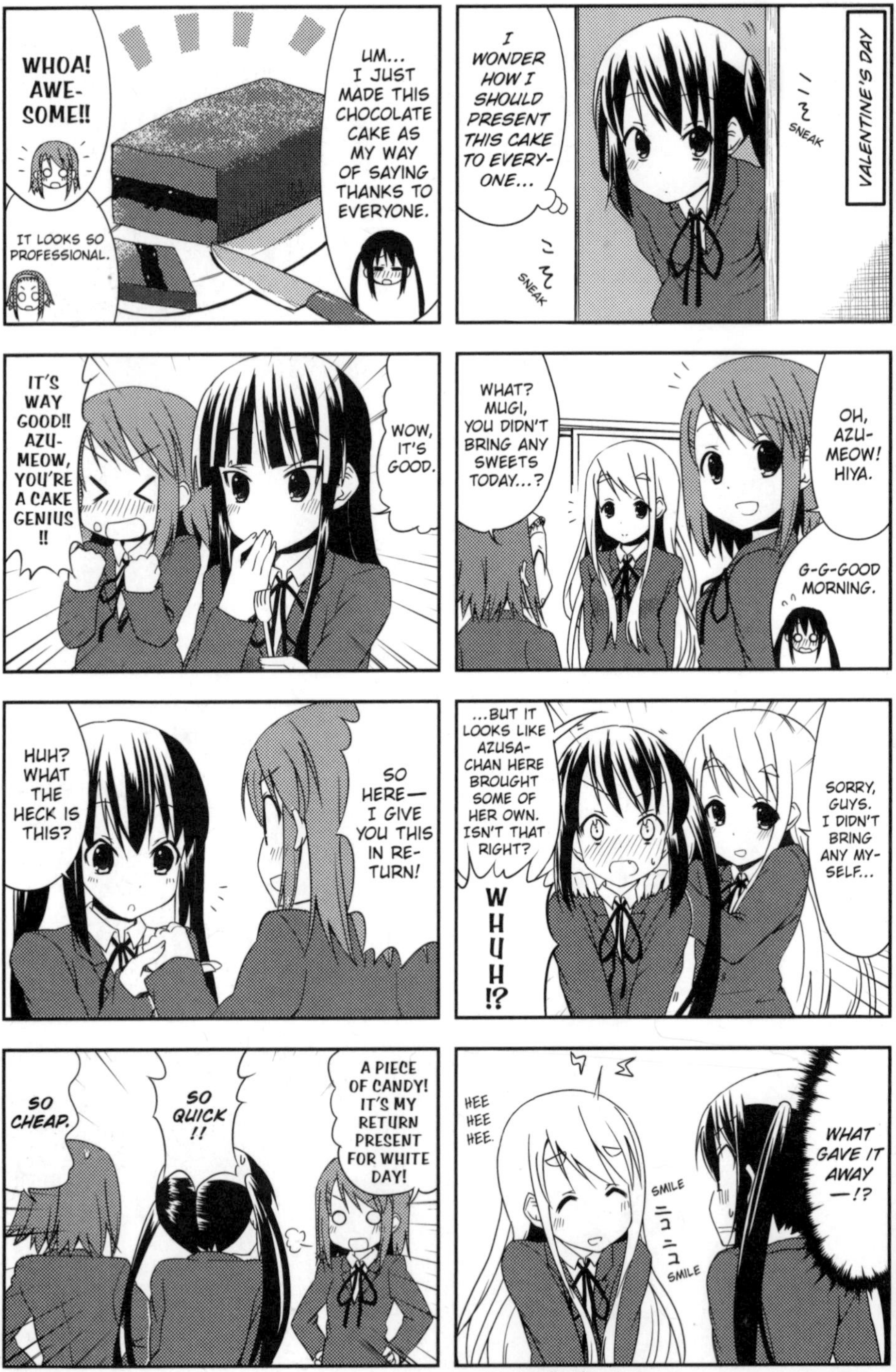
VALENTINE'S DAY
SNEAK
I WONDER HOW I SHOULD PRESENT THIS CAKE TO EVERYONE...
SNEAK
OH, AZU-MEOW! HIYA.
G-G-GOOD MORNING.
WHAT? MUGI, YOU DIDN'T BRING ANY SWEETS TODAY...?
SORRY, GUYS. I DIDN'T BRING ANY MYSELF...
...BUT IT LOOKS LIKE AZUSA-CHAN HERE BROUGHT SOME OF HER OWN. ISN'T THAT RIGHT?
WHUH!?
WHAT GAVE IT AWAY—!?
SMILE
SMILE
HEE HEE HEE.
UM... I JUST MADE THIS CHOCOLATE CAKE AS MY WAY OF SAYING THANKS TO EVERYONE.
WHOA! AWE-SOME!!
IT LOOKS SO PROFESSIONAL.
WOW, IT'S GOOD.
IT'S WAY GOOD!! AZU-MEOW, YOU'RE A CAKE GENIUS!!
SO HERE—I GIVE YOU THIS IN RE-TURN!
HUH? WHAT THE HECK IS THIS?
A PIECE OF CANDY! IT'S MY RETURN PRESENT FOR WHITE DAY!
SO QUICK!!
SO CHEAP.

GIRLS' MIND RADIO RECEPTION

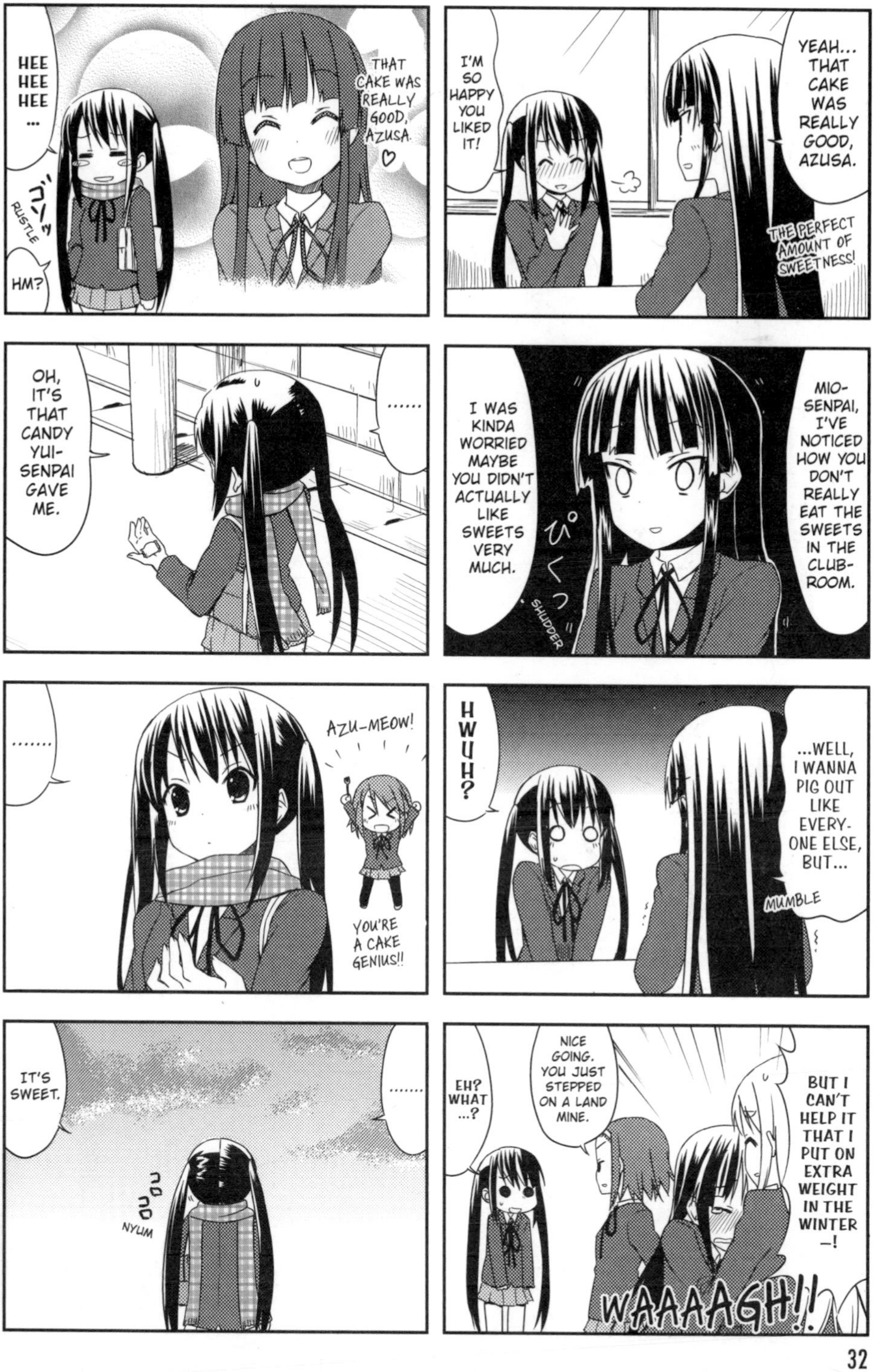
YEAH... THAT CAKE WAS REALLY GOOD, AZUSA.
THE PERFECT AMOUNT OF SWEETNESS!
I'M SO HAPPY YOU LIKED IT!
THAT CAKE WAS REALLY GOOD, AZUSA. ♡
HEE HEE HEE ...
ゴソッ
RUSTLE
HM?
MIO-SENPAI, I'VE NOTICED HOW YOU DON'T REALLY EAT THE SWEETS IN THE CLUB-ROOM.
I WAS KINDA WORRIED MAYBE YOU DIDN'T ACTUALLY LIKE SWEETS VERY MUCH.
ぴくっ
SHUDDER
......
OH, IT'S THAT CANDY YUI-SENPAI GAVE ME.
...WELL, I WANNA PIG OUT LIKE EVERY-ONE ELSE, BUT...
MUMBLE
HWUH?
AZU-MEOW!
YOU'RE A CAKE GENIUS!!
....
BUT I CAN'T HELP IT THAT I PUT ON EXTRA WEIGHT IN THE WINTER—!
NICE GOING. YOU JUST STEPPED ON A LAND MINE.
EH? WHAT ...?
WAAAAGH!!
....
IT'S SWEET.
コロコロ
NYUM

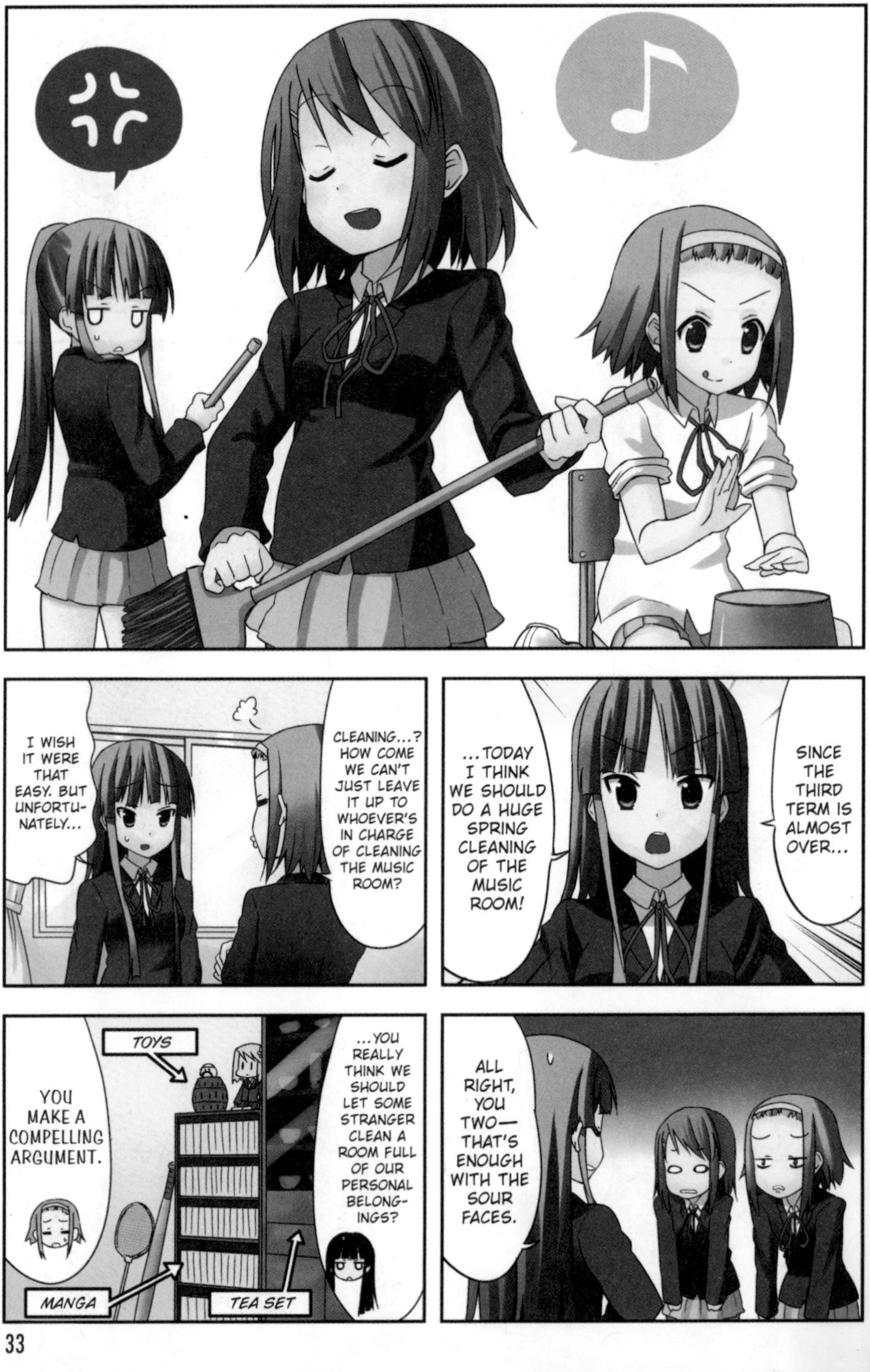
SINCE THE THIRD TERM IS ALMOST OVER...
...TODAY I THINK WE SHOULD DO A HUGE SPRING CLEANING OF THE MUSIC ROOM!
CLEANING...? HOW COME WE CAN'T JUST LEAVE IT UP TO WHOEVER'S IN CHARGE OF CLEANING THE MUSIC ROOM?
I WISH IT WERE THAT EASY. BUT UNFORTUNATELY...
ALL RIGHT, YOU TWO—THAT'S ENOUGH WITH THE SOUR FACES.
...YOU REALLY THINK WE SHOULD LET SOME STRANGER CLEAN A ROOM FULL OF OUR PERSONAL BELONGINGS?
TOYS
YOU MAKE A COMPELLING ARGUMENT.
TEA SET
MANGA

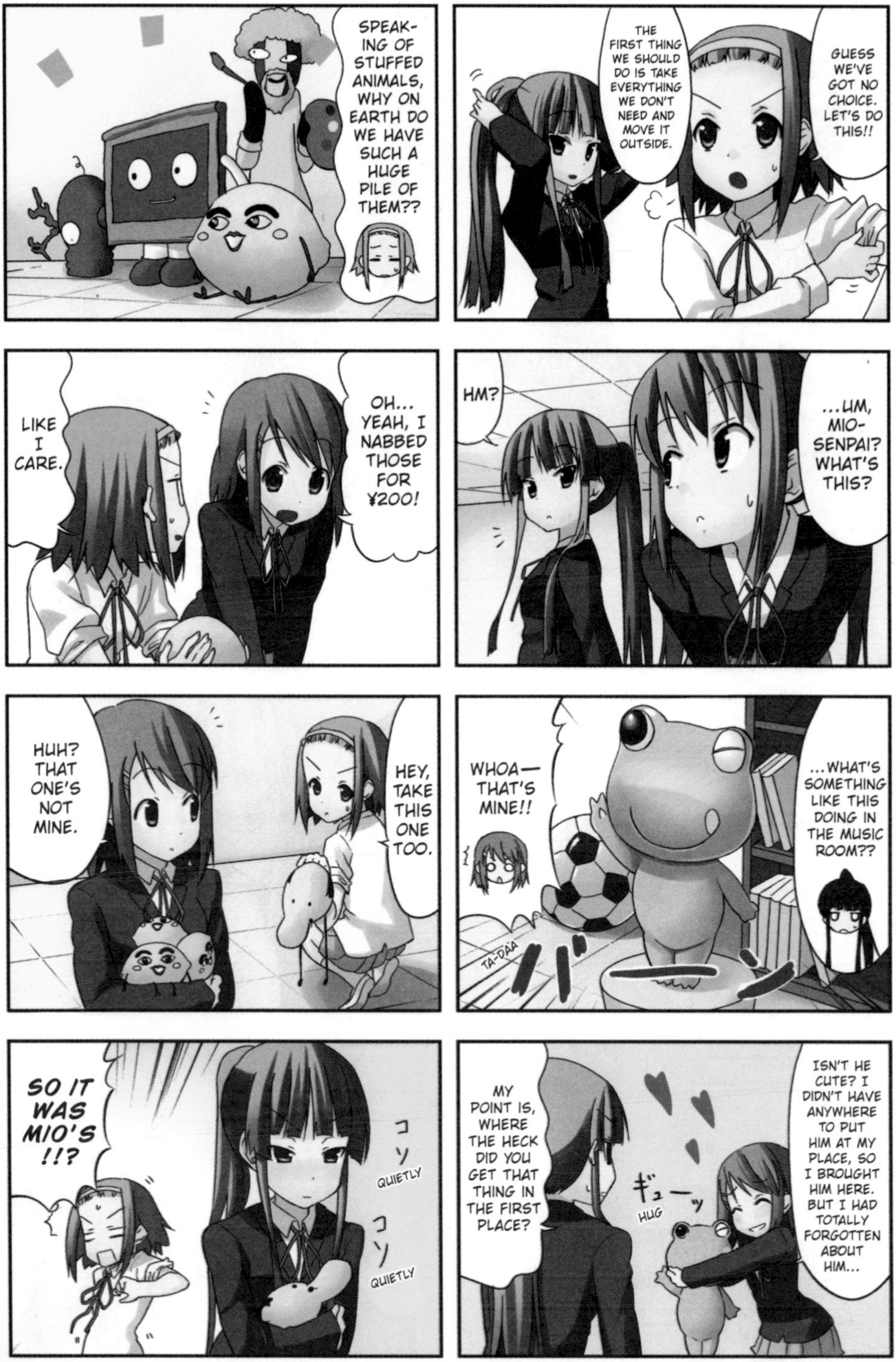
GUESS WE'VE GOT NO CHOICE. LET'S DO THIS!!
THE FIRST THING WE SHOULD DO IS TAKE EVERYTHING WE DON'T NEED AND MOVE IT OUTSIDE.
SPEAK-ING OF STUFFED ANIMALS, WHY ON EARTH DO WE HAVE SUCH A HUGE PILE OF THEM??
...UM, MIO-SENPAI? WHAT'S THIS?
HM?
OH... YEAH, I NABBED THOSE FOR ¥200!
LIKE I CARE.
...WHAT'S SOMETHING LIKE THIS DOING IN THE MUSIC ROOM??
WHOA— THAT'S MINE!!
TA-DAA
HEY, TAKE THIS ONE TOO.
HUH? THAT ONE'S NOT MINE.
ISN'T HE CUTE? I DIDN'T HAVE ANYWHERE TO PUT HIM AT MY PLACE, SO I BROUGHT HIM HERE. BUT I HAD TOTALLY FORGOTTEN ABOUT HIM...
ギューッ
HUG
MY POINT IS, WHERE THE HECK DID YOU GET THAT THING IN THE FIRST PLACE?
コソ
QUIETLY
コソ
QUIETLY
SO IT WAS MIO'S!!?

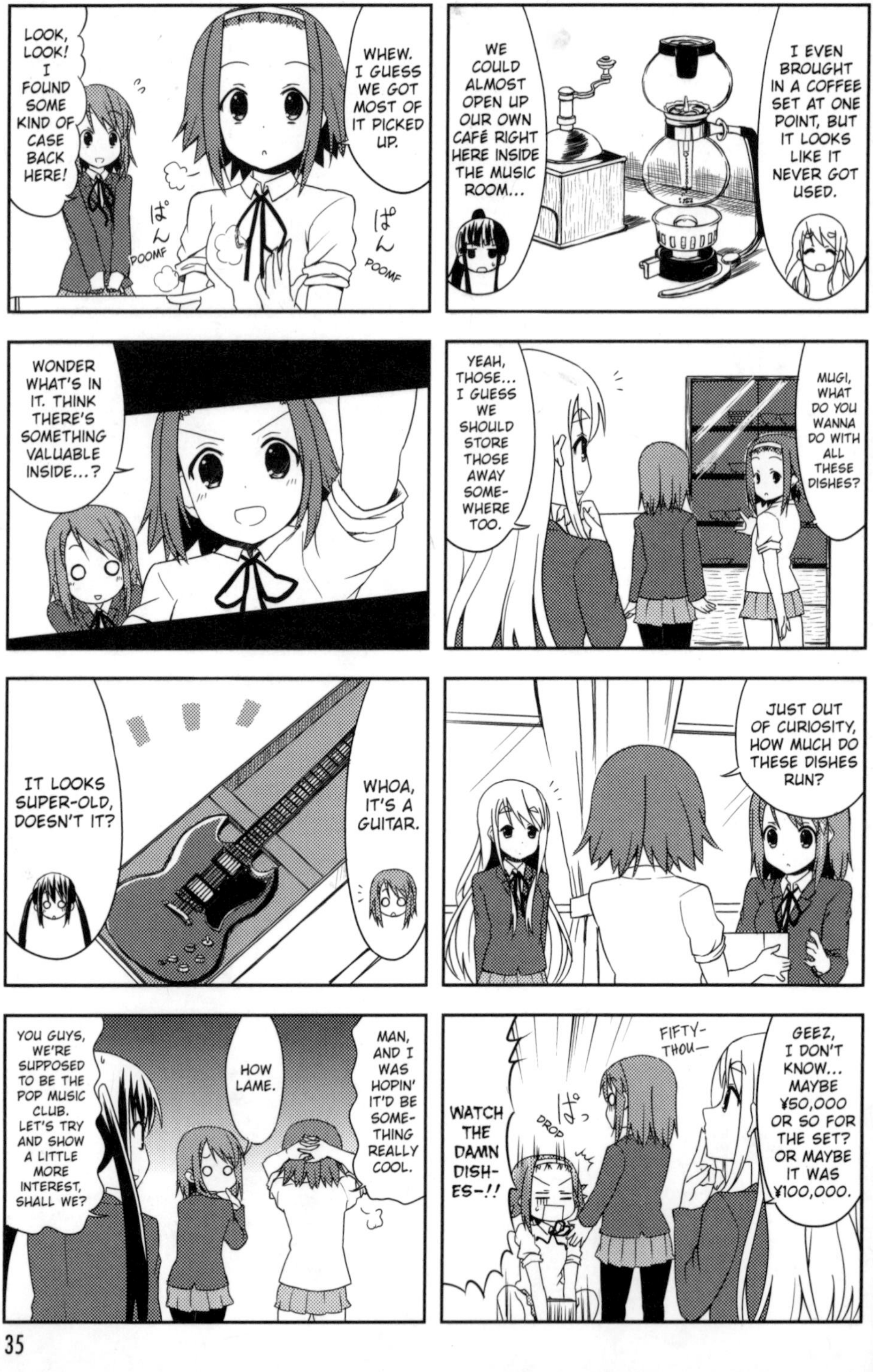
I EVEN BROUGHT IN A COFFEE SET AT ONE POINT, BUT IT LOOKS LIKE IT NEVER GOT USED.
WE COULD ALMOST OPEN UP OUR OWN CAFÉ RIGHT HERE INSIDE THE MUSIC ROOM...
WHEW. I GUESS WE GOT MOST OF IT PICKED UP.
ぱん POOMF
ぱん POOMF
LOOK, LOOK! I FOUND SOME KIND OF CASE BACK HERE!
MUGI, WHAT DO YOU WANNA DO WITH ALL THESE DISHES?
YEAH, THOSE... I GUESS WE SHOULD STORE THOSE AWAY SOME-WHERE TOO.
WONDER WHAT'S IN IT. THINK THERE'S SOMETHING VALUABLE INSIDE...?
JUST OUT OF CURIOSITY, HOW MUCH DO THESE DISHES RUN?
WHOA, IT'S A GUITAR.
IT LOOKS SUPER-OLD, DOESN'T IT?
GEEZ, I DON'T KNOW... MAYBE ¥50,000 OR SO FOR THE SET? OR MAYBE IT WAS ¥100,000.
FIFTY-THOU—
ぱっ DROP
WATCH THE DAMN DISH-ES—!!
MAN, AND I WAS HOPIN' IT'D BE SOME-THING REALLY COOL.
HOW LAME.
YOU GUYS, WE'RE SUPPOSED TO BE THE POP MUSIC CLUB. LET'S TRY AND SHOW A LITTLE MORE INTEREST, SHALL WE?

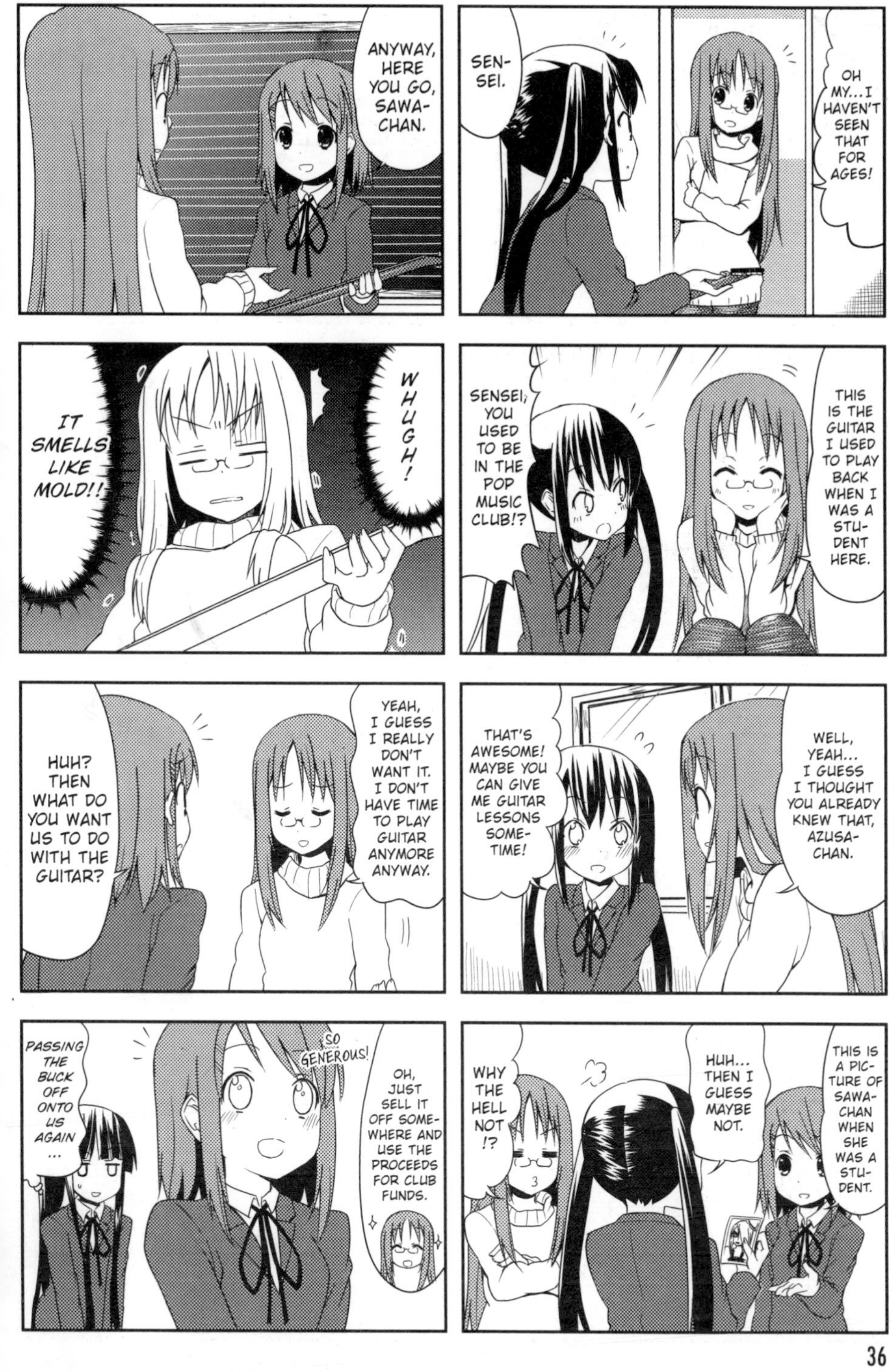
OH MY... I HAVEN'T SEEN THAT FOR AGES!
SEN-SEI.
THIS IS THE GUITAR I USED TO PLAY BACK WHEN I WAS A STU-DENT HERE.
SENSEI, YOU USED TO BE IN THE POP MUSIC CLUB!?
WELL, YEAH... I GUESS I THOUGHT YOU ALREADY KNEW THAT, AZUSA-CHAN.
THAT'S AWESOME! MAYBE YOU CAN GIVE ME GUITAR LESSONS SOME-TIME!
THIS IS A PIC-TURE OF SAWA-CHAN WHEN SHE WAS A STU-DENT.
HUH... THEN I GUESS MAYBE NOT.
WHY THE HELL NOT !?
ANYWAY, HERE YOU GO, SAWA-CHAN.
WHUGH!
IT SMELLS LIKE MOLD!!
YEAH, I GUESS I REALLY DON'T WANT IT. I DON'T HAVE TIME TO PLAY GUITAR ANYMORE ANYWAY.
HUH? THEN WHAT DO YOU WANT US TO DO WITH THE GUITAR?
SO GENEROUS!
OH, JUST SELL IT OFF SOME-WHERE AND USE THE PROCEEDS FOR CLUB FUNDS.
PASSING THE BUCK OFF ONTO US AGAIN ...

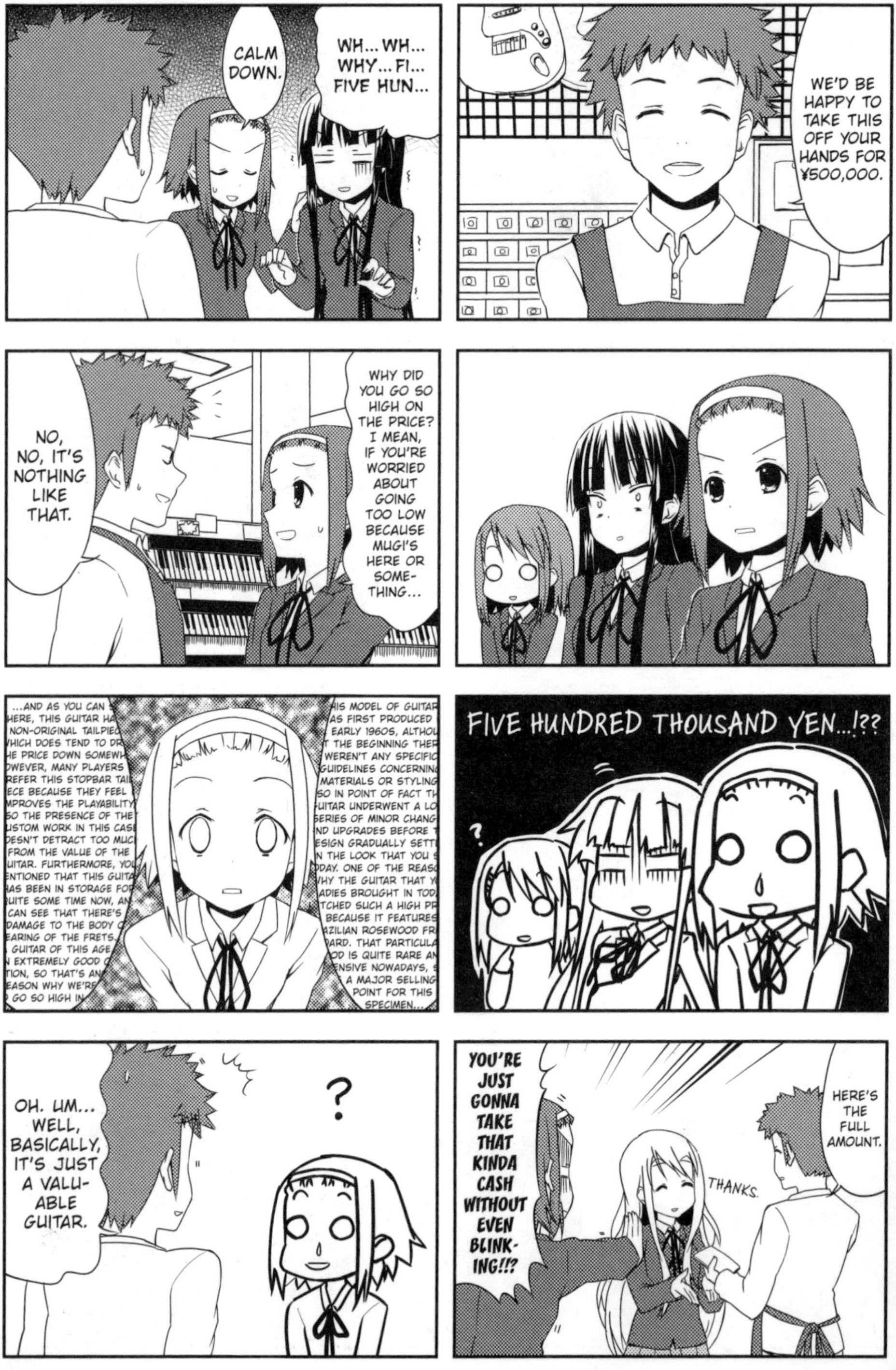
WE'D BE HAPPY TO TAKE THIS OFF YOUR HANDS FOR ¥500,000.
WH... WH... WHY... FI... FIVE HUN...
CALM DOWN.
WHY DID YOU GO SO HIGH ON THE PRICE? I MEAN, IF YOU'RE WORRIED ABOUT GOING TOO LOW BECAUSE MUGI'S HERE OR SOME-THING...
NO, NO, IT'S NOTHING LIKE THAT.
FIVE HUNDRED THOUSAND YEN...!??
?
IS MODEL OF GUITAR AS FIRST PRODUCED EARLY 1960S, ALTHOU T THE BEGINNING THER WEREN'T ANY SPECIFIC GUIDELINES CONCERNING MATERIALS OR STYLING SO IN POINT OF FACT TH UITAR UNDERWENT A LO SERIES OF MINOR CHANG ND UPGRADES BEFORE ESIGN GRADUALLY SETT N THE LOOK THAT YOU DAY. ONE OF THE REAS HY THE GUITAR THAT Y ADIES BROUGHT IN TOD TCHED SUCH A HIGH PR BECAUSE IT FEATURES AZILIAN ROSEWOOD FR ARD. THAT PARTICULA OD IS QUITE RARE AN NSIVE NOWADAYS, A MAJOR SELLING POINT FOR THIS SPECIMEN...
...AND AS YOU CAN HERE, THIS GUITAR HA NON-ORIGINAL TAILPIEC HICH DOES TEND TO DR E PRICE DOWN SOMEWH WEVER, MANY PLAYERS REFER THIS STOPBAR TAI ECE BECAUSE THEY FEEL MPROVES THE PLAYABILITY SO THE PRESENCE OF THE USTOM WORK IN THIS CAS ESN'T DETRACT TOO MUC FROM THE VALUE OF THE UITAR. FURTHERMORE, YO ENTIONED THAT THIS GUITA HAS BEEN IN STORAGE FO UITE SOME TIME NOW, AN CAN SEE THAT THERE'S DAMAGE TO THE BODY EARING OF THE FRETS. GUITAR OF THIS AGE EXTREMELY GOOD TION, SO THAT'S AN EASON WHY WE'R GO SO HIGH IN
HERE'S THE FULL AMOUNT.
THANKS.
YOU'RE JUST GONNA TAKE THAT KINDA CASH WITHOUT EVEN BLINK-ING!!?
?
OH. UM... WELL, BASICALLY, IT'S JUST A VALU-ABLE GUITAR.

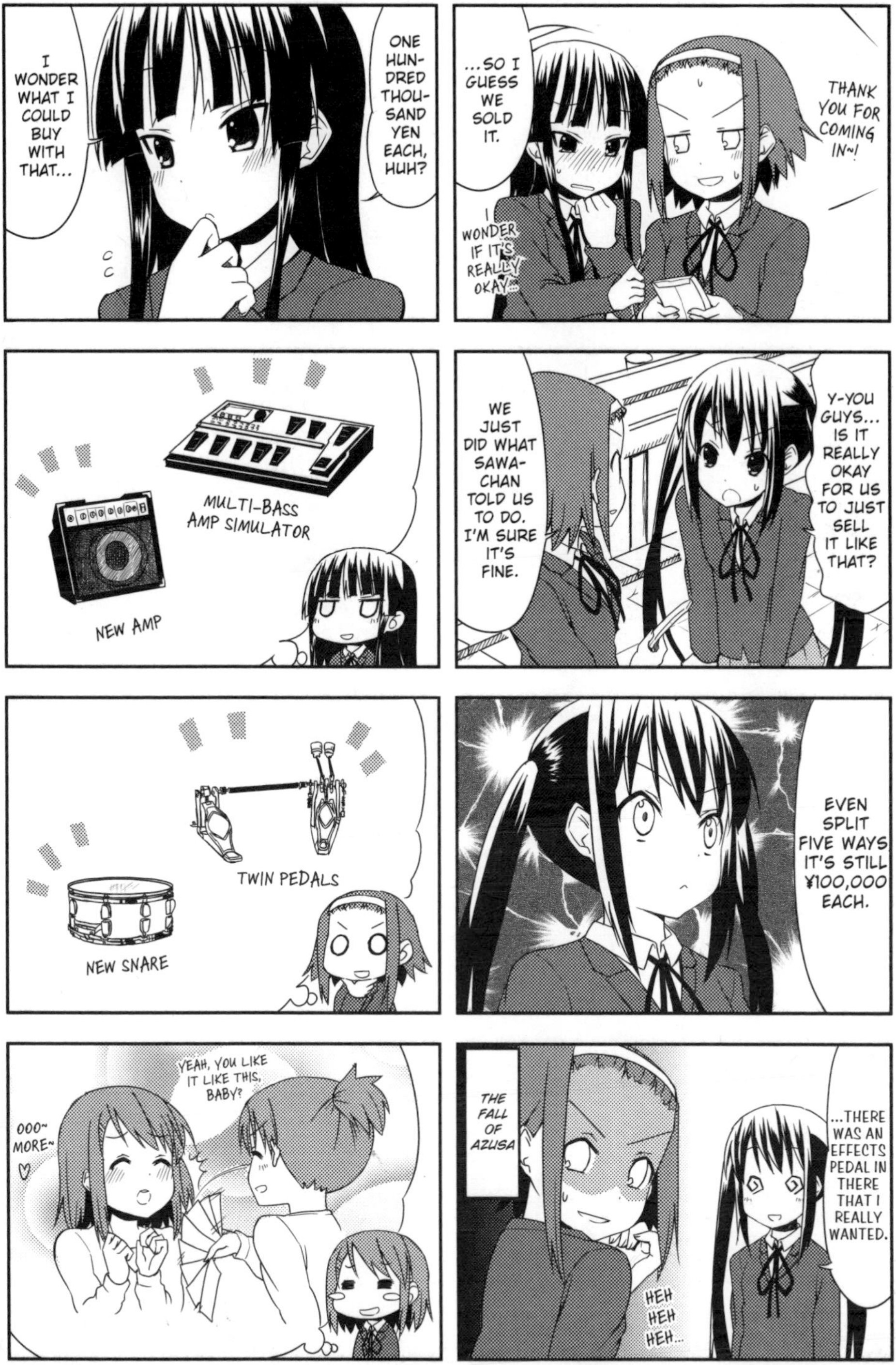
THANK YOU FOR COMING IN~!
...SO I GUESS WE SOLD IT.
I WONDER IF IT'S REALLY OKAY...
ONE HUNDRED THOUSAND YEN EACH, HUH?
I WONDER WHAT I COULD BUY WITH THAT...
Y-YOU GUYS... IS IT REALLY OKAY FOR US TO JUST SELL IT LIKE THAT?
WE JUST DID WHAT SAWA-CHAN TOLD US TO DO. I'M SURE IT'S FINE.
MULTI-BASS AMP SIMULATOR
NEW AMP
EVEN SPLIT FIVE WAYS IT'S STILL ¥100,000 EACH.
TWIN PEDALS
NEW SNARE
...THERE WAS AN EFFECTS PEDAL IN THERE THAT I REALLY WANTED.
THE FALL OF AZUSA
HEH HEH HEH...
YEAH, YOU LIKE IT LIKE THIS, BABY?
OOO~ MORE~ ♥

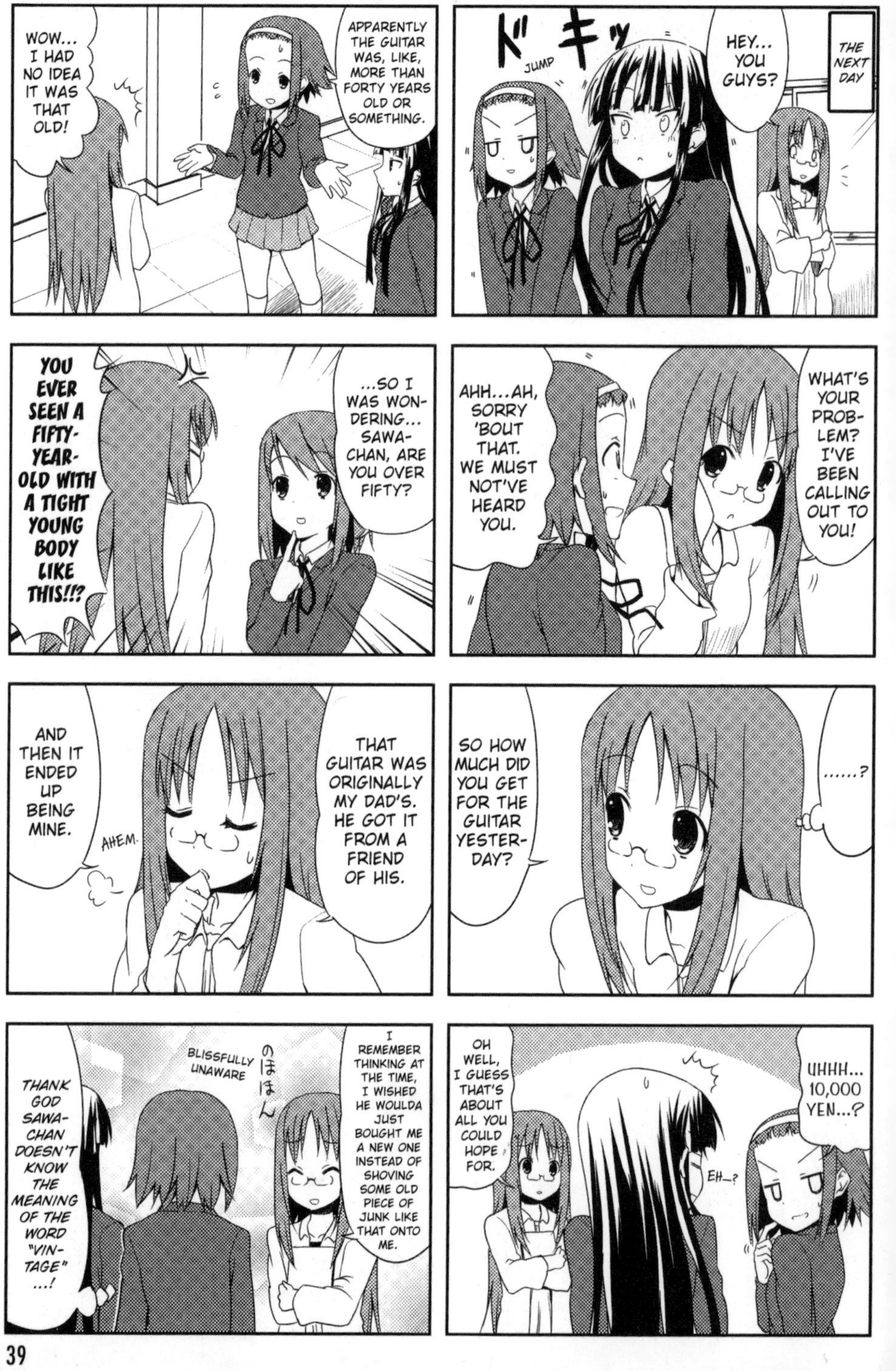
THE NEXT DAY
ドキッ
JUMP
HEY... YOU GUYS?
APPARENTLY THE GUITAR WAS, LIKE, MORE THAN FORTY YEARS OLD OR SOMETHING.
WOW... I HAD NO IDEA IT WAS THAT OLD!
WHAT'S YOUR PROBLEM? I'VE BEEN CALLING OUT TO YOU!
AHH...AH, SORRY 'BOUT THAT. WE MUST NOT'VE HEARD YOU.
...SO I WAS WONDERING... SAWA-CHAN, ARE YOU OVER FIFTY?
YOU EVER SEEN A FIFTY-YEAR-OLD WITH A TIGHT YOUNG BODY LIKE THIS!!?
......?
SO HOW MUCH DID YOU GET FOR THE GUITAR YESTERDAY?
THAT GUITAR WAS ORIGINALLY MY DAD'S. HE GOT IT FROM A FRIEND OF HIS.
AHEM.
AND THEN IT ENDED UP BEING MINE.
UHHH... 10,000 YEN...?
EH...?
OH WELL, I GUESS THAT'S ABOUT ALL YOU COULD HOPE FOR.
I REMEMBER THINKING AT THE TIME, I WISHED HE WOULDA JUST BOUGHT ME A NEW ONE INSTEAD OF SHOVING SOME OLD PIECE OF JUNK LIKE THAT ONTO ME.
のほほん
BLISSFULLY UNAWARE
THANK GOD SAWA-CHAN DOESN'T KNOW THE MEANING OF THE WORD "VINTAGE"...!

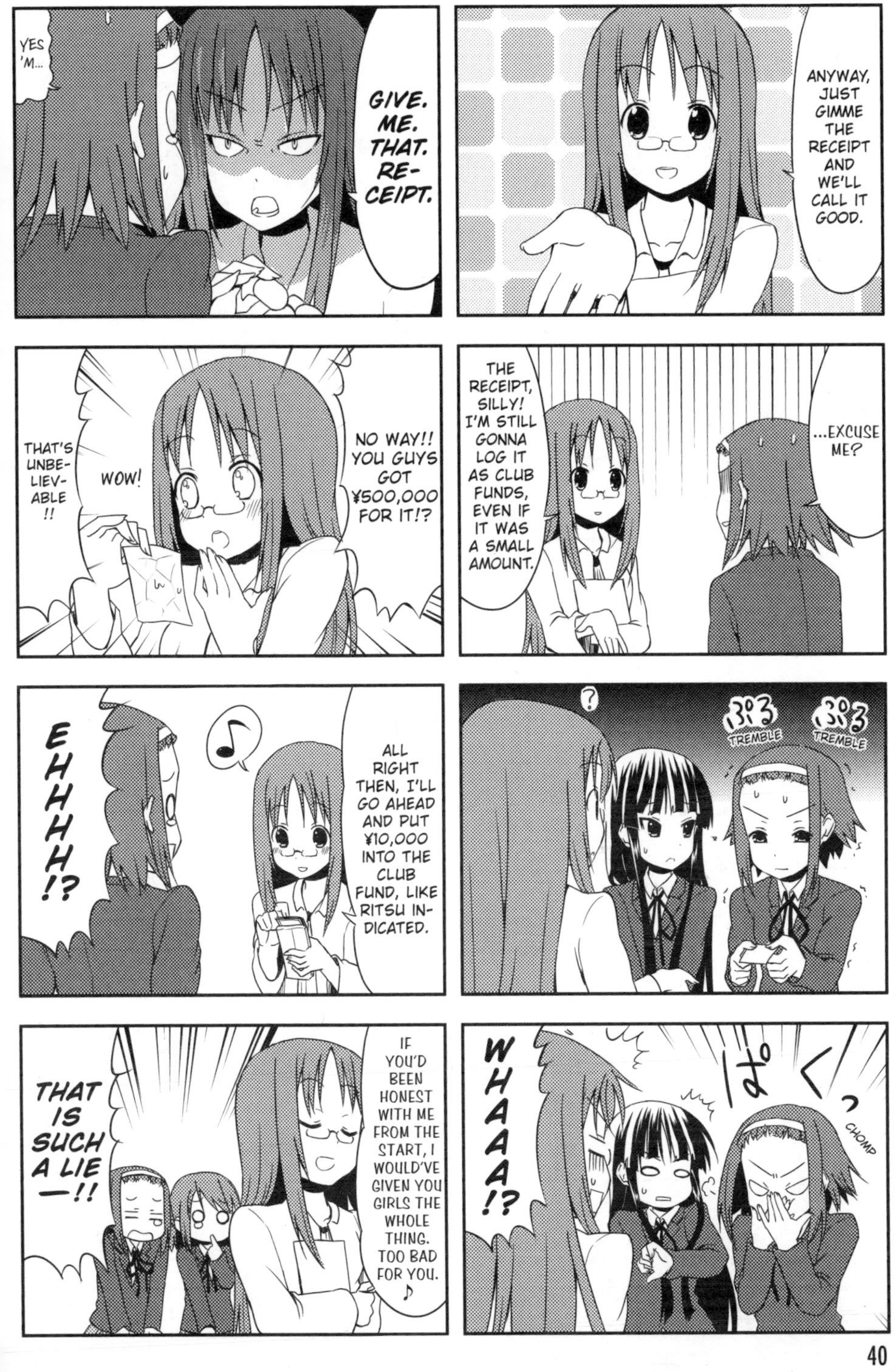
ANYWAY, JUST GIMME THE RECEIPT AND WE'LL CALL IT GOOD.
GIVE. ME. THAT. RE-CEIPT.
YES 'M...
...EXCUSE ME?
THE RECEIPT, SILLY! I'M STILL GONNA LOG IT AS CLUB FUNDS, EVEN IF IT WAS A SMALL AMOUNT.
NO WAY!! YOU GUYS GOT ¥500,000 FOR IT!?
WOW!
THAT'S UNBE-LIEV-ABLE !!
ぷる
TREMBLE
ぷる
TREMBLE
?
ALL RIGHT THEN, I'LL GO AHEAD AND PUT ¥10,000 INTO THE CLUB FUND, LIKE RITSU IN-DICATED.
EHHHHH!?
ぱくっ
CHOMP
WHAAAA!?
IF YOU'D BEEN HONEST WITH ME FROM THE START, I WOULD'VE GIVEN YOU GIRLS THE WHOLE THING. TOO BAD FOR YOU. ♪
THAT IS SUCH A LIE—!!

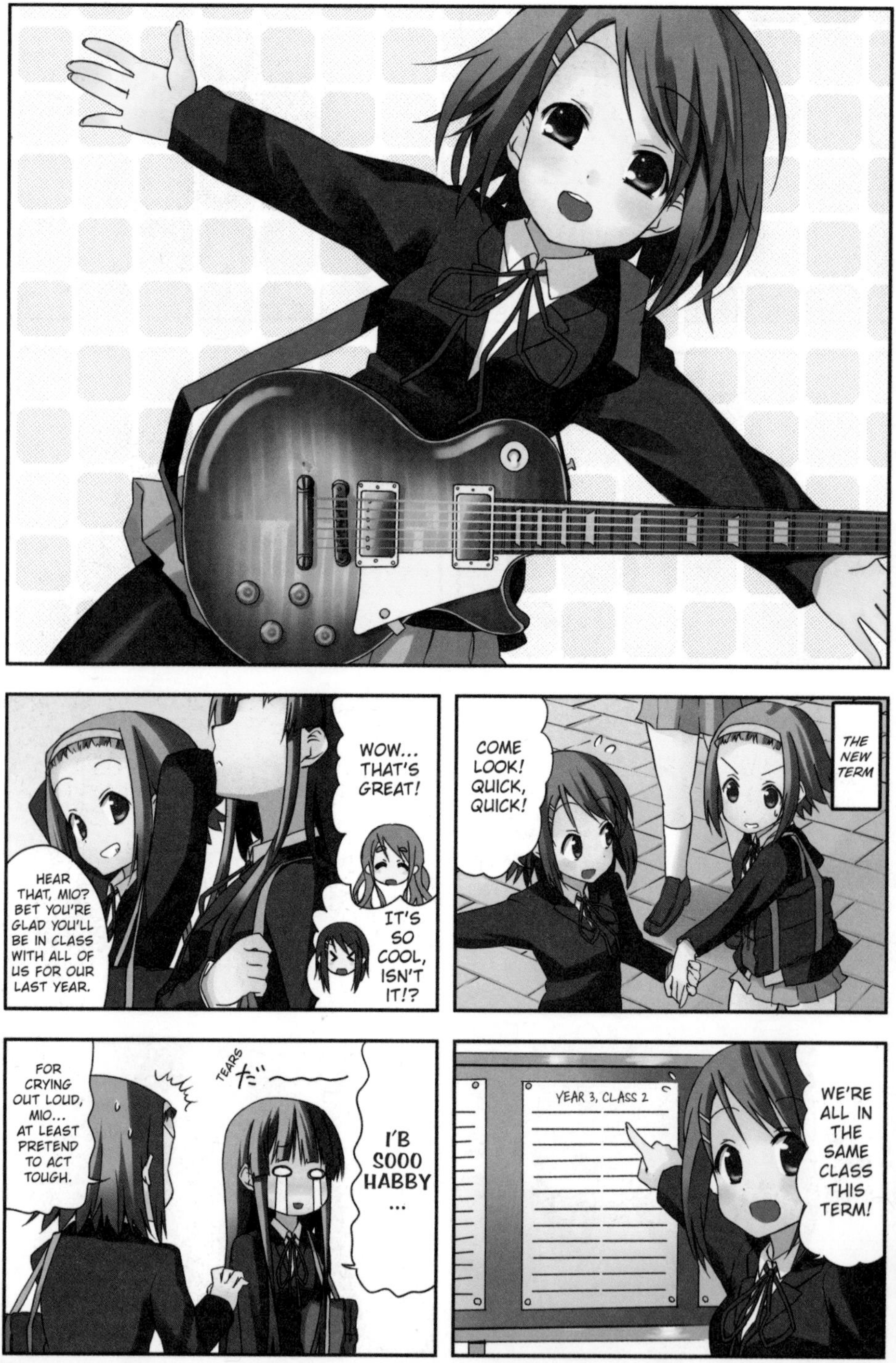
THE NEW TERM
COME LOOK! QUICK, QUICK!
WOW... THAT'S GREAT!
IT'S SO COOL, ISN'T IT!?
HEAR THAT, MIO? BET YOU'RE GLAD YOU'LL BE IN CLASS WITH ALL OF US FOR OUR LAST YEAR.
YEAR 3, CLASS 2
WE'RE ALL IN THE SAME CLASS THIS TERM!
I'B SOOO HABBY ...
TEARS だ〜〜〜
FOR CRYING OUT LOUD, MIO... AT LEAST PRETEND TO ACT TOUGH.

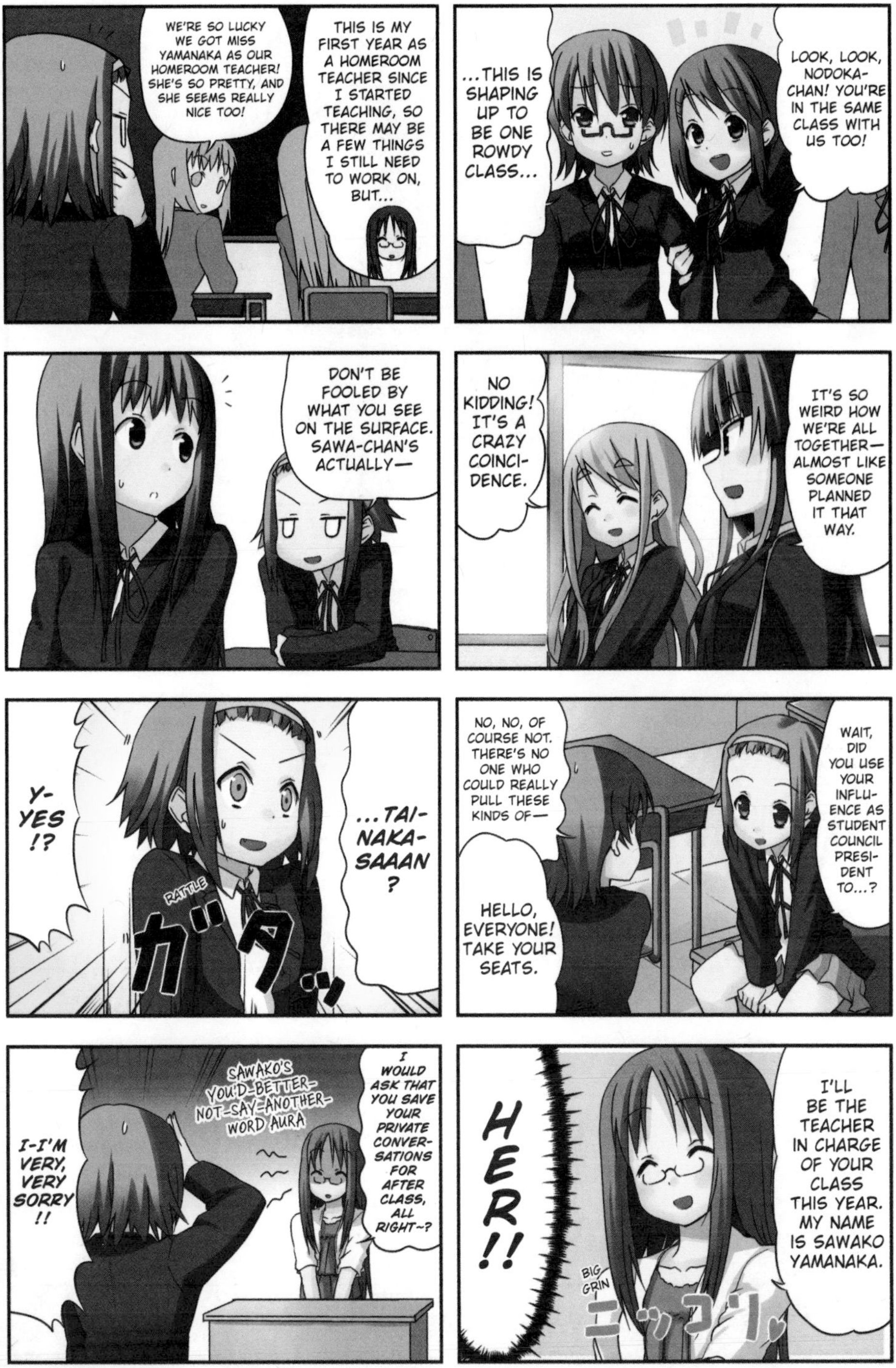

LOOK, LOOK, NODOKA-CHAN! YOU'RE IN THE SAME CLASS WITH US TOO!
...THIS IS SHAPING UP TO BE ONE ROWDY CLASS...
THIS IS MY FIRST YEAR AS A HOMEROOM TEACHER SINCE I STARTED TEACHING, SO THERE MAY BE A FEW THINGS I STILL NEED TO WORK ON, BUT...
WE'RE SO LUCKY WE GOT MISS YAMANAKA AS OUR HOMEROOM TEACHER! SHE'S SO PRETTY, AND SHE SEEMS REALLY NICE TOO!
IT'S SO WEIRD HOW WE'RE ALL TOGETHER—ALMOST LIKE SOMEONE PLANNED IT THAT WAY.
NO KIDDING! IT'S A CRAZY COINCI-DENCE.
DON'T BE FOOLED BY WHAT YOU SEE ON THE SURFACE. SAWA-CHAN'S ACTUALLY—
WAIT, DID YOU USE YOUR INFLU-ENCE AS STUDENT COUNCIL PRESI-DENT TO...?
NO, NO, OF COURSE NOT. THERE'S NO ONE WHO COULD REALLY PULL THESE KINDS OF—
HELLO, EVERYONE! TAKE YOUR SEATS.
...TAI-NAKA-SAAAN?
Y-YES!?
RATTLE
ガタッ
I'LL BE THE TEACHER IN CHARGE OF YOUR CLASS THIS YEAR. MY NAME IS SAWAKO YAMANAKA.
HER!!
BIG GRIN
ニッコリ
I WOULD ASK THAT YOU SAVE YOUR PRIVATE CONVER-SATIONS FOR AFTER CLASS, ALL RIGHT~?
SAWAKO'S YOU'D-BETTER-NOT-SAY-ANOTHER-WORD AURA
I-I'M VERY, VERY SORRY!!

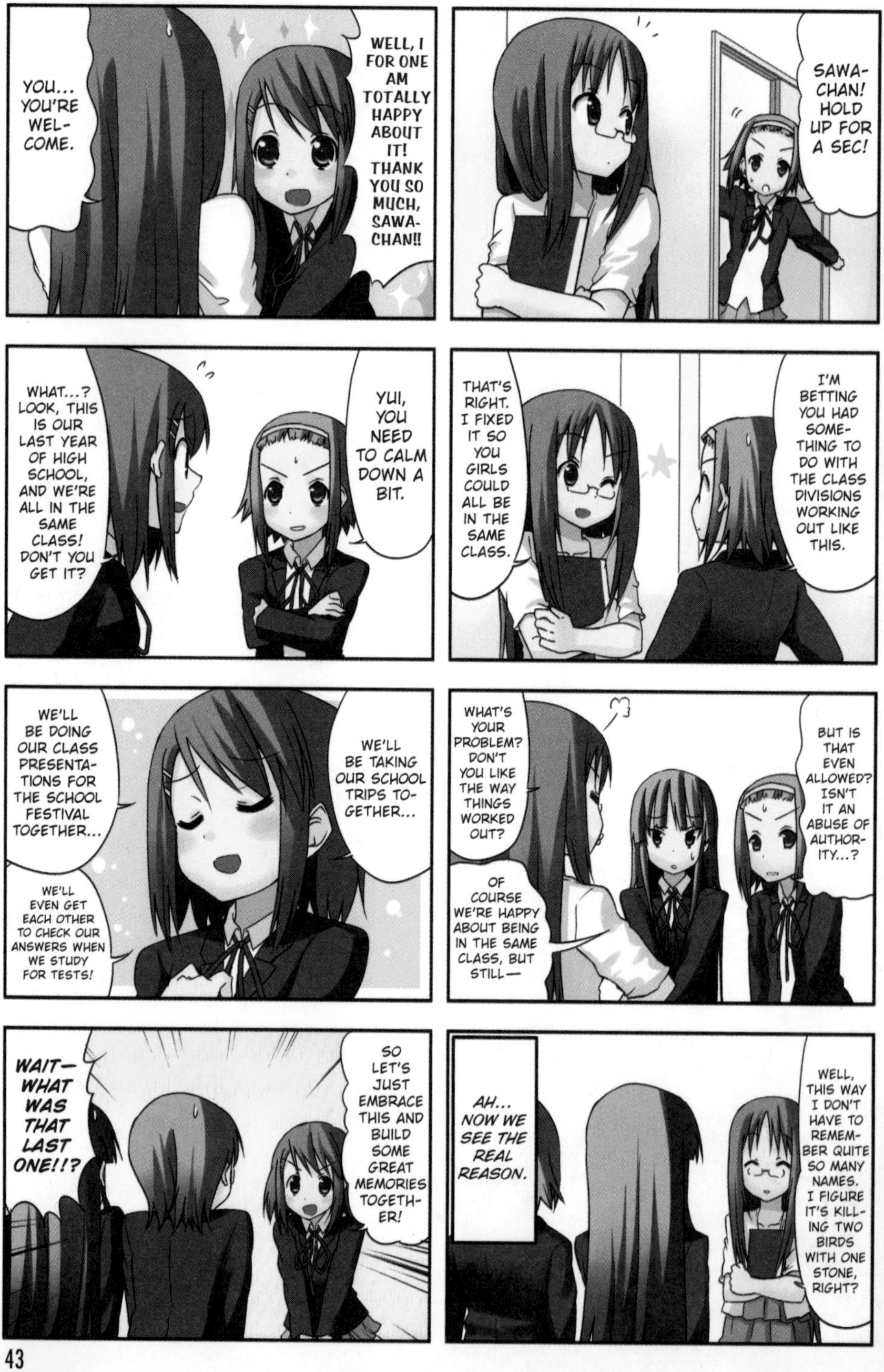
SAWA-CHAN! HOLD UP FOR A SEC!
I'M BETTING YOU HAD SOMETHING TO DO WITH THE CLASS DIVISIONS WORKING OUT LIKE THIS.
THAT'S RIGHT. I FIXED IT SO YOU GIRLS COULD ALL BE IN THE SAME CLASS.
BUT IS THAT EVEN ALLOWED? ISN'T IT AN ABUSE OF AUTHORITY...?
WHAT'S YOUR PROBLEM? DON'T YOU LIKE THE WAY THINGS WORKED OUT?
OF COURSE WE'RE HAPPY ABOUT BEING IN THE SAME CLASS, BUT STILL—
WELL, THIS WAY I DON'T HAVE TO REMEMBER QUITE SO MANY NAMES. I FIGURE IT'S KILLING TWO BIRDS WITH ONE STONE, RIGHT?
AH... NOW WE SEE THE REAL REASON.
WELL, I FOR ONE AM TOTALLY HAPPY ABOUT IT! THANK YOU SO MUCH, SAWA-CHAN!!
YOU... YOU'RE WELCOME.
YUI, YOU NEED TO CALM DOWN A BIT.
WHAT...? LOOK, THIS IS OUR LAST YEAR OF HIGH SCHOOL, AND WE'RE ALL IN THE SAME CLASS! DON'T YOU GET IT?
WE'LL BE TAKING OUR SCHOOL TRIPS TOGETHER...
WE'LL BE DOING OUR CLASS PRESENTATIONS FOR THE SCHOOL FESTIVAL TOGETHER...
WE'LL EVEN GET EACH OTHER TO CHECK OUR ANSWERS WHEN WE STUDY FOR TESTS!
SO LET'S JUST EMBRACE THIS AND BUILD SOME GREAT MEMORIES TOGETHER!
WAIT—WHAT WAS THAT LAST ONE!!?

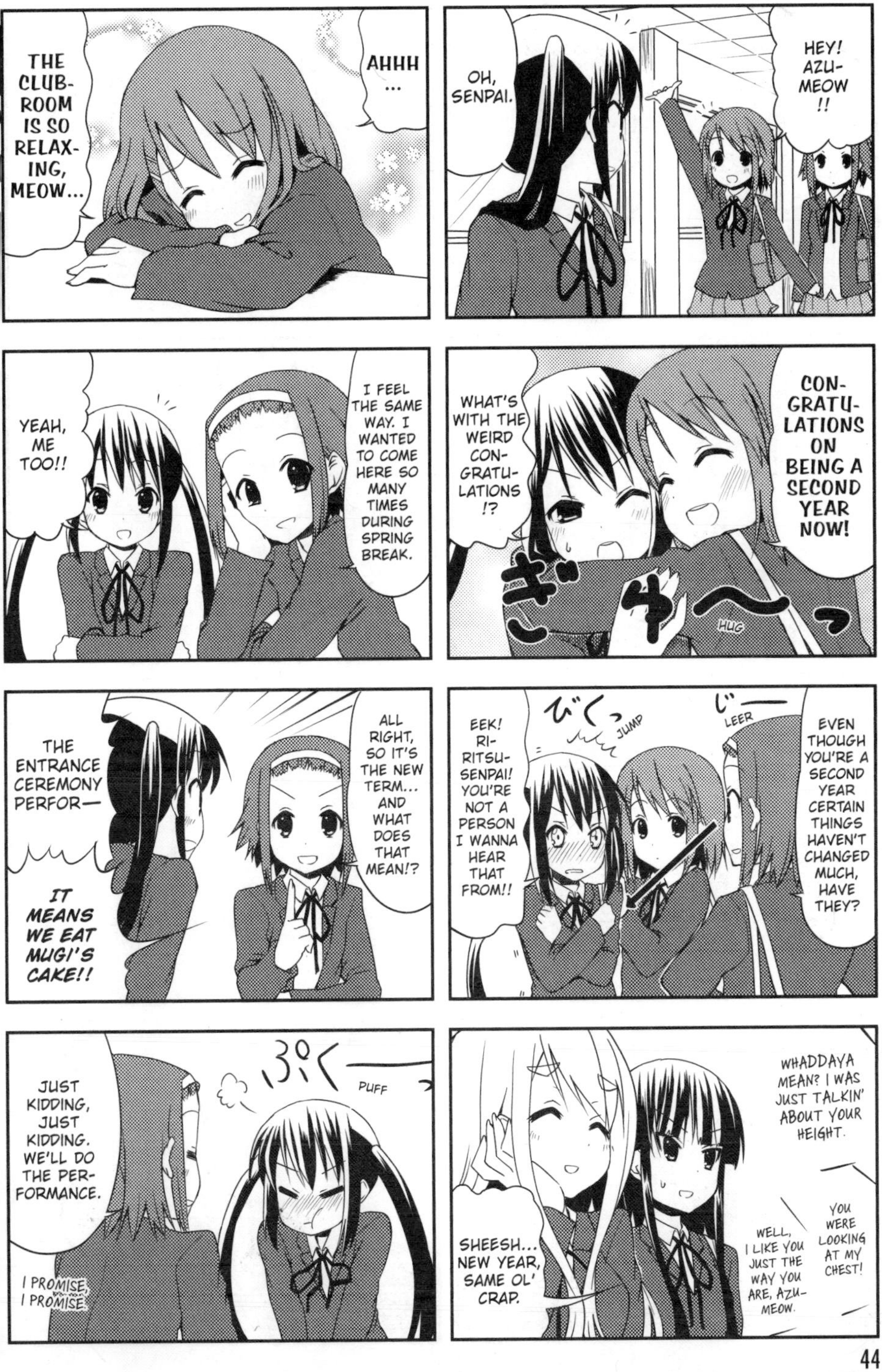
HEY! AZU-MEOW!!
OH, SENPAI.
AHHH...
THE CLUB-ROOM IS SO RELAX-ING, MEOW...
CON-GRATU-LATIONS ON BEING A SECOND YEAR NOW!
WHAT'S WITH THE WEIRD CON-GRATU-LATIONS!?
ぎゅ〜っ
HUG
I FEEL THE SAME WAY. I WANTED TO COME HERE SO MANY TIMES DURING SPRING BREAK.
YEAH, ME TOO!!
EVEN THOUGH YOU'RE A SECOND YEAR CERTAIN THINGS HAVEN'T CHANGED MUCH, HAVE THEY?
じー
LEER
びくっ
JUMP
EEK! RI-RITSU-SENPAI! YOU'RE NOT A PERSON I WANNA HEAR THAT FROM!!
ALL RIGHT, SO IT'S THE NEW TERM... AND WHAT DOES THAT MEAN!?
THE ENTRANCE CEREMONY PERFOR—
IT MEANS WE EAT MUGI'S CAKE!!
WHADDAYA MEAN? I WAS JUST TALKIN' ABOUT YOUR HEIGHT.
YOU WERE LOOKING AT MY CHEST!
WELL, I LIKE YOU JUST THE WAY YOU ARE, AZU-MEOW.
SHEESH... NEW YEAR, SAME OL' CRAP.
ぷく〜
PUFF
JUST KIDDING, JUST KIDDING. WE'LL DO THE PER-FORMANCE.
I PROMISE, I PROMISE.

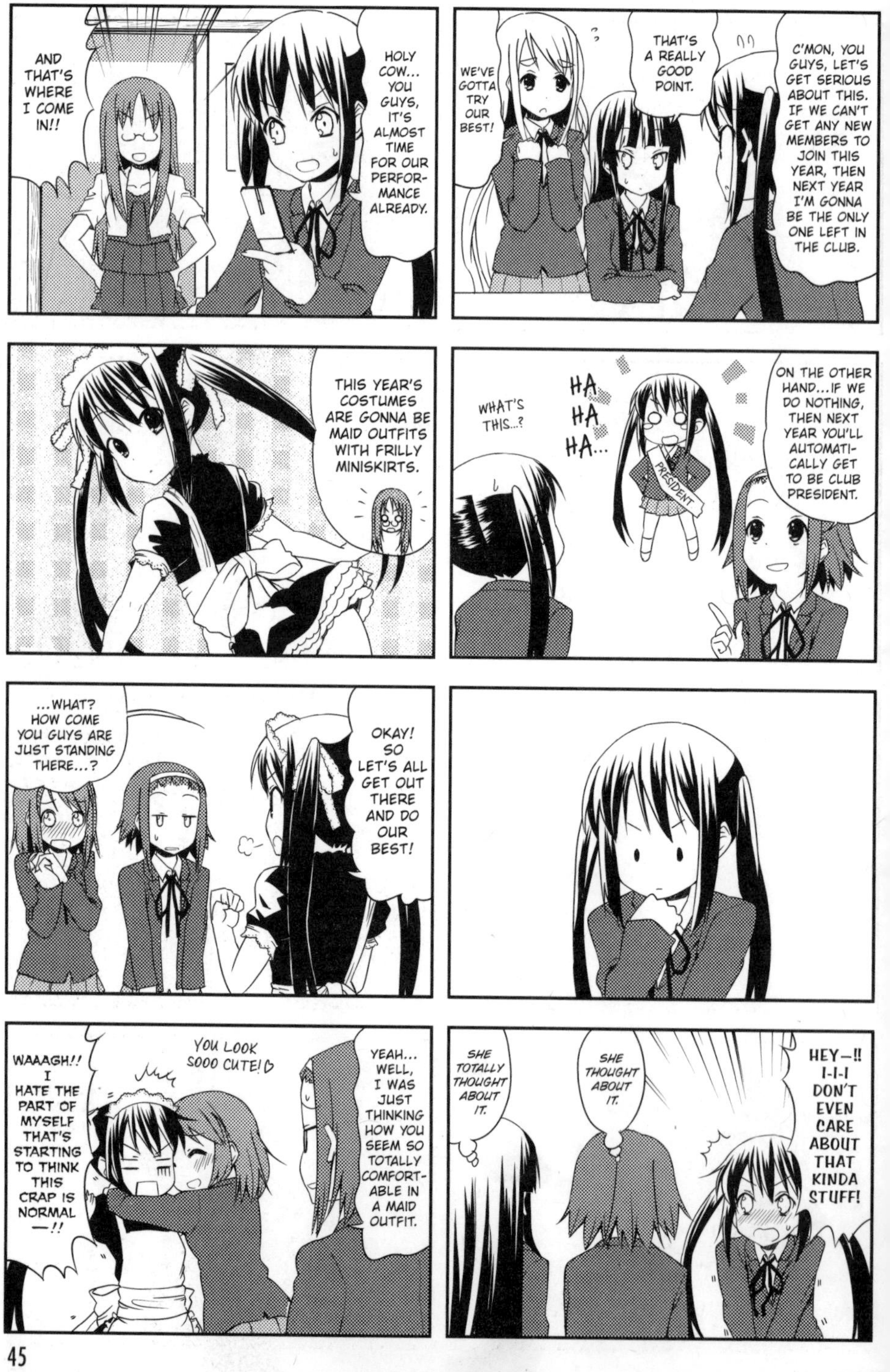
C'MON, YOU GUYS, LET'S GET SERIOUS ABOUT THIS. IF WE CAN'T GET ANY NEW MEMBERS TO JOIN THIS YEAR, THEN NEXT YEAR I'M GONNA BE THE ONLY ONE LEFT IN THE CLUB.
THAT'S A REALLY GOOD POINT.
WE'VE GOTTA TRY OUR BEST!
HOLY COW... YOU GUYS, IT'S ALMOST TIME FOR OUR PERFORMANCE ALREADY.
AND THAT'S WHERE I COME IN!!
ON THE OTHER HAND...IF WE DO NOTHING, THEN NEXT YEAR YOU'LL AUTOMATICALLY GET TO BE CLUB PRESIDENT.
HA HA HA...
PRESIDENT
WHAT'S THIS...?
THIS YEAR'S COSTUMES ARE GONNA BE MAID OUTFITS WITH FRILLY MINISKIRTS.
OKAY! SO LET'S ALL GET OUT THERE AND DO OUR BEST!
...WHAT? HOW COME YOU GUYS ARE JUST STANDING THERE...?
HEY—!! I-I-I DON'T EVEN CARE ABOUT THAT KINDA STUFF!
SHE THOUGHT ABOUT IT.
SHE TOTALLY THOUGHT ABOUT IT.
YEAH... WELL, I WAS JUST THINKING HOW YOU SEEM SO TOTALLY COMFORTABLE IN A MAID OUTFIT.
YOU LOOK SOOO CUTE!♡
WAAAGH!! I HATE THE PART OF MYSELF THAT'S STARTING TO THINK THIS CRAP IS NORMAL—!!

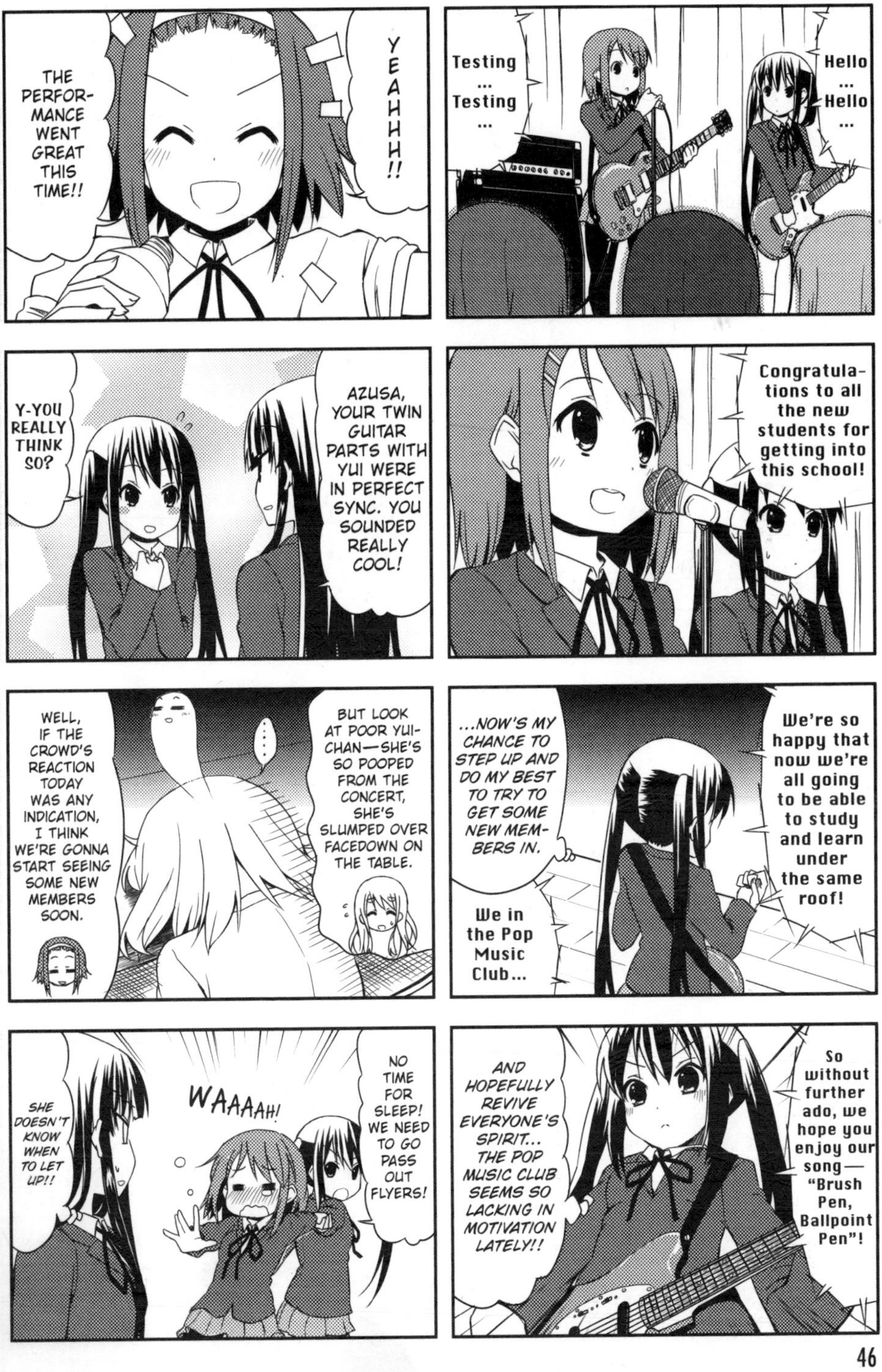
Hello ... Hello ...
Testing ... Testing ...
Congratulations to all the new students for getting into this school!
We're so happy that now we're all going to be able to study and learn under the same roof!
...NOW'S MY CHANCE TO STEP UP AND DO MY BEST TO TRY TO GET SOME NEW MEMBERS IN.
We in the Pop Music Club...
So without further ado, we hope you enjoy our song—"Brush Pen, Ballpoint Pen"!
AND HOPEFULLY REVIVE EVERYONE'S SPIRIT... THE POP MUSIC CLUB SEEMS SO LACKING IN MOTIVATION LATELY!!
YEAHHH!!
THE PERFORMANCE WENT GREAT THIS TIME!!
AZUSA, YOUR TWIN GUITAR PARTS WITH YUI WERE IN PERFECT SYNC. YOU SOUNDED REALLY COOL!
Y-YOU REALLY THINK SO?
BUT LOOK AT POOR YUI-CHAN—SHE'S SO POOPED FROM THE CONCERT, SHE'S SLUMPED OVER FACEDOWN ON THE TABLE.
...
WELL, IF THE CROWD'S REACTION TODAY WAS ANY INDICATION, I THINK WE'RE GONNA START SEEING SOME NEW MEMBERS SOON.
NO TIME FOR SLEEP! WE NEED TO GO PASS OUT FLYERS!
WAAAAAH!
SHE DOESN'T KNOW WHEN TO LET UP!!

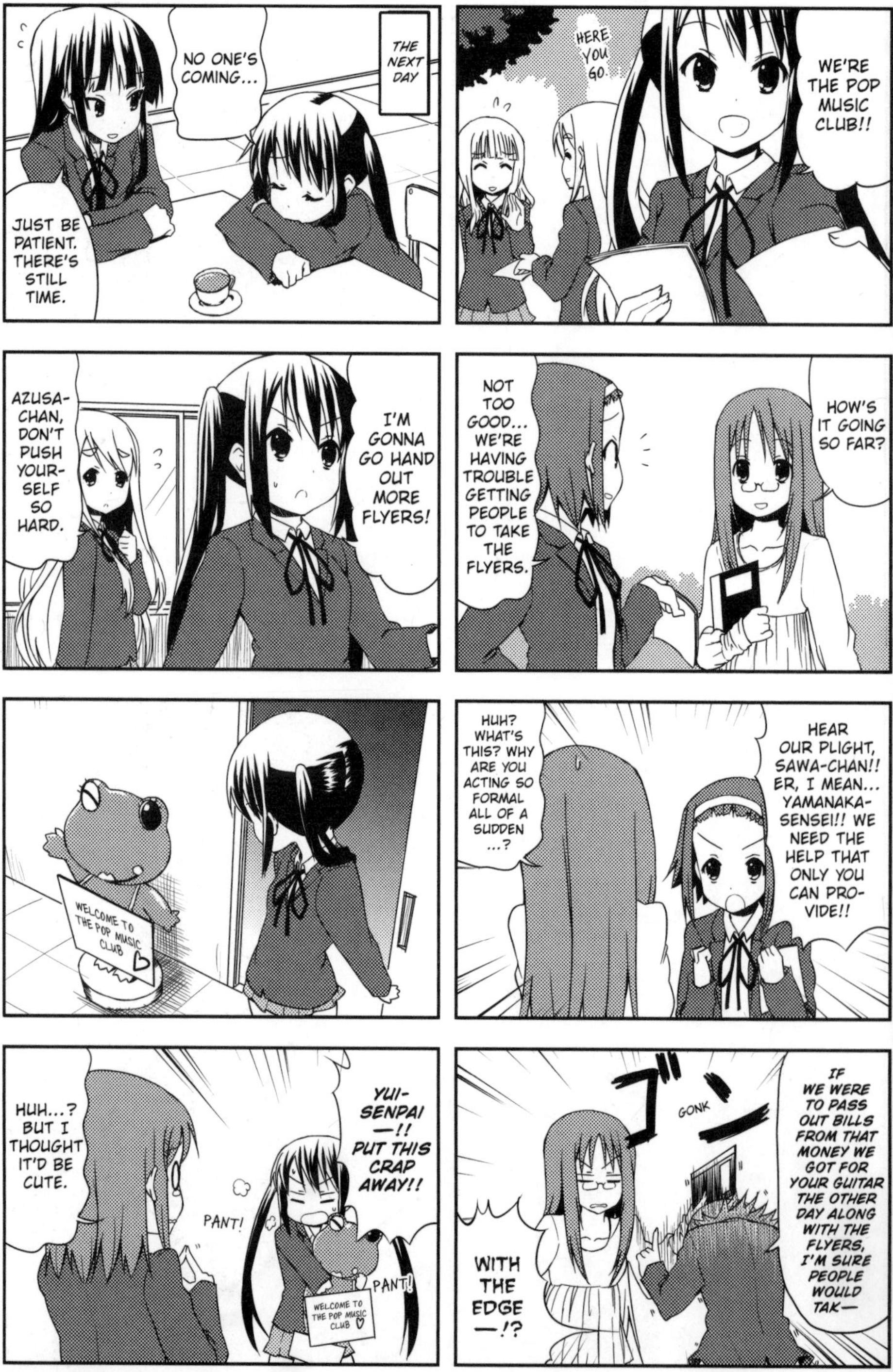
WE'RE THE POP MUSIC CLUB!!
HERE YOU GO.
HOW'S IT GOING SO FAR?
NOT TOO GOOD... WE'RE HAVING TROUBLE GETTING PEOPLE TO TAKE THE FLYERS.
HEAR OUR PLIGHT, SAWA-CHAN!! ER, I MEAN... YAMANAKA-SENSEI!! WE NEED THE HELP THAT ONLY YOU CAN PROVIDE!!
HUH? WHAT'S THIS? WHY ARE YOU ACTING SO FORMAL ALL OF A SUDDEN ...?
IF WE WERE TO PASS OUT BILLS FROM THAT MONEY WE GOT FOR YOUR GUITAR THE OTHER DAY ALONG WITH THE FLYERS, I'M SURE PEOPLE WOULD TAK—
GONK
WITH THE EDGE —!?
THE NEXT DAY
NO ONE'S COMING...
JUST BE PATIENT. THERE'S STILL TIME.
I'M GONNA GO HAND OUT MORE FLYERS!
AZUSA-CHAN, DON'T PUSH YOURSELF SO HARD.
WELCOME TO THE POP MUSIC CLUB
YUI-SENPAI —!! PUT THIS CRAP AWAY!!
PANT!
PANT!
HUH...? BUT I THOUGHT IT'D BE CUTE.
WELCOME TO THE POP MUSIC CLUB

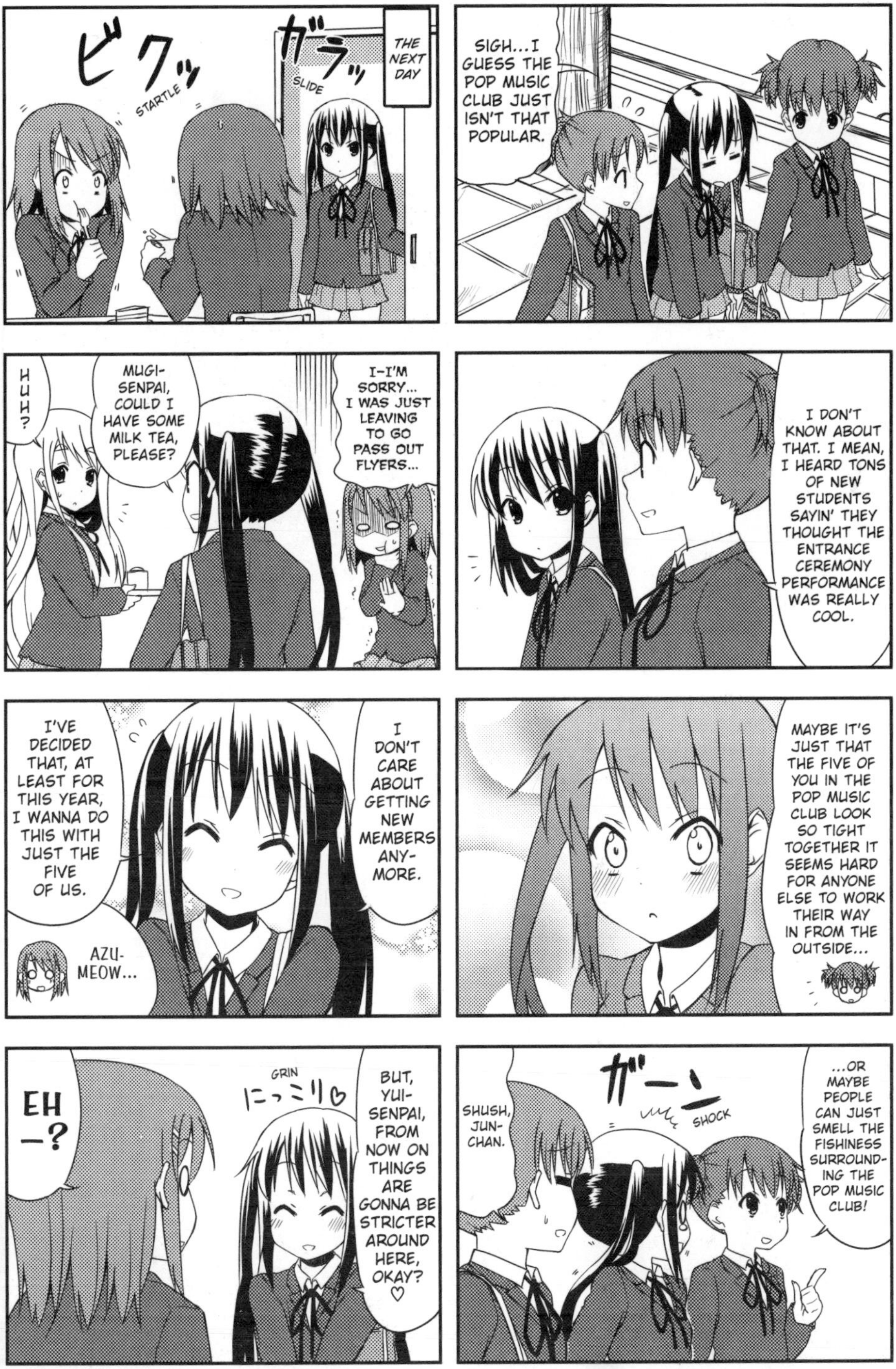
SIGH...I GUESS THE POP MUSIC CLUB JUST ISN'T THAT POPULAR.
THE NEXT DAY
ガラッ
SLIDE
ビクッ
STARTLE
I DON'T KNOW ABOUT THAT. I MEAN, I HEARD TONS OF NEW STUDENTS SAYIN' THEY THOUGHT THE ENTRANCE CEREMONY PERFORMANCE WAS REALLY COOL.
I-I'M SORRY... I WAS JUST LEAVING TO GO PASS OUT FLYERS...
MUGI-SENPAI, COULD I HAVE SOME MILK TEA, PLEASE?
HUH?
MAYBE IT'S JUST THAT THE FIVE OF YOU IN THE POP MUSIC CLUB LOOK SO TIGHT TOGETHER IT SEEMS HARD FOR ANYONE ELSE TO WORK THEIR WAY IN FROM THE OUTSIDE...
I DON'T CARE ABOUT GETTING NEW MEMBERS ANYMORE.
I'VE DECIDED THAT, AT LEAST FOR THIS YEAR, I WANNA DO THIS WITH JUST THE FIVE OF US.
AZU-MEOW...
...OR MAYBE PEOPLE CAN JUST SMELL THE FISHINESS SURROUNDING THE POP MUSIC CLUB!
ガーン
SHOCK
SHUSH, JUN-CHAN.
BUT, YUI-SENPAI, FROM NOW ON THINGS ARE GONNA BE STRICTER AROUND HERE, OKAY? ♡
にっこり♡
GRIN
EH—?

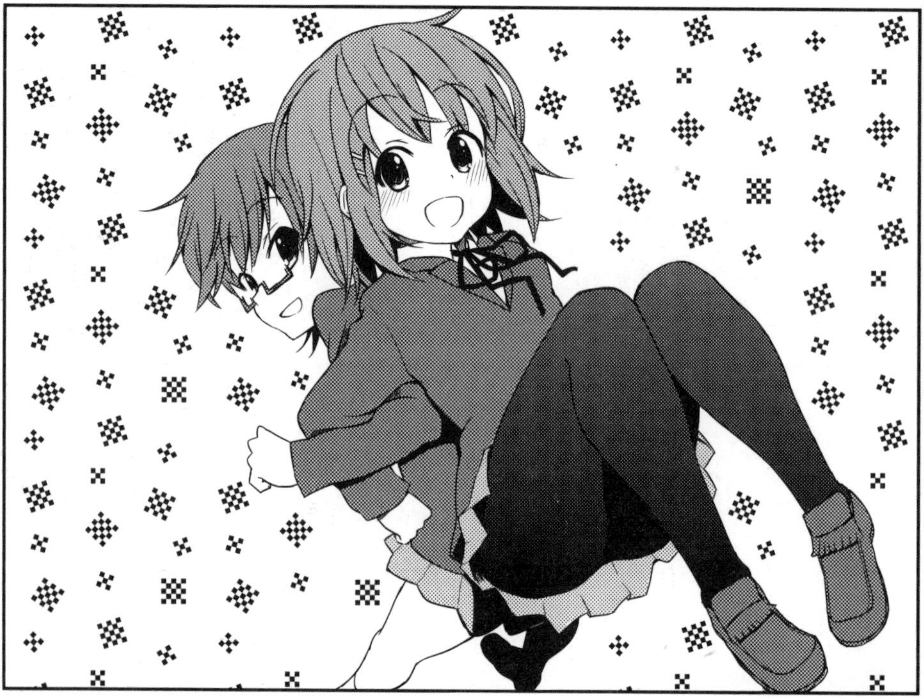

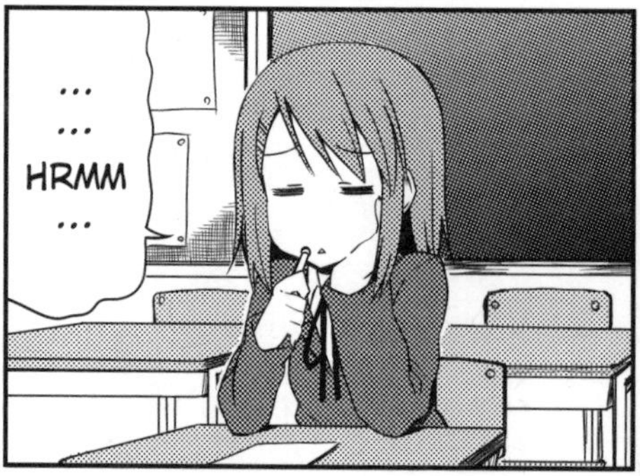
...
...
HRMM
...

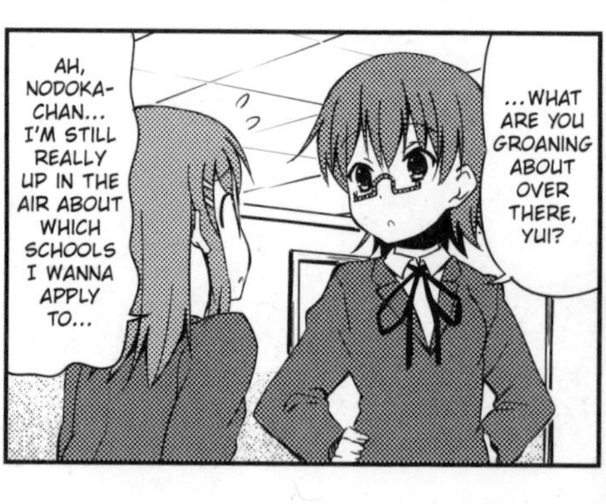
...WHAT ARE YOU GROANING ABOUT OVER THERE, YUI?
AH, NODOKA-CHAN... I'M STILL REALLY UP IN THE AIR ABOUT WHICH SCHOOLS I WANNA APPLY TO...

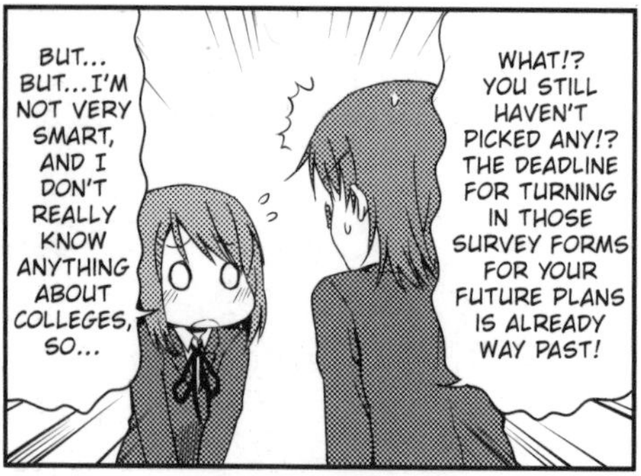
WHAT!? YOU STILL HAVEN'T PICKED ANY!? THE DEADLINE FOR TURNING IN THOSE SURVEY FORMS FOR YOUR FUTURE PLANS IS ALREADY WAY PAST!
BUT... BUT...I'M NOT VERY SMART, AND I DON'T REALLY KNOW ANYTHING ABOUT COLLEGES, SO...

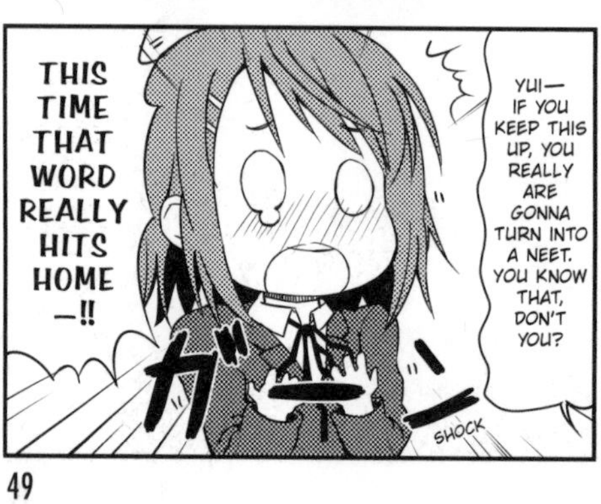
YUI— IF YOU KEEP THIS UP, YOU REALLY ARE GONNA TURN INTO A NEET. YOU KNOW THAT, DON'T YOU?
THIS TIME THAT WORD REALLY HITS HOME —!!
SHOCK

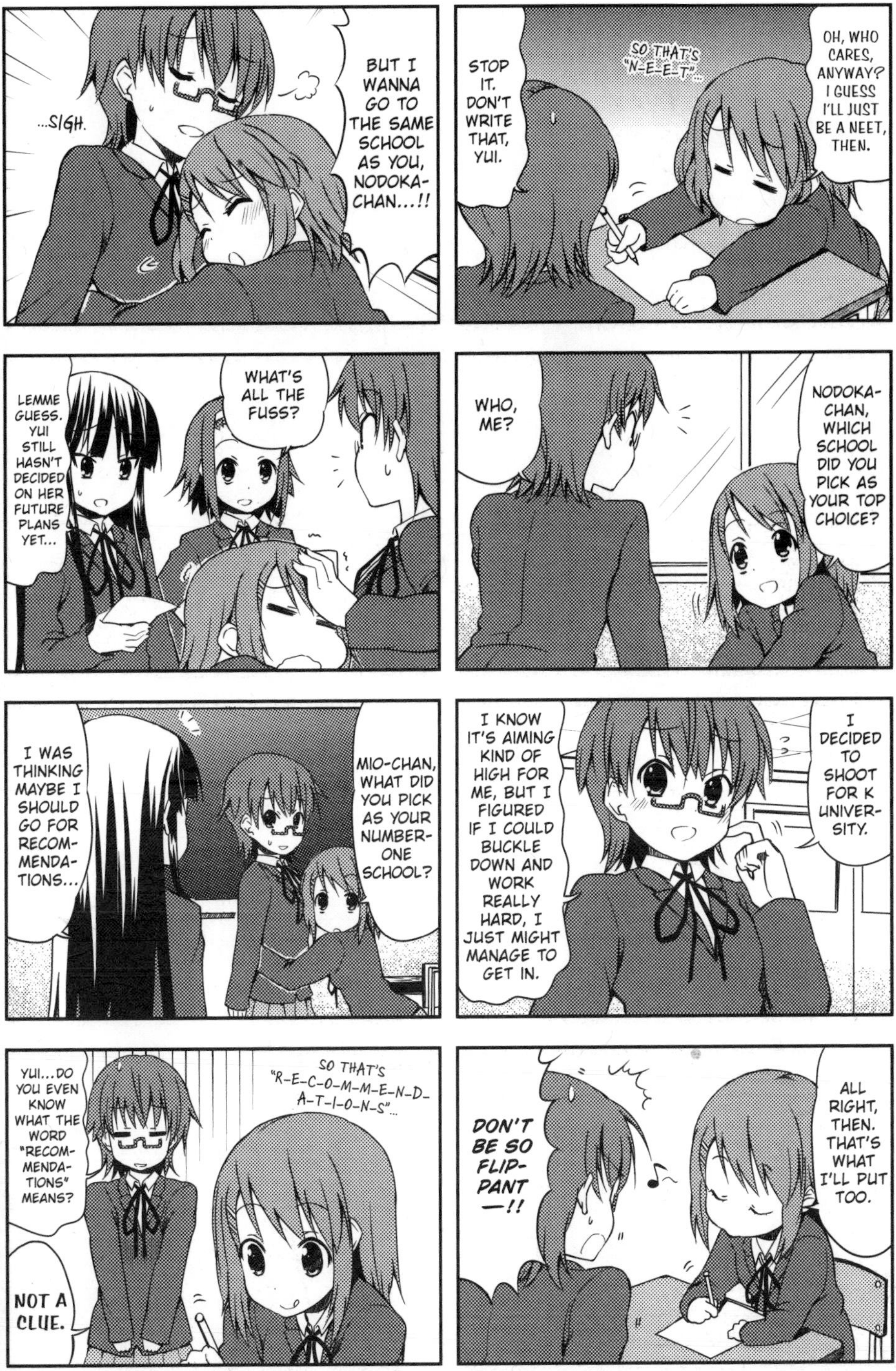
OH, WHO CARES, ANYWAY? I GUESS I'LL JUST BE A NEET, THEN.
SO THAT'S "N-E-E-T"...
STOP IT. DON'T WRITE THAT, YUI.
NODOKA-CHAN, WHICH SCHOOL DID YOU PICK AS YOUR TOP CHOICE?
WHO, ME?
I DECIDED TO SHOOT FOR K UNIVERSITY.
I KNOW IT'S AIMING KIND OF HIGH FOR ME, BUT I FIGURED IF I COULD BUCKLE DOWN AND WORK REALLY HARD, I JUST MIGHT MANAGE TO GET IN.
ALL RIGHT, THEN. THAT'S WHAT I'LL PUT TOO.
DON'T BE SO FLIPPANT—!!
BUT I WANNA GO TO THE SAME SCHOOL AS YOU, NODOKA-CHAN...!!
...SIGH.
WHAT'S ALL THE FUSS?
LEMME GUESS. YUI STILL HASN'T DECIDED ON HER FUTURE PLANS YET...
MIO-CHAN, WHAT DID YOU PICK AS YOUR NUMBER-ONE SCHOOL?
I WAS THINKING MAYBE I SHOULD GO FOR RECOMMENDATIONS...
SO THAT'S "R-E-C-O-M-M-E-N-D-A-T-I-O-N-S"...
YUI...DO YOU EVEN KNOW WHAT THE WORD "RECOMMENDATIONS" MEANS?
NOT A CLUE.

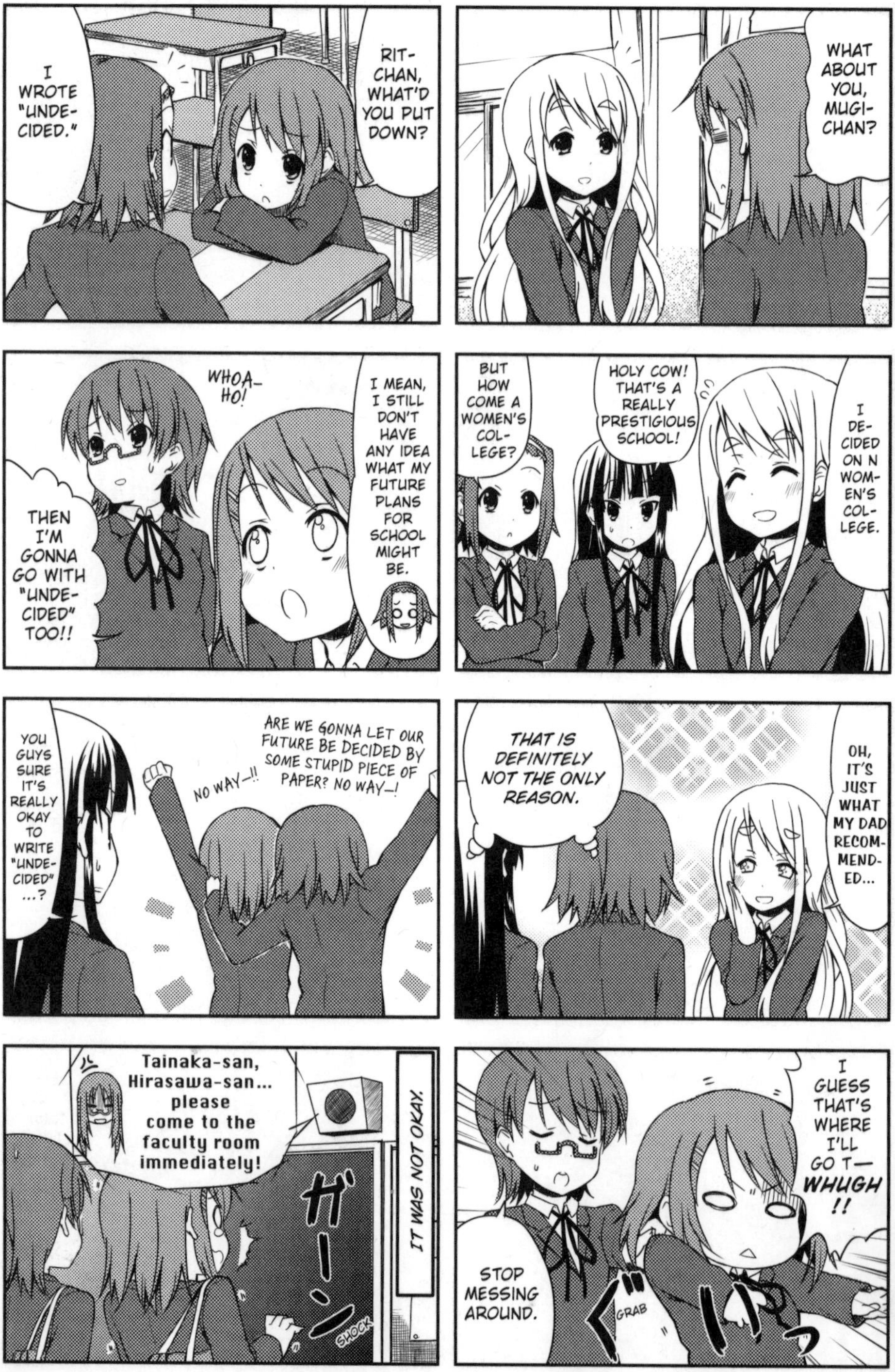
WHAT ABOUT YOU, MUGI-CHAN?
I DECIDED ON N WOMEN'S COLLEGE.
HOLY COW! THAT'S A REALLY PRESTIGIOUS SCHOOL!
BUT HOW COME A WOMEN'S COLLEGE?
OH, IT'S JUST WHAT MY DAD RECOMMENDED...
THAT IS DEFINITELY NOT THE ONLY REASON.
I GUESS THAT'S WHERE I'LL GO T— WHUGH!!
STOP MESSING AROUND.
GRAB
RIT-CHAN, WHAT'D YOU PUT DOWN?
I WROTE "UNDECIDED."
I MEAN, I STILL DON'T HAVE ANY IDEA WHAT MY FUTURE PLANS FOR SCHOOL MIGHT BE.
WHOA-HO!
THEN I'M GONNA GO WITH "UNDECIDED" TOO!!
ARE WE GONNA LET OUR FUTURE BE DECIDED BY SOME STUPID PIECE OF PAPER? NO WAY—!
NO WAY—!!
YOU GUYS SURE IT'S REALLY OKAY TO WRITE "UNDECIDED"...?
IT WAS NOT OKAY.
Tainaka-san, Hirasawa-san... please come to the faculty room immediately!
SHOCK

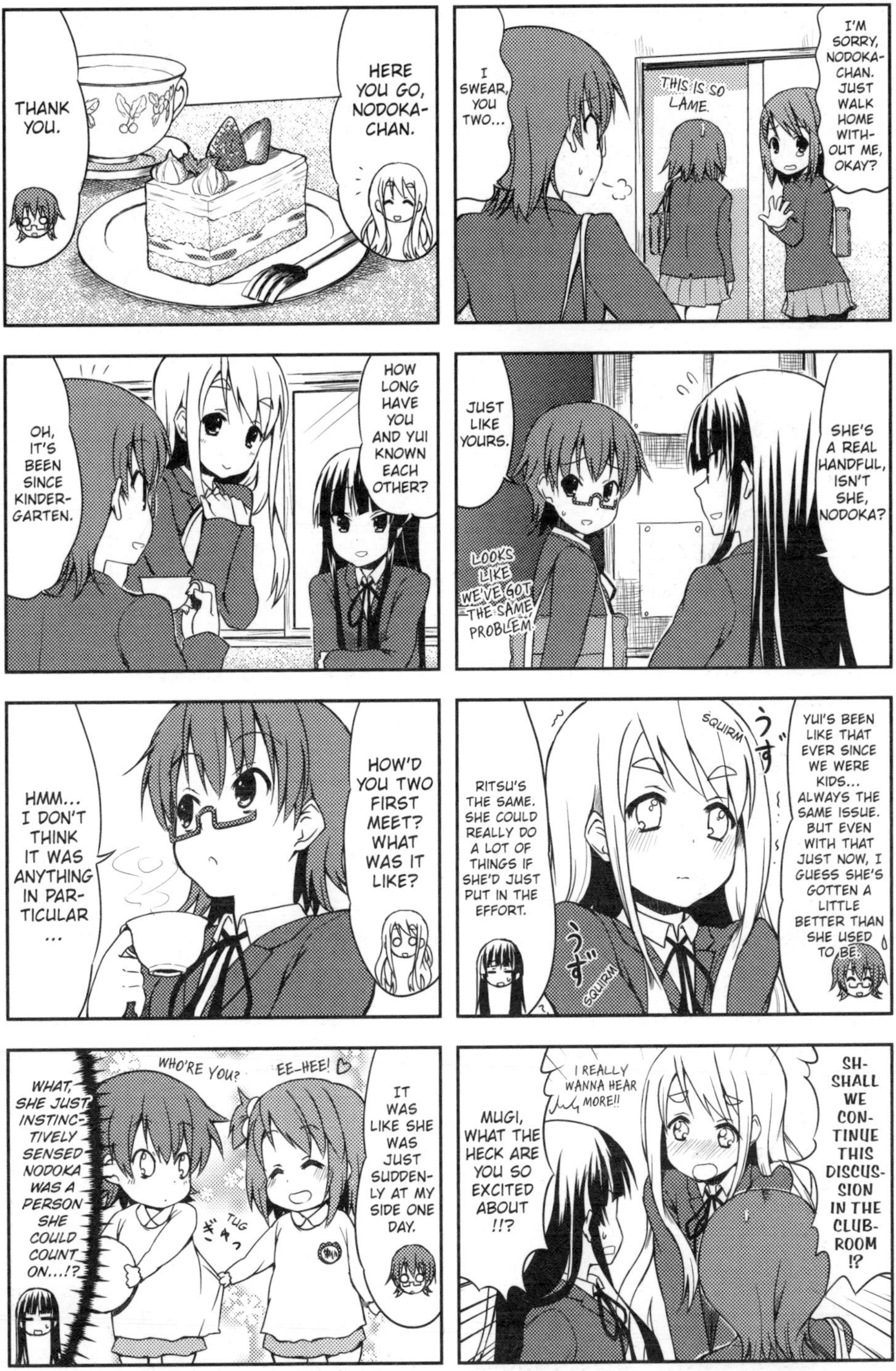
I'M SORRY, NODOKA-CHAN. JUST WALK HOME WITHOUT ME, OKAY?
THIS IS SO LAME.
I SWEAR, YOU TWO...
HERE YOU GO, NODOKA-CHAN.
THANK YOU.
SHE'S A REAL HANDFUL, ISN'T SHE, NODOKA?
JUST LIKE YOURS.
LOOKS LIKE WE'VE GOT THE SAME PROBLEM.
HOW LONG HAVE YOU AND YUI KNOWN EACH OTHER?
OH, IT'S BEEN SINCE KINDERGARTEN.
YUI'S BEEN LIKE THAT EVER SINCE WE WERE KIDS... ALWAYS THE SAME ISSUE. BUT EVEN WITH THAT JUST NOW, I GUESS SHE'S GOTTEN A LITTLE BETTER THAN SHE USED TO BE.
うず SQUIRM
RITSU'S THE SAME. SHE COULD REALLY DO A LOT OF THINGS IF SHE'D JUST PUT IN THE EFFORT.
うず SQUIRM
HOW'D YOU TWO FIRST MEET? WHAT WAS IT LIKE?
HMM... I DON'T THINK IT WAS ANYTHING IN PARTICULAR...
SH-SHALL WE CONTINUE THIS DISCUSSION IN THE CLUBROOM!?
I REALLY WANNA HEAR MORE!!
MUGI, WHAT THE HECK ARE YOU SO EXCITED ABOUT!!?
IT WAS LIKE SHE WAS JUST SUDDENLY AT MY SIDE ONE DAY.
EE-HEE! ♡
WHO'RE YOU?
ぎゅっ TUG
WHAT, SHE JUST INSTINCTIVELY SENSED NODOKA WAS A PERSON SHE COULD COUNT ON...!?

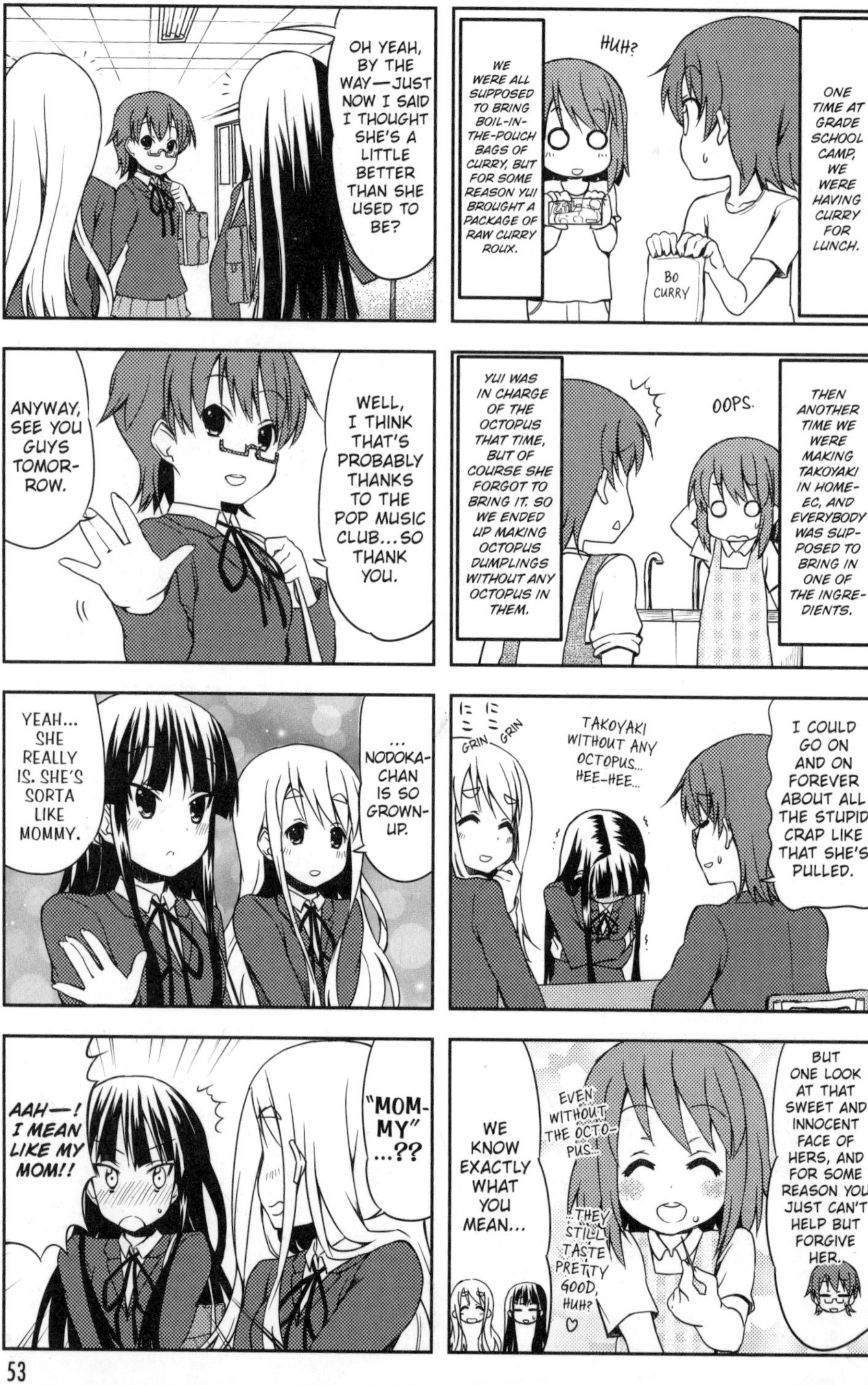
ONE TIME AT GRADE SCHOOL CAMP, WE WERE HAVING CURRY FOR LUNCH.
HUH?
WE WERE ALL SUPPOSED TO BRING BOIL-IN-THE-POUCH BAGS OF CURRY, BUT FOR SOME REASON YUI BROUGHT A PACKAGE OF RAW CURRY ROUX.
BO CURRY
THEN ANOTHER TIME WE WERE MAKING TAKOYAKI IN HOME-EC, AND EVERYBODY WAS SUPPOSED TO BRING IN ONE OF THE INGREDIENTS.
OOPS.
YUI WAS IN CHARGE OF THE OCTOPUS THAT TIME, BUT OF COURSE SHE FORGOT TO BRING IT. SO WE ENDED UP MAKING OCTOPUS DUMPLINGS WITHOUT ANY OCTOPUS IN THEM.
I COULD GO ON AND ON FOREVER ABOUT ALL THE STUPID CRAP LIKE THAT SHE'S PULLED.
TAKOYAKI WITHOUT ANY OCTOPUS... HEE-HEE...
GRIN GRIN
BUT ONE LOOK AT THAT SWEET AND INNOCENT FACE OF HERS, AND FOR SOME REASON YOU JUST CAN'T HELP BUT FORGIVE HER.
EVEN WITHOUT THE OCTOPUS...
...THEY STILL TASTE PRETTY GOOD, HUH?
WE KNOW EXACTLY WHAT YOU MEAN...
OH YEAH, BY THE WAY—JUST NOW I SAID I THOUGHT SHE'S A LITTLE BETTER THAN SHE USED TO BE?
WELL, I THINK THAT'S PROBABLY THANKS TO THE POP MUSIC CLUB... SO THANK YOU.
ANYWAY, SEE YOU GUYS TOMORROW.
...NODOKA-CHAN IS SO GROWN-UP.
YEAH... SHE REALLY IS. SHE'S SORTA LIKE MOMMY.
"MOMMY"...??
AAH—! I MEAN LIKE MY MOM!!

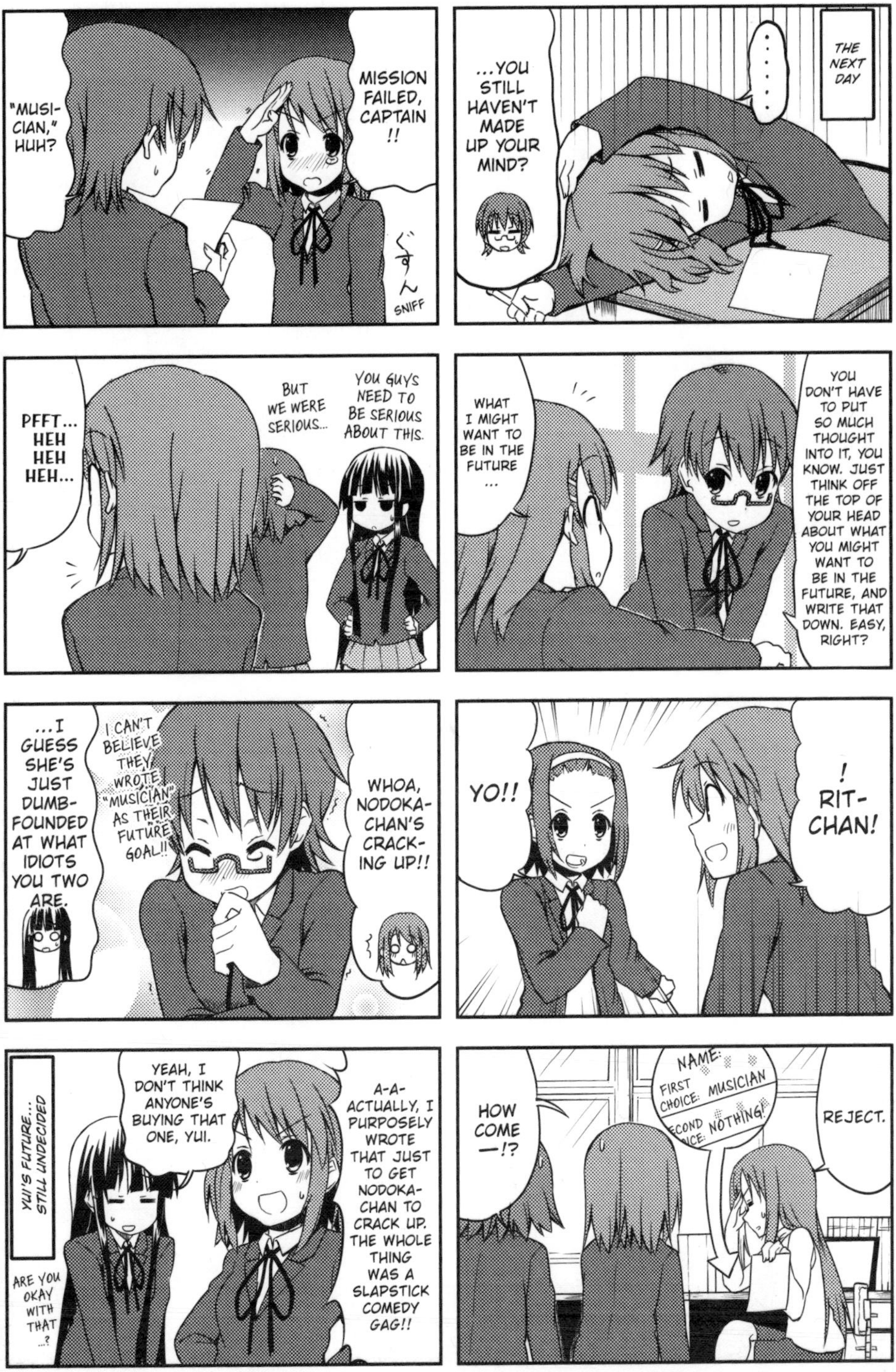
THE NEXT DAY
. . . . . .
...YOU STILL HAVEN'T MADE UP YOUR MIND?
YOU DON'T HAVE TO PUT SO MUCH THOUGHT INTO IT, YOU KNOW. JUST THINK OFF THE TOP OF YOUR HEAD ABOUT WHAT YOU MIGHT WANT TO BE IN THE FUTURE, AND WRITE THAT DOWN. EASY, RIGHT?
WHAT I MIGHT WANT TO BE IN THE FUTURE ...
! RIT-CHAN!
YO!!
NAME:
FIRST CHOICE: MUSICIAN
NOTHING!
REJECT.
HOW COME—!?
MISSION FAILED, CAPTAIN!!
"MUSI-CIAN," HUH?
ぐすん
SNIFF
YOU GUYS NEED TO BE SERIOUS ABOUT THIS.
BUT WE WERE SERIOUS...
PFFT... HEH HEH HEH...
WHOA, NODOKA-CHAN'S CRACKING UP!!
I CAN'T BELIEVE THEY WROTE "MUSICIAN" AS THEIR FUTURE GOAL!!
...I GUESS SHE'S JUST DUMB-FOUNDED AT WHAT IDIOTS YOU TWO ARE.
A-A-ACTUALLY, I PURPOSELY WROTE THAT JUST TO GET NODOKA-CHAN TO CRACK UP. THE WHOLE THING WAS A SLAPSTICK COMEDY GAG!!
YEAH, I DON'T THINK ANYONE'S BUYING THAT ONE, YUI.
YUI'S FUTURE... STILL UNDECIDED
ARE YOU OKAY WITH THAT ...?

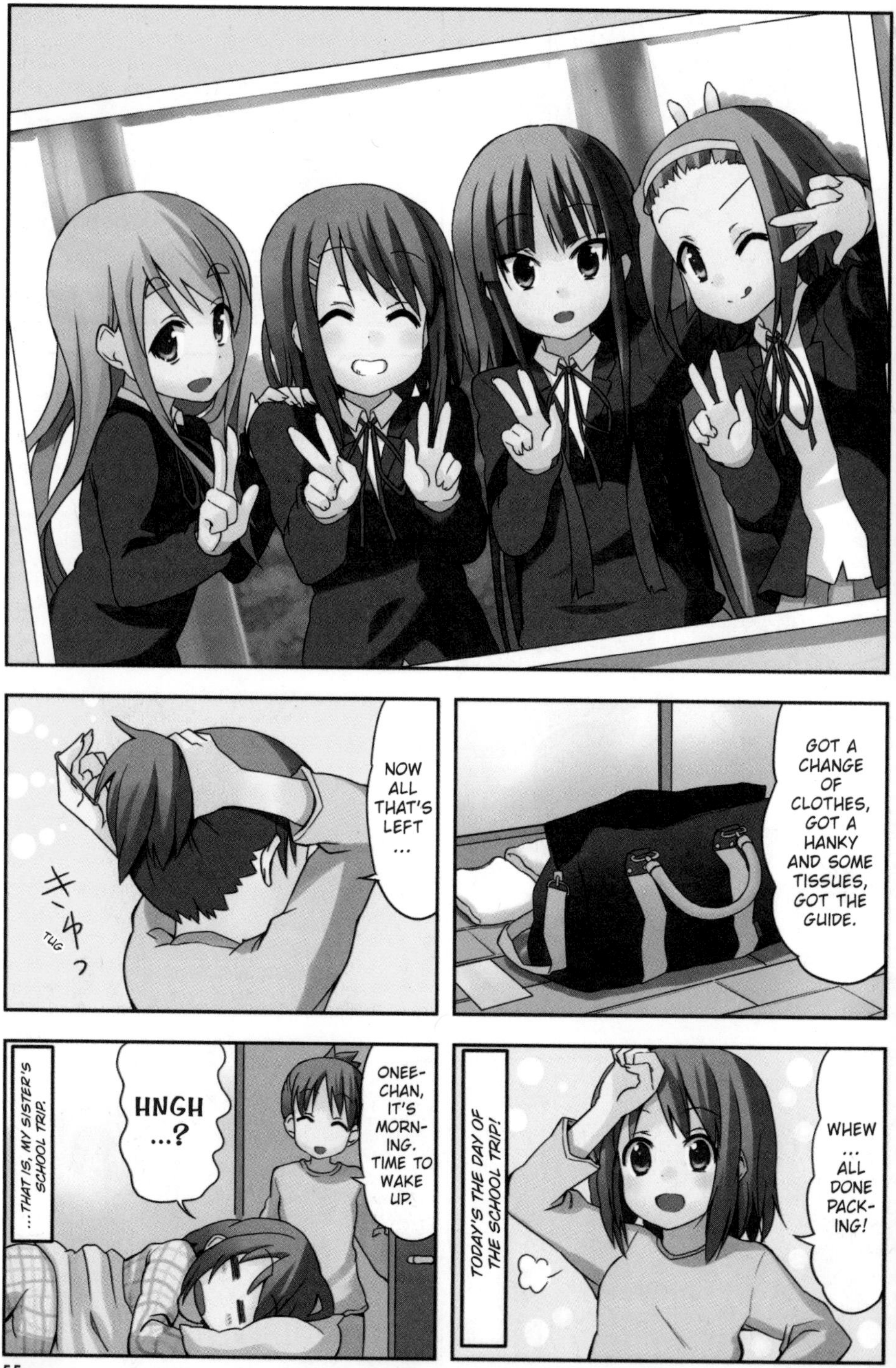
GOT A CHANGE OF CLOTHES, GOT A HANKY AND SOME TISSUES, GOT THE GUIDE.
NOW ALL THAT'S LEFT ...
TUG
WHEW ... ALL DONE PACK-ING!
TODAY'S THE DAY OF THE SCHOOL TRIP!
ONEE-CHAN, IT'S MORN-ING. TIME TO WAKE UP.
HNGH ...?
...THAT IS, MY SISTER'S SCHOOL TRIP.

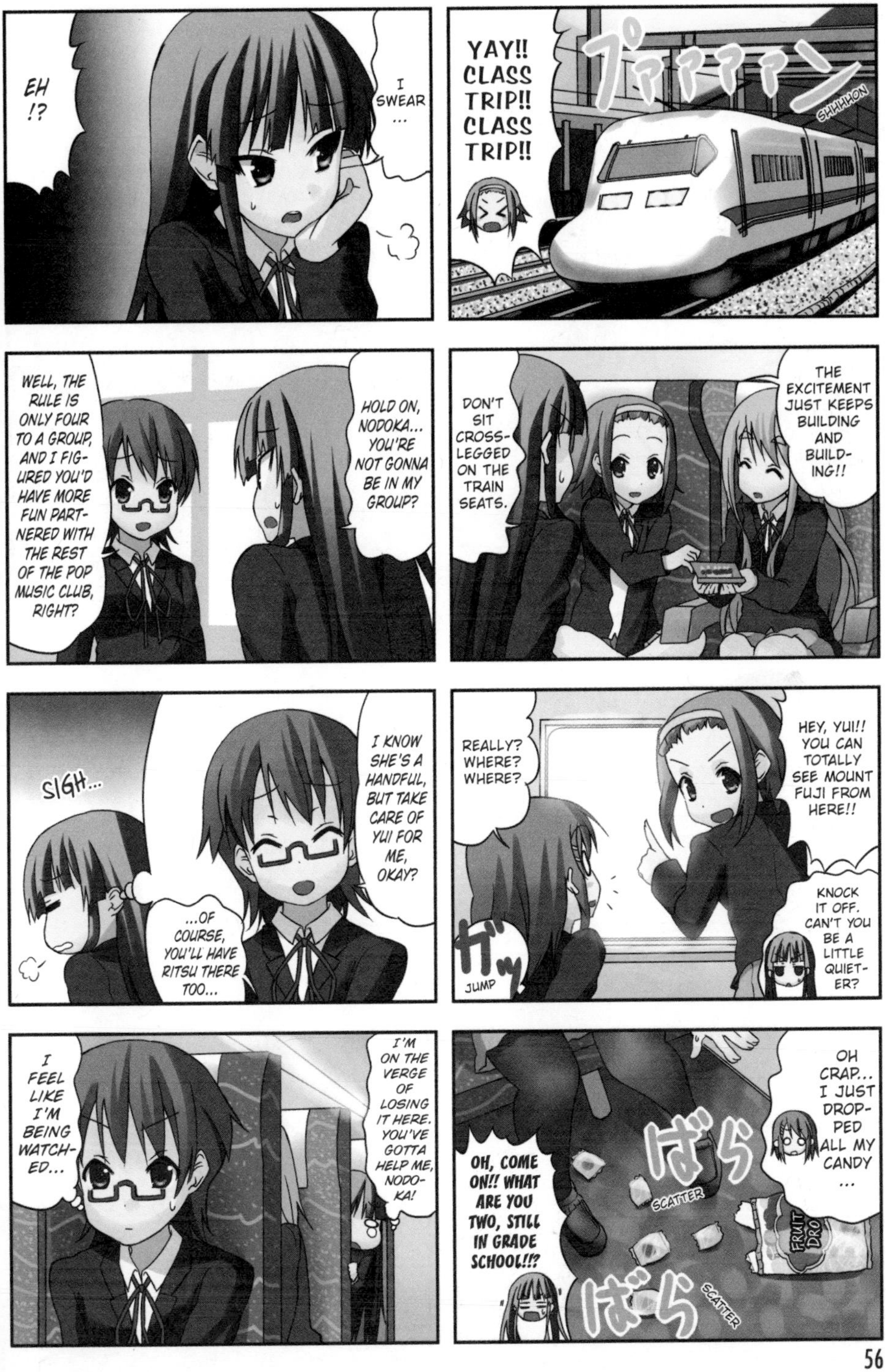
YAY!! CLASS TRIP!! CLASS TRIP!!
SHHHHON
I SWEAR ...
EH !?
THE EXCITEMENT JUST KEEPS BUILDING AND BUILDING!!
DON'T SIT CROSS-LEGGED ON THE TRAIN SEATS.
HOLD ON, NODOKA... YOU'RE NOT GONNA BE IN MY GROUP?
WELL, THE RULE IS ONLY FOUR TO A GROUP, AND I FIGURED YOU'D HAVE MORE FUN PARTNERED WITH THE REST OF THE POP MUSIC CLUB, RIGHT?
HEY, YUI!! YOU CAN TOTALLY SEE MOUNT FUJI FROM HERE!!
REALLY? WHERE? WHERE?
JUMP
KNOCK IT OFF. CAN'T YOU BE A LITTLE QUIETER?
I KNOW SHE'S A HANDFUL, BUT TAKE CARE OF YUI FOR ME, OKAY?
SIGH...
...OF COURSE, YOU'LL HAVE RITSU THERE TOO...
OH CRAP... I JUST DROPPED ALL MY CANDY ...
ばら
SCATTER
OH, COME ON!! WHAT ARE YOU TWO, STILL IN GRADE SCHOOL!!?
ばら
SCATTER
I'M ON THE VERGE OF LOSING IT HERE. YOU'VE GOTTA HELP ME, NODOKA!
I FEEL LIKE I'M BEING WATCHED...

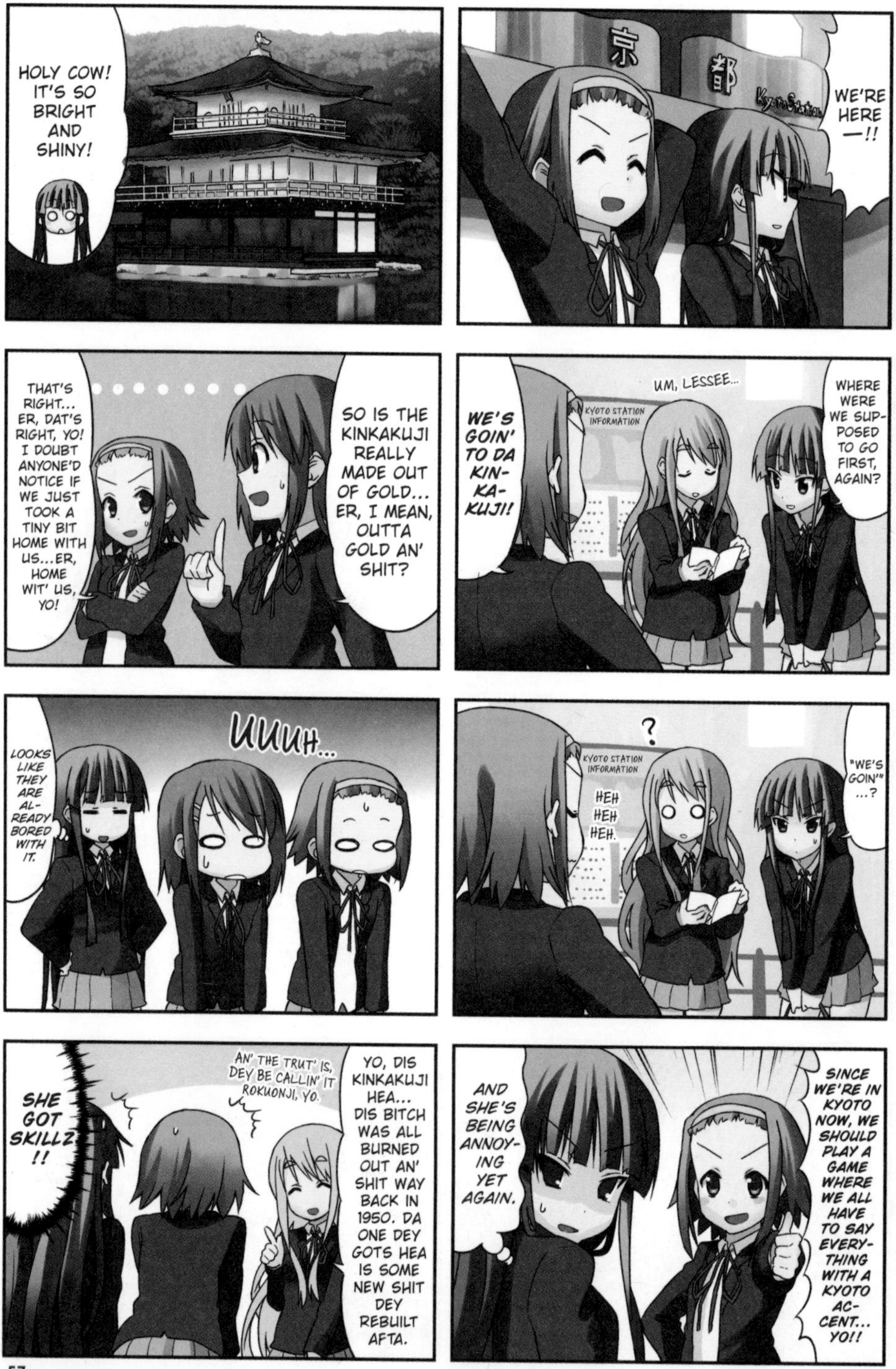

WE'RE HERE—!!
WHERE WERE WE SUPPOSED TO GO FIRST, AGAIN?
UM, LESSEE...
KYOTO STATION INFORMATION
WE'S GOIN' TO DA KIN-KA-KUJI!
"WE'S GOIN'"...?
?
HEH HEH HEH.
KYOTO STATION INFORMATION
SINCE WE'RE IN KYOTO NOW, WE SHOULD PLAY A GAME WHERE WE ALL HAVE TO SAY EVERYTHING WITH A KYOTO ACCENT... YO!!
AND SHE'S BEING ANNOYING YET AGAIN.
HOLY COW! IT'S SO BRIGHT AND SHINY!
SO IS THE KINKAKUJI REALLY MADE OUT OF GOLD... ER, I MEAN, OUTTA GOLD AN' SHIT?
THAT'S RIGHT... ER, DAT'S RIGHT, YO! I DOUBT ANYONE'D NOTICE IF WE JUST TOOK A TINY BIT HOME WITH US...ER, HOME WIT' US, YO!
UUUH...
LOOKS LIKE THEY ARE ALREADY BORED WITH IT.
YO, DIS KINKAKUJI HEA... DIS BITCH WAS ALL BURNED OUT AN' SHIT WAY BACK IN 1950. DA ONE DEY GOTS HEA IS SOME NEW SHIT DEY REBUILT AFTA.
AN' THE TRUT' IS, DEY BE CALLIN' IT ROKUONJI, YO.
SHE GOT SKILLZ!!

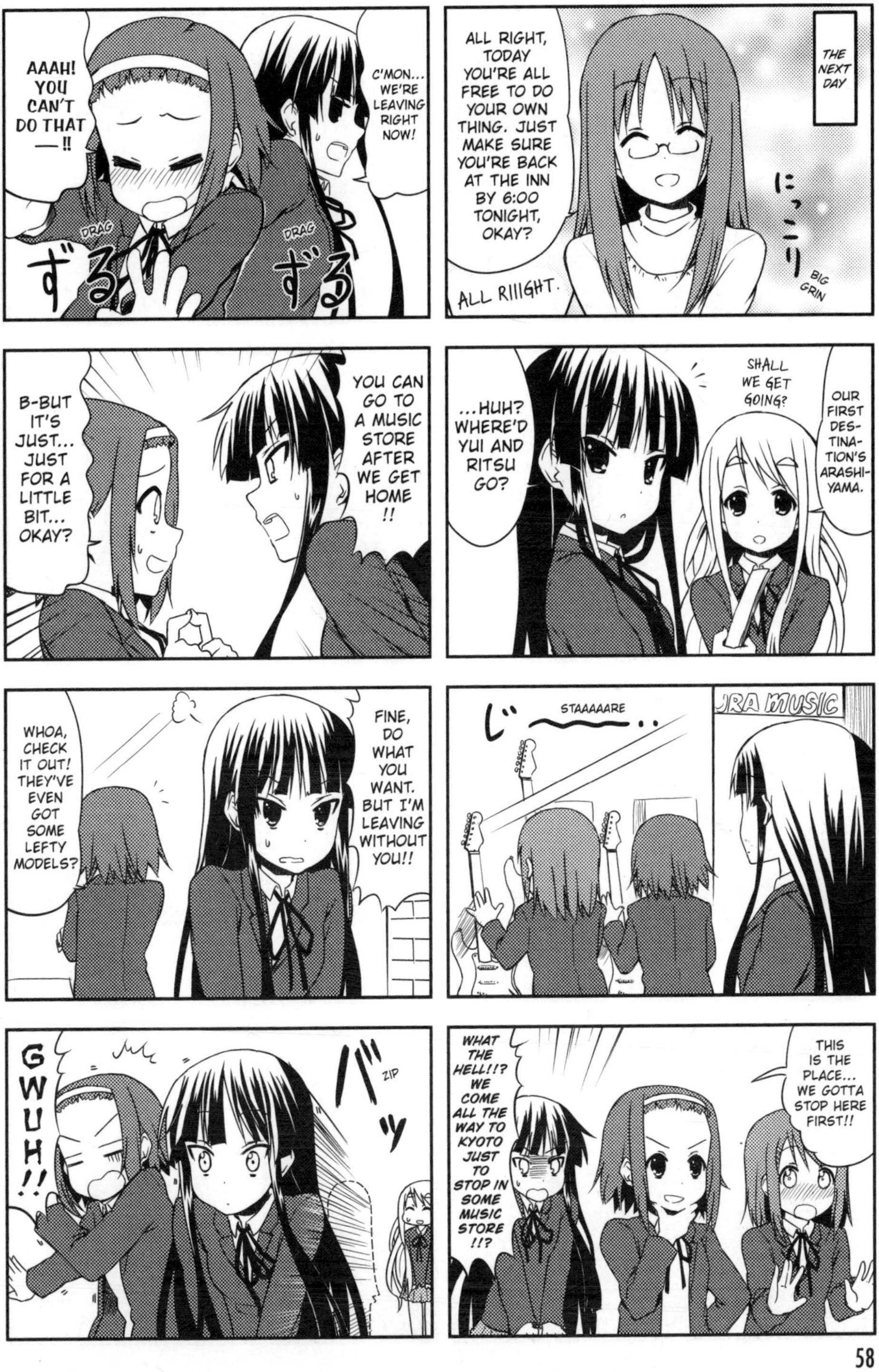
THE NEXT DAY
ALL RIGHT, TODAY YOU'RE ALL FREE TO DO YOUR OWN THING. JUST MAKE SURE YOU'RE BACK AT THE INN BY 6:00 TONIGHT, OKAY?
にっこり
BIG GRIN
ALL RIIIGHT.
C'MON... WE'RE LEAVING RIGHT NOW!
AAAH! YOU CAN'T DO THAT—!!
DRAG
ずる
DRAG
ずる
OUR FIRST DESTINATION'S ARASHIYAMA.
SHALL WE GET GOING?
...HUH? WHERE'D YUI AND RITSU GO?
YOU CAN GO TO A MUSIC STORE AFTER WE GET HOME!!
B-BUT IT'S JUST... JUST FOR A LITTLE BIT... OKAY?
RA MUSIC
じ〜〜〜..
STAAAAARE
FINE, DO WHAT YOU WANT. BUT I'M LEAVING WITHOUT YOU!!
WHOA, CHECK IT OUT! THEY'VE EVEN GOT SOME LEFTY MODELS?
THIS IS THE PLACE... WE GOTTA STOP HERE FIRST!!
WHAT THE HELL!!? WE COME ALL THE WAY TO KYOTO JUST TO STOP IN SOME MUSIC STORE!!?
バッ
ZIP
GWUH!!

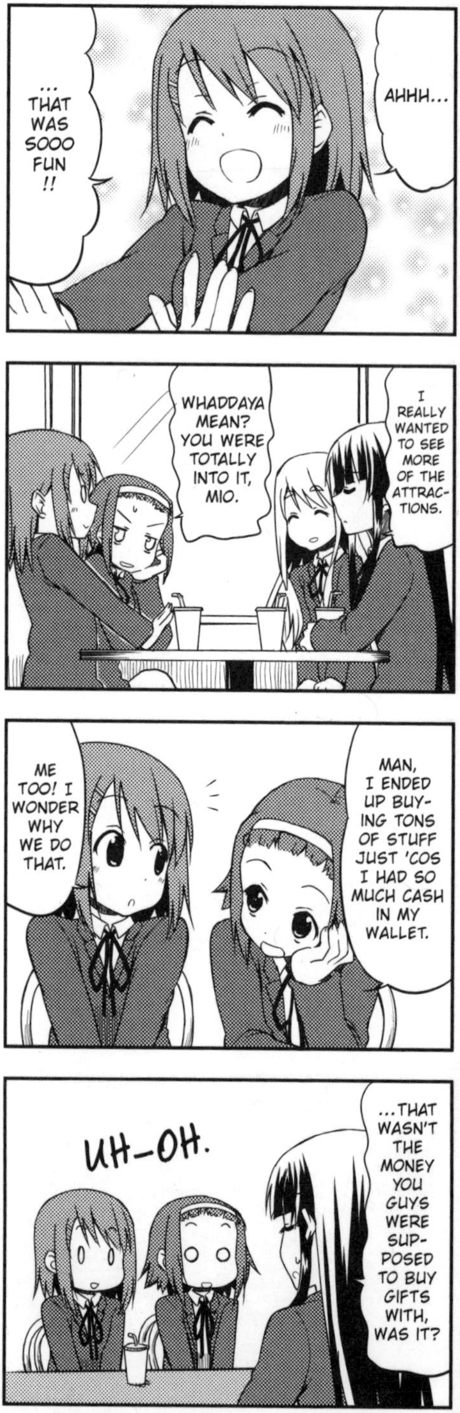
AHHH...
...THAT WAS SOOO FUN!!
I REALLY WANTED TO SEE MORE OF THE ATTRACTIONS.
WHADDAYA MEAN? YOU WERE TOTALLY INTO IT, MIO.
MAN, I ENDED UP BUYING TONS OF STUFF JUST 'COS I HAD SO MUCH CASH IN MY WALLET.
ME TOO! I WONDER WHY WE DO THAT.
...THAT WASN'T THE MONEY YOU GUYS WERE SUPPOSED TO BUY GIFTS WITH, WAS IT?
UH-OH.

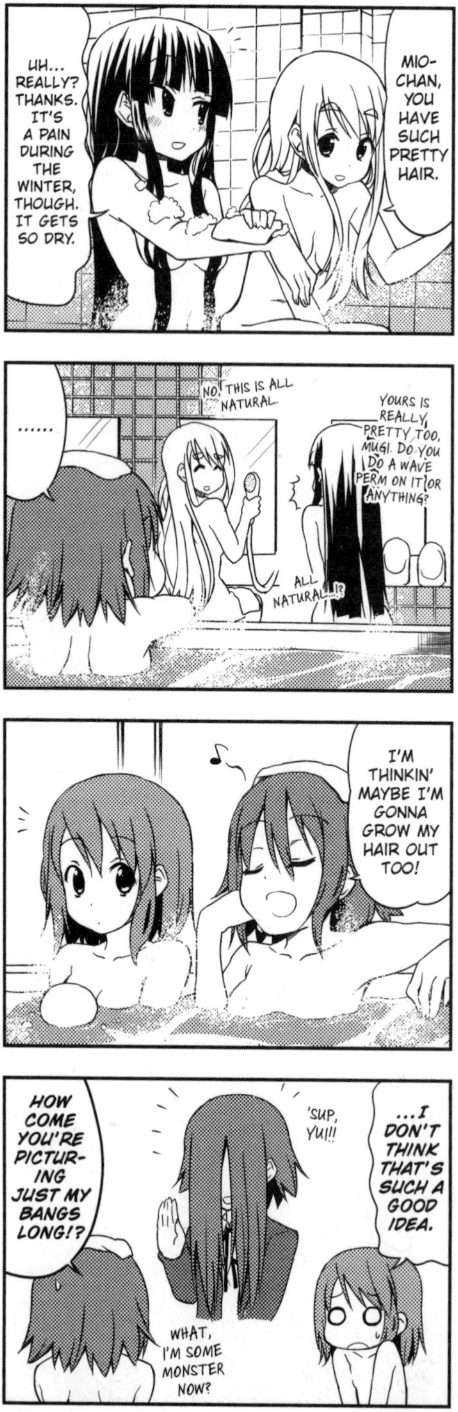
MIO-CHAN, YOU HAVE SUCH PRETTY HAIR.
UH... REALLY? THANKS. IT'S A PAIN DURING THE WINTER, THOUGH. IT GETS SO DRY.
YOURS IS REALLY PRETTY TOO, MUGI. DO YOU DO A WAVE PERM ON IT OR ANYTHING?
NO, THIS IS ALL NATURAL.
ALL NATURAL...!?
......
I'M THINKIN' MAYBE I'M GONNA GROW MY HAIR OUT TOO!
...I DON'T THINK THAT'S SUCH A GOOD IDEA.
'SUP, YUI!!
HOW COME YOU'RE PICTURING JUST MY BANGS LONG!?
WHAT, I'M SOME MONSTER NOW?

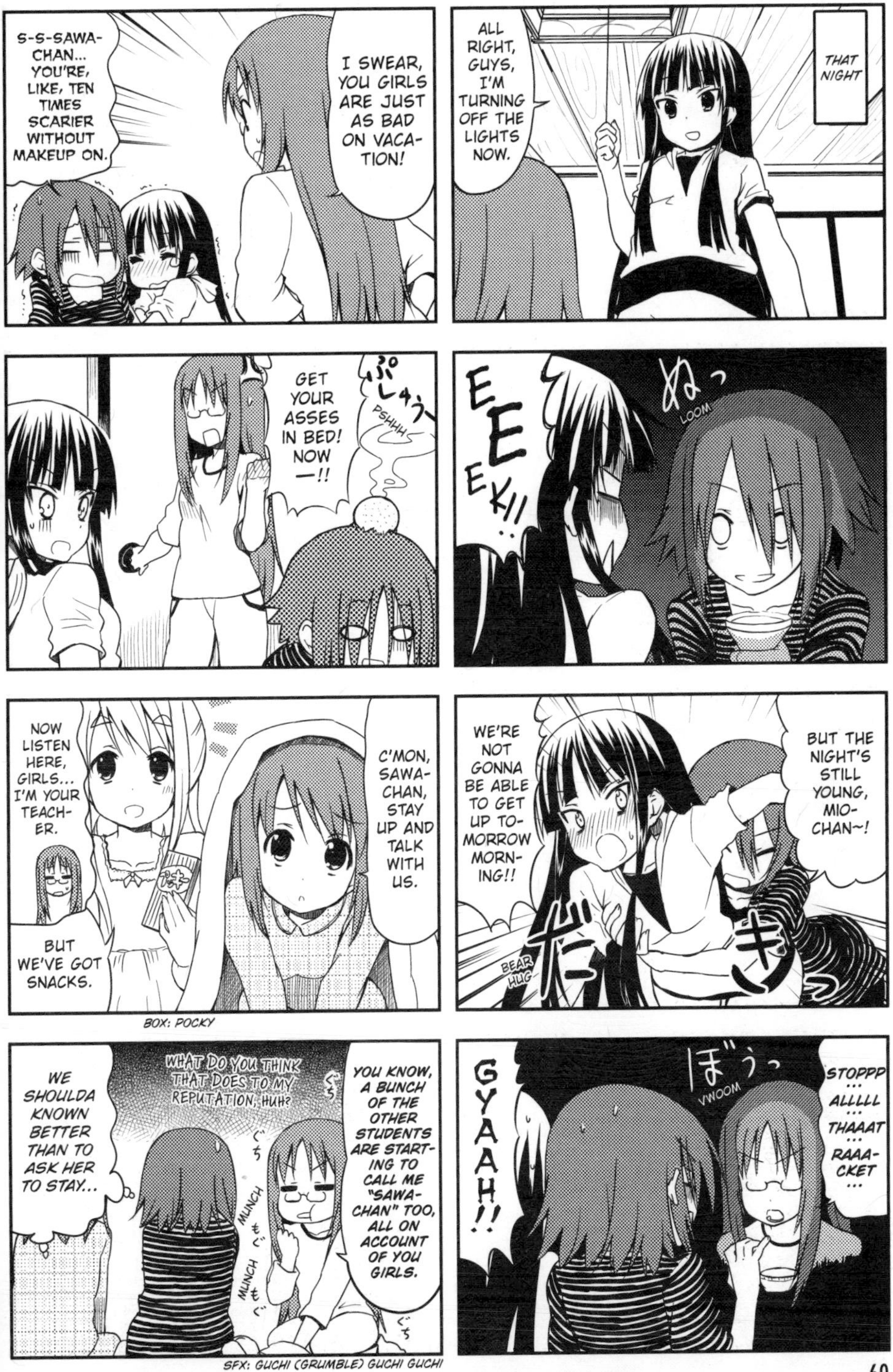
THAT NIGHT
ALL RIGHT, GUYS, I'M TURNING OFF THE LIGHTS NOW.
ぬっ
LOOM
EEEK!!
ぎゅっ
BEAR HUG
BUT THE NIGHT'S STILL YOUNG, MIO-CHAN~!
WE'RE NOT GONNA BE ABLE TO GET UP TOMORROW MORNING!!
ぼうっ
VWOOM
STOPPP... ALLLLL... THAAAT... RAAACKET...
GYAAH!!
I SWEAR, YOU GIRLS ARE JUST AS BAD ON VACATION!
S-S-SAWA-CHAN... YOU'RE, LIKE, TEN TIMES SCARIER WITHOUT MAKEUP ON.
ぷしゅう
PSHHH
GET YOUR ASSES IN BED! NOW—!!
C'MON, SAWA-CHAN, STAY UP AND TALK WITH US.
NOW LISTEN HERE, GIRLS... I'M YOUR TEACHER.
BUT WE'VE GOT SNACKS.
BOX: POCKY
YOU KNOW, A BUNCH OF THE OTHER STUDENTS ARE STARTING TO CALL ME "SAWA-CHAN" TOO, ALL ON ACCOUNT OF YOU GIRLS.
WHAT DO YOU THINK THAT DOES TO MY REPUTATION, HUH?
MUNCH MUNCH
WE SHOULDA KNOWN BETTER THAN TO ASK HER TO STAY...

SFX: GUCHI (GRUMBLE) GUCHI GUCHI

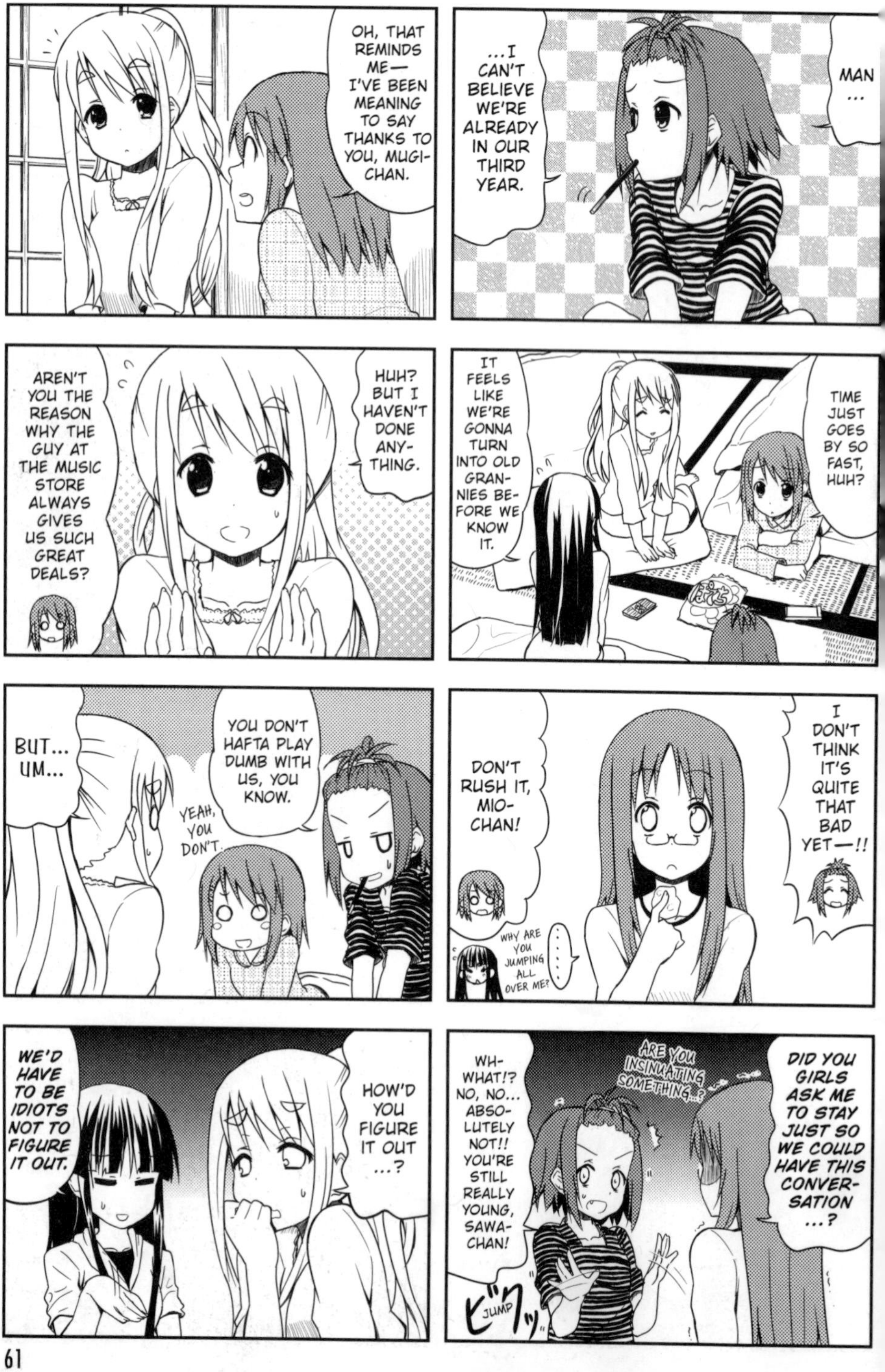
MAN ...
...I CAN'T BELIEVE WE'RE ALREADY IN OUR THIRD YEAR.
TIME JUST GOES BY SO FAST, HUH?
IT FEELS LIKE WE'RE GONNA TURN INTO OLD GRANNIES BEFORE WE KNOW IT.
I DON'T THINK IT'S QUITE THAT BAD YET—!!
DON'T RUSH IT, MIO-CHAN!
...
WHY ARE YOU JUMPING ALL OVER ME?
DID YOU GIRLS ASK ME TO STAY JUST SO WE COULD HAVE THIS CONVERSATION ...?
ARE YOU INSINUATING SOMETHING...?
WH-WHAT!? NO, NO... ABSOLUTELY NOT!! YOU'RE STILL REALLY YOUNG, SAWA-CHAN!
JUMP
OH, THAT REMINDS ME— I'VE BEEN MEANING TO SAY THANKS TO YOU, MUGI-CHAN.
HUH? BUT I HAVEN'T DONE ANYTHING.
AREN'T YOU THE REASON WHY THE GUY AT THE MUSIC STORE ALWAYS GIVES US SUCH GREAT DEALS?
YOU DON'T HAFTA PLAY DUMB WITH US, YOU KNOW.
YEAH, YOU DON'T.
BUT... UM...
HOW'D YOU FIGURE IT OUT ...?
WE'D HAVE TO BE IDIOTS NOT TO FIGURE IT OUT.

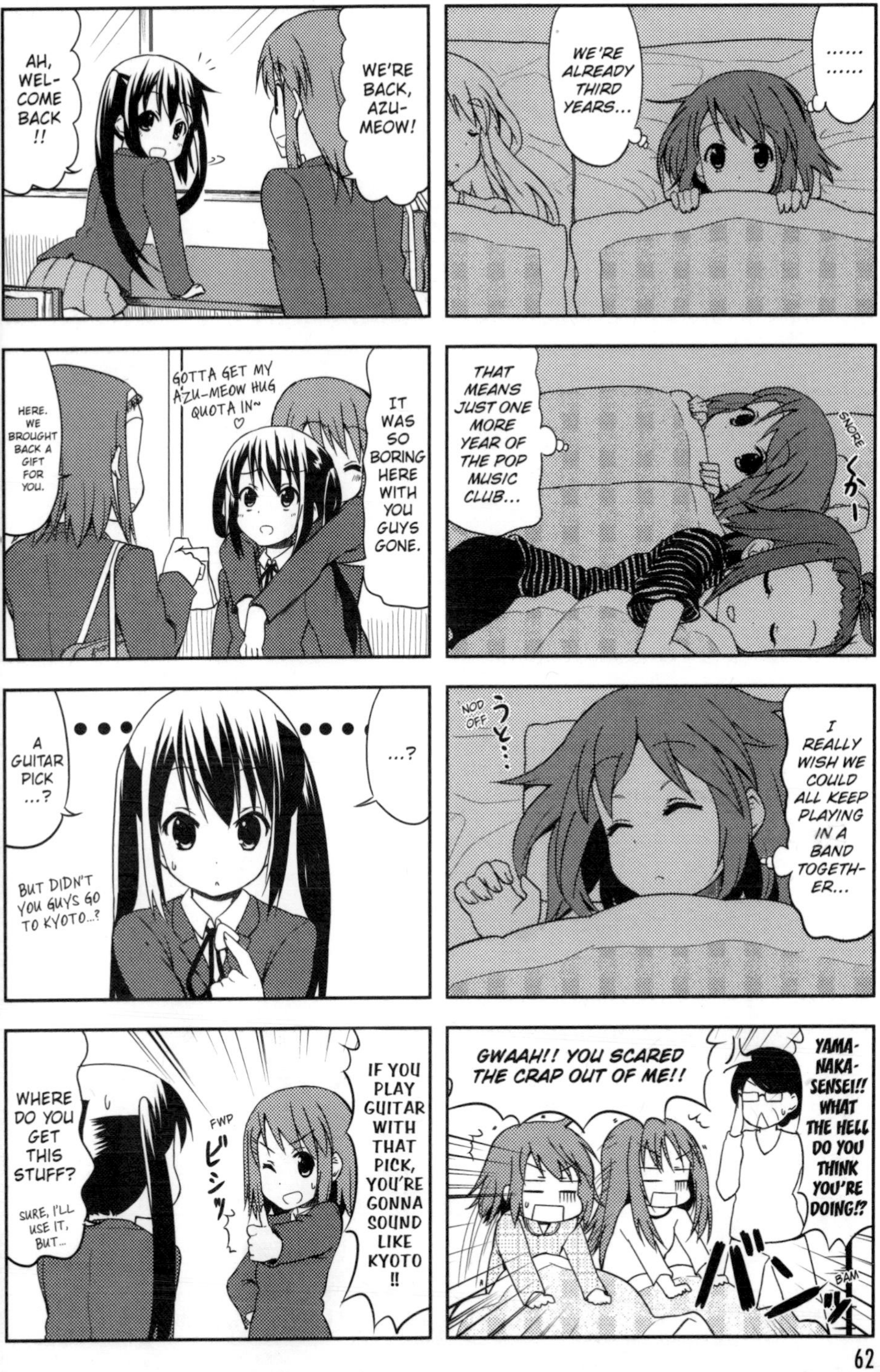
......
......
WE'RE ALREADY THIRD YEARS...
THAT MEANS JUST ONE MORE YEAR OF THE POP MUSIC CLUB...
SNORE
NOD OFF
I REALLY WISH WE COULD ALL KEEP PLAYING IN A BAND TOGETHER...
YAMA-NAKA-SENSEI!! WHAT THE HELL DO YOU THINK YOU'RE DOING!?
GWAAH!! YOU SCARED THE CRAP OUT OF ME!!
BAM
WE'RE BACK, AZU-MEOW!
AH, WEL-COME BACK!!
IT WAS SO BORING HERE WITH YOU GUYS GONE.
GOTTA GET MY AZU-MEOW HUG QUOTA IN~ ♡
HERE. WE BROUGHT BACK A GIFT FOR YOU.
...?
A GUITAR PICK ...?
BUT DIDN'T YOU GUYS GO TO KYOTO...?
IF YOU PLAY GUITAR WITH THAT PICK, YOU'RE GONNA SOUND LIKE KYOTO!!
FWP
WHERE DO YOU GET THIS STUFF?
SURE, I'LL USE IT, BUT...

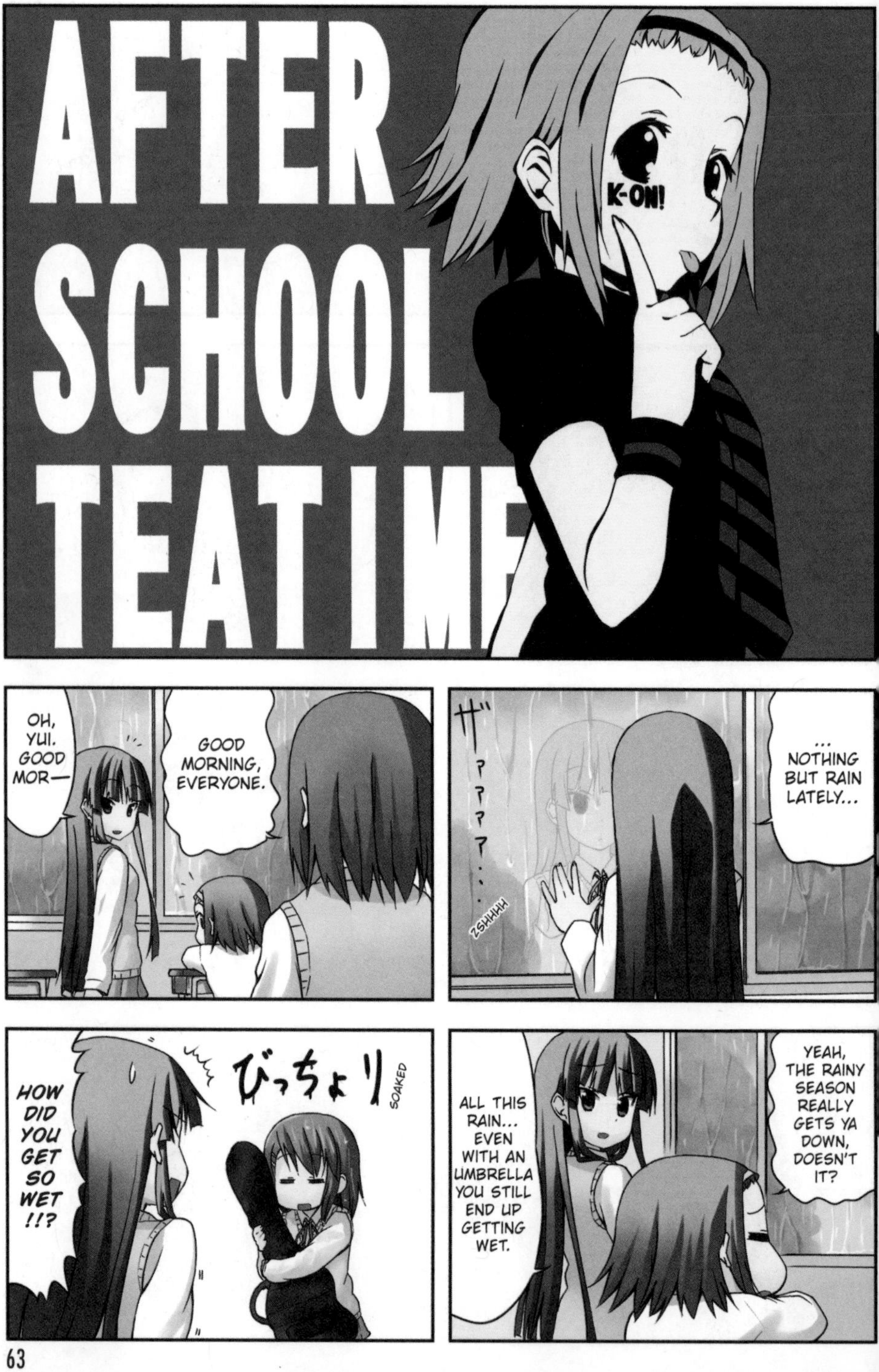
AFTER SCHOOL TEATIME
K-ON!
...NOTHING BUT RAIN LATELY...
ザァァァァ・・・
ZSHHHH
GOOD MORNING, EVERYONE.
OH, YUI. GOOD MOR—
YEAH, THE RAINY SEASON REALLY GETS YA DOWN, DOESN'T IT?
ALL THIS RAIN... EVEN WITH AN UMBRELLA YOU STILL END UP GETTING WET.
びっちょり
SOAKED
HOW DID YOU GET SO WET!!?

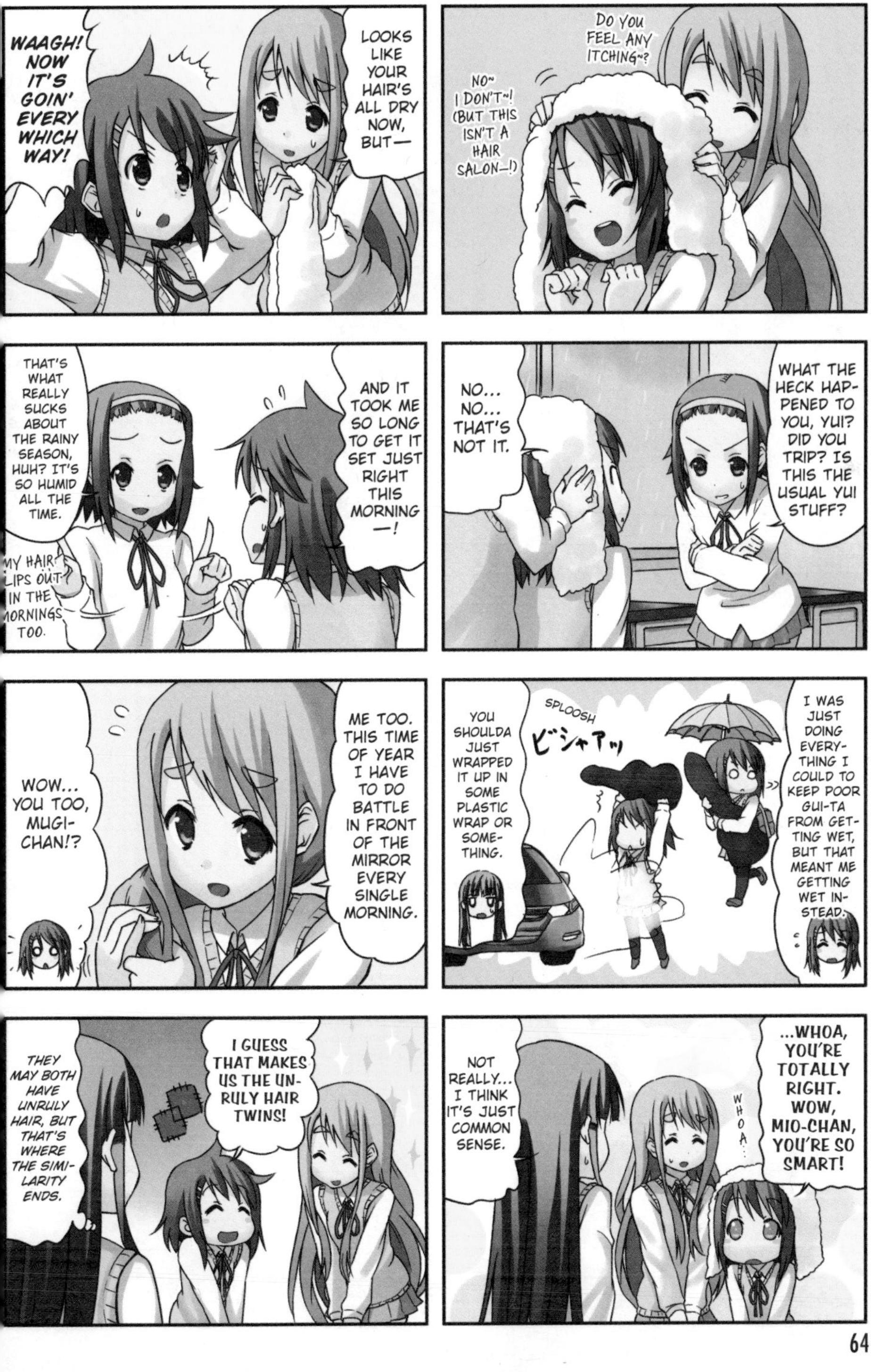
DO YOU FEEL ANY ITCHING~?
NO~ I DON'T~! (BUT THIS ISN'T A HAIR SALON—!)
LOOKS LIKE YOUR HAIR'S ALL DRY NOW, BUT—
WAAGH! NOW IT'S GOIN' EVERY WHICH WAY!
WHAT THE HECK HAPPENED TO YOU, YUI? DID YOU TRIP? IS THIS THE USUAL YUI STUFF?
NO... NO... THAT'S NOT IT.
AND IT TOOK ME SO LONG TO GET IT SET JUST RIGHT THIS MORNING—!
THAT'S WHAT REALLY SUCKS ABOUT THE RAINY SEASON, HUH? IT'S SO HUMID ALL THE TIME.
MY HAIR FLIPS OUT IN THE MORNINGS TOO.
I WAS JUST DOING EVERYTHING I COULD TO KEEP POOR GUI-TA FROM GETTING WET, BUT THAT MEANT ME GETTING WET INSTEAD.
SPLOOSH
ビシャアッ
YOU SHOULDA JUST WRAPPED IT UP IN SOME PLASTIC WRAP OR SOMETHING.
ME TOO. THIS TIME OF YEAR I HAVE TO DO BATTLE IN FRONT OF THE MIRROR EVERY SINGLE MORNING.
WOW... YOU TOO, MUGI-CHAN!?
...WHOA, YOU'RE TOTALLY RIGHT. WOW, MIO-CHAN, YOU'RE SO SMART!
WHOA...
NOT REALLY... I THINK IT'S JUST COMMON SENSE.
I GUESS THAT MAKES US THE UNRULY HAIR TWINS!
THEY MAY BOTH HAVE UNRULY HAIR, BUT THAT'S WHERE THE SIMILARITY ENDS.

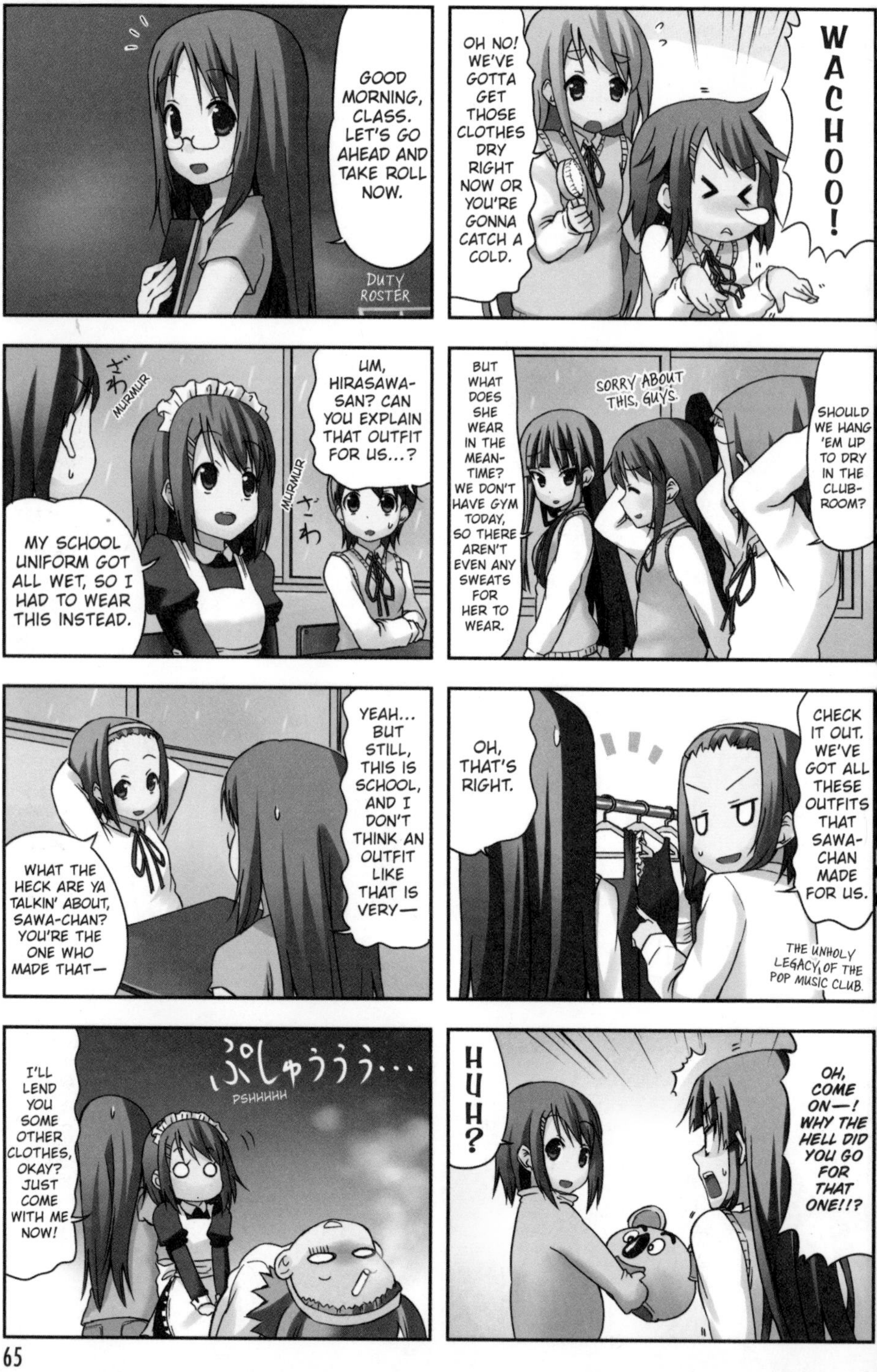
WACHOO!
OH NO! WE'VE GOTTA GET THOSE CLOTHES DRY RIGHT NOW OR YOU'RE GONNA CATCH A COLD.
SHOULD WE HANG 'EM UP TO DRY IN THE CLUB-ROOM?
SORRY ABOUT THIS, GUYS.
BUT WHAT DOES SHE WEAR IN THE MEAN-TIME? WE DON'T HAVE GYM TODAY, SO THERE AREN'T EVEN ANY SWEATS FOR HER TO WEAR.
CHECK IT OUT. WE'VE GOT ALL THESE OUTFITS THAT SAWA-CHAN MADE FOR US.
OH, THAT'S RIGHT.
THE UNHOLY LEGACY OF THE POP MUSIC CLUB.
OH, COME ON—! WHY THE HELL DID YOU GO FOR THAT ONE!!?
HUH?
GOOD MORNING, CLASS. LET'S GO AHEAD AND TAKE ROLL NOW.
DUTY ROSTER
UM, HIRASAWA-SAN? CAN YOU EXPLAIN THAT OUTFIT FOR US...?
ざわ
MURMUR
ざわ
MURMUR
MY SCHOOL UNIFORM GOT ALL WET, SO I HAD TO WEAR THIS INSTEAD.
YEAH... BUT STILL, THIS IS SCHOOL, AND I DON'T THINK AN OUTFIT LIKE THAT IS VERY—
WHAT THE HECK ARE YA TALKIN' ABOUT, SAWA-CHAN? YOU'RE THE ONE WHO MADE THAT—
ぷしゅううう…
PSHHHHH
I'LL LEND YOU SOME OTHER CLOTHES, OKAY? JUST COME WITH ME NOW!

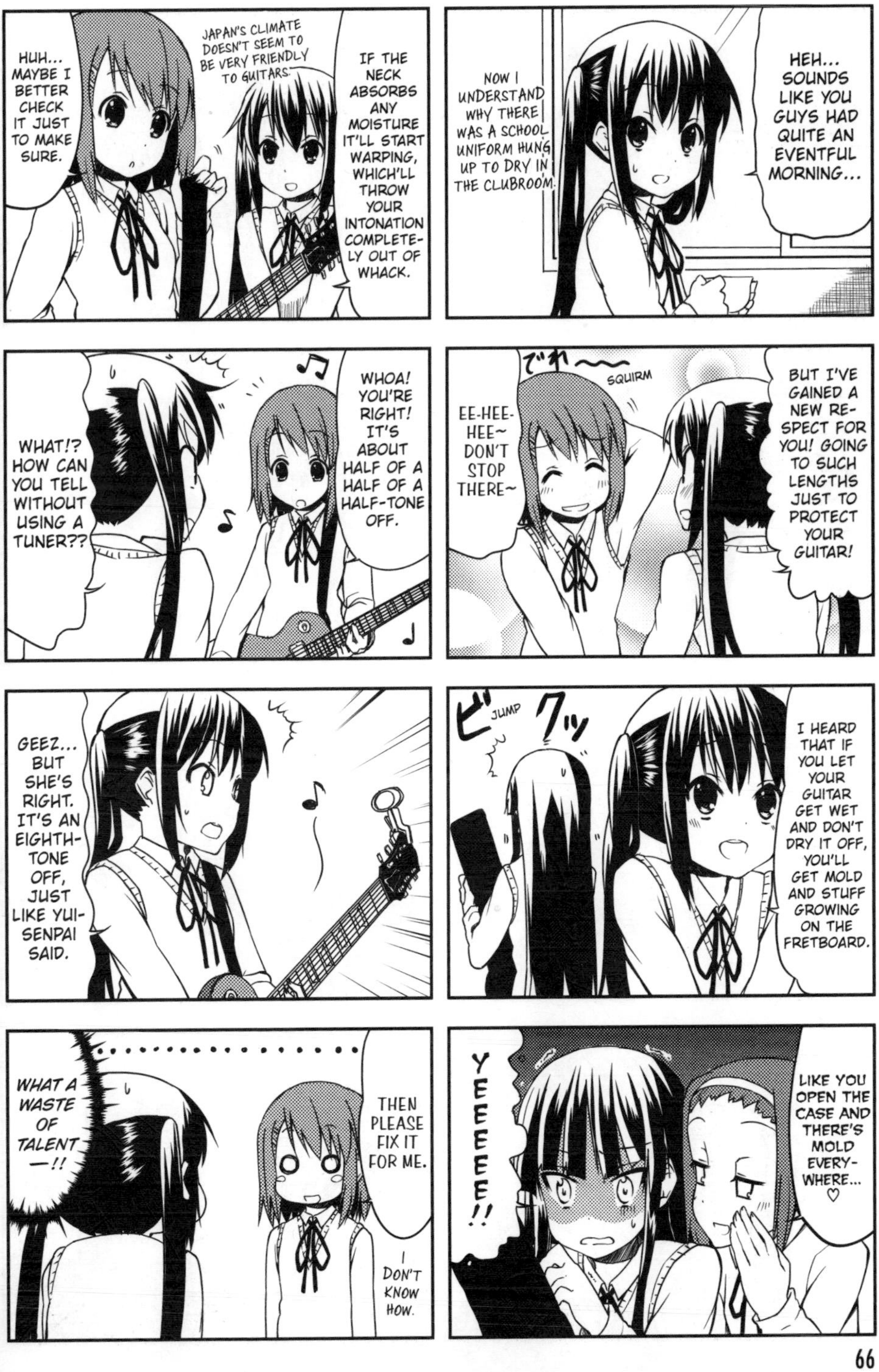

HEH... SOUNDS LIKE YOU GUYS HAD QUITE AN EVENTFUL MORNING...
NOW I UNDERSTAND WHY THERE WAS A SCHOOL UNIFORM HUNG UP TO DRY IN THE CLUBROOM.
IF THE NECK ABSORBS ANY MOISTURE IT'LL START WARPING, WHICH'LL THROW YOUR INTONATION COMPLETELY OUT OF WHACK.
JAPAN'S CLIMATE DOESN'T SEEM TO BE VERY FRIENDLY TO GUITARS.
HUH... MAYBE I BETTER CHECK IT JUST TO MAKE SURE.
BUT I'VE GAINED A NEW RESPECT FOR YOU! GOING TO SUCH LENGTHS JUST TO PROTECT YOUR GUITAR!
でれ~~ SQUIRM
EE-HEE-HEE~ DON'T STOP THERE~
WHOA! YOU'RE RIGHT! IT'S ABOUT HALF OF A HALF OF A HALF-TONE OFF.
WHAT!? HOW CAN YOU TELL WITHOUT USING A TUNER??
I HEARD THAT IF YOU LET YOUR GUITAR GET WET AND DON'T DRY IT OFF, YOU'LL GET MOLD AND STUFF GROWING ON THE FRETBOARD.
クッ
ビ JUMP
GEEZ... BUT SHE'S RIGHT. IT'S AN EIGHTH-TONE OFF, JUST LIKE YUI-SENPAI SAID.
LIKE YOU OPEN THE CASE AND THERE'S MOLD EVERYWHERE... ♡
YEEEEEE!!
THEN PLEASE FIX IT FOR ME.
I DON'T KNOW HOW.
....
WHAT A WASTE OF TALENT—!!

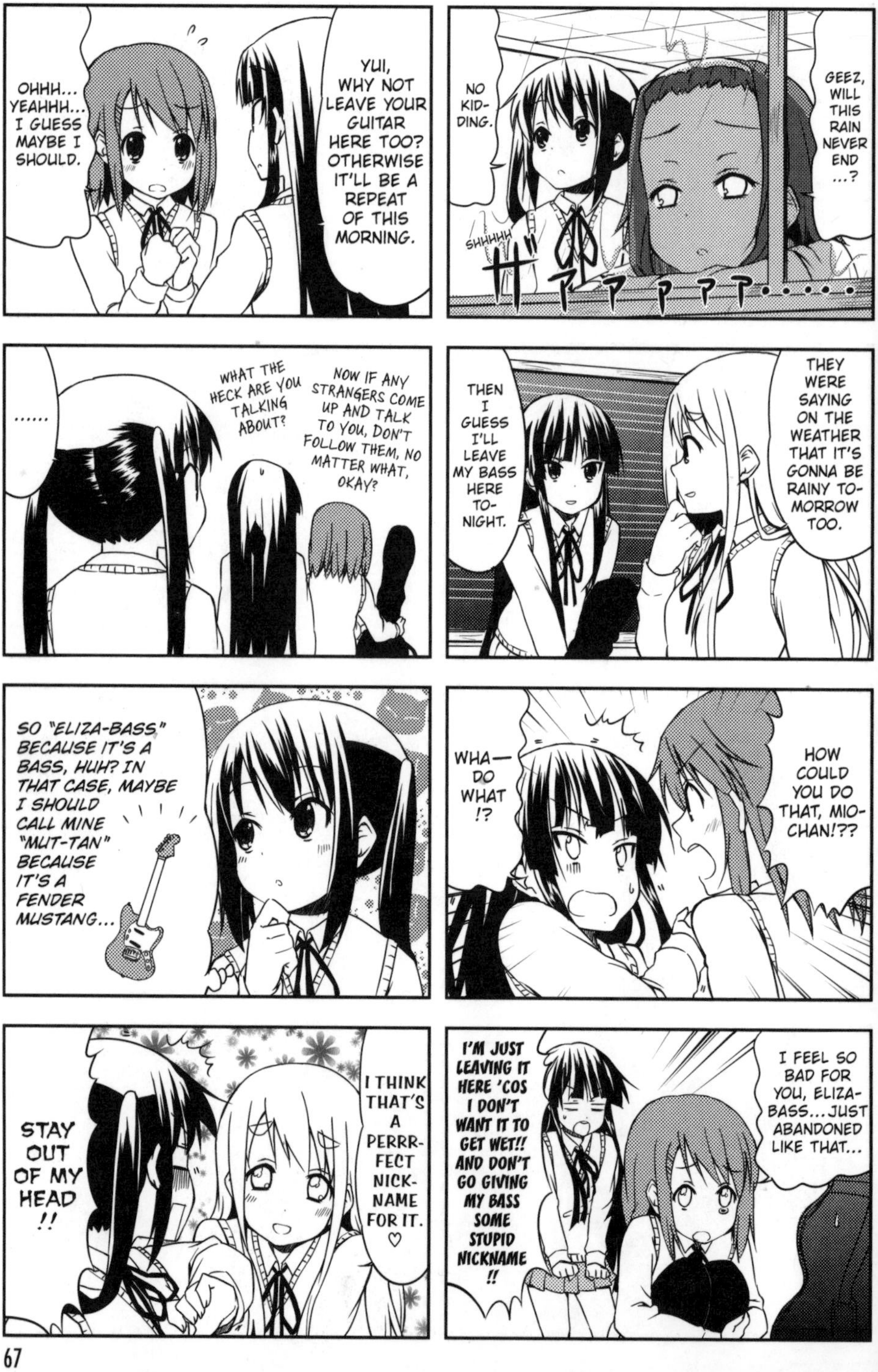
GEEZ, WILL THIS RAIN NEVER END ...?
NO KIDDING.
SHHHHH
ザァァァァァ.....
YUI, WHY NOT LEAVE YOUR GUITAR HERE TOO? OTHERWISE IT'LL BE A REPEAT OF THIS MORNING.
OHHH... YEAHHH... I GUESS MAYBE I SHOULD.
THEY WERE SAYING ON THE WEATHER THAT IT'S GONNA BE RAINY TOMORROW TOO.
THEN I GUESS I'LL LEAVE MY BASS HERE TONIGHT.
NOW IF ANY STRANGERS COME UP AND TALK TO YOU, DON'T FOLLOW THEM, NO MATTER WHAT, OKAY?
WHAT THE HECK ARE YOU TALKING ABOUT?
......
HOW COULD YOU DO THAT, MIO-CHAN!??
WHA— DO WHAT!?
SO "ELIZA-BASS" BECAUSE IT'S A BASS, HUH? IN THAT CASE, MAYBE I SHOULD CALL MINE "MUT-TAN" BECAUSE IT'S A FENDER MUSTANG...
I FEEL SO BAD FOR YOU, ELIZA-BASS... JUST ABANDONED LIKE THAT...
I'M JUST LEAVING IT HERE 'COS I DON'T WANT IT TO GET WET!! AND DON'T GO GIVING MY BASS SOME STUPID NICKNAME!!
I THINK THAT'S A PERRRFECT NICKNAME FOR IT. ♡
STAY OUT OF MY HEAD!!

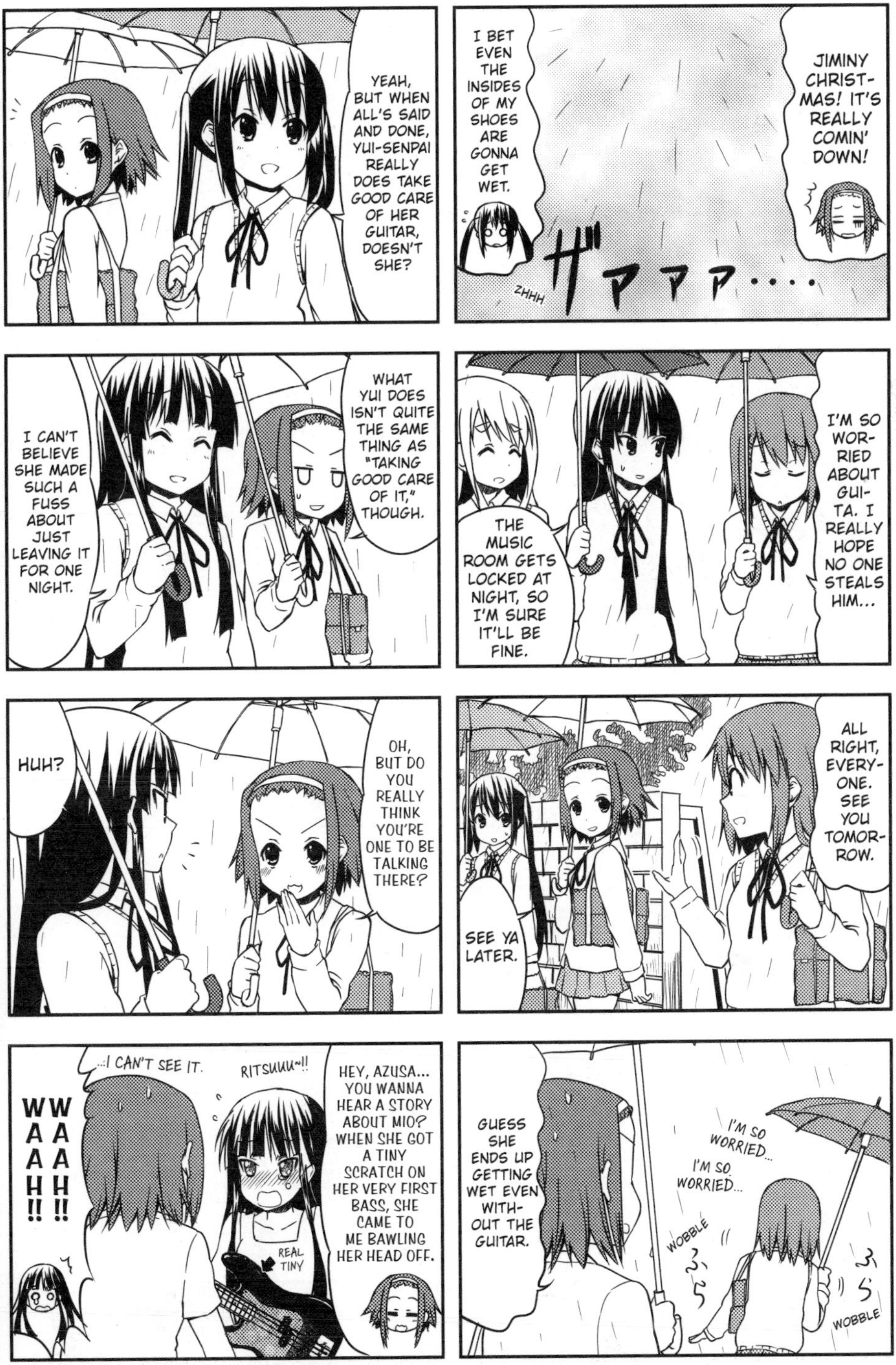

JIMINY CHRIST-MAS! IT'S REALLY COMIN' DOWN!
I BET EVEN THE INSIDES OF MY SHOES ARE GONNA GET WET.
ザァァァ....
ZHHH
YEAH, BUT WHEN ALL'S SAID AND DONE, YUI-SENPAI REALLY DOES TAKE GOOD CARE OF HER GUITAR, DOESN'T SHE?
I'M SO WOR-RIED ABOUT GUI-TA. I REALLY HOPE NO ONE STEALS HIM...
THE MUSIC ROOM GETS LOCKED AT NIGHT, SO I'M SURE IT'LL BE FINE.
WHAT YUI DOES ISN'T QUITE THE SAME THING AS "TAKING GOOD CARE OF IT," THOUGH.
I CAN'T BELIEVE SHE MADE SUCH A FUSS ABOUT JUST LEAVING IT FOR ONE NIGHT.
ALL RIGHT, EVERY-ONE. SEE YOU TOMOR-ROW.
SEE YA LATER.
OH, BUT DO YOU REALLY THINK YOU'RE ONE TO BE TALKING THERE?
HUH?
GUESS SHE ENDS UP GETTING WET EVEN WITH-OUT THE GUITAR.
I'M SO WORRIED...
I'M SO. WORRIED...
WOBBLE
ふら
ふら
WOBBLE
HEY, AZUSA... YOU WANNA HEAR A STORY ABOUT MIO? WHEN SHE GOT A TINY SCRATCH ON HER VERY FIRST BASS, SHE CAME TO ME BAWLING HER HEAD OFF.
RITSUUU~!!
...I CAN'T SEE IT.
WAAAH!!
WAAAH!!
REAL TINY

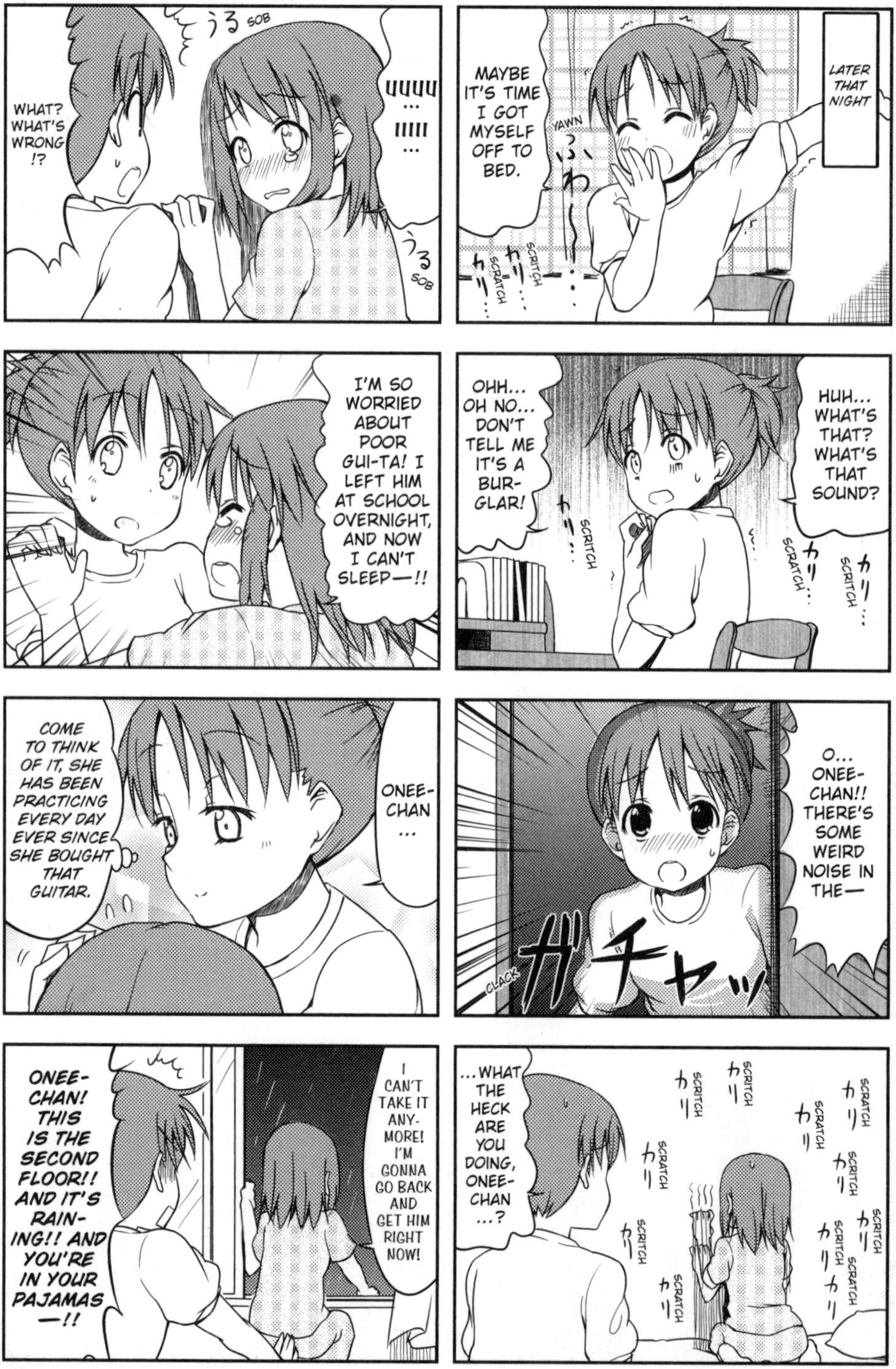
LATER THAT NIGHT
MAYBE IT'S TIME I GOT MYSELF OFF TO BED.
ふわ~…
YAWN
カリ…
SCRITCH
カリ…
SCRITCH
HUH... WHAT'S THAT? WHAT'S THAT SOUND?
カリ…
SCRITCH
カリ…
SCRITCH
OHH... OH NO... DON'T TELL ME IT'S A BUR-GLAR!
カリ…
SCRITCH
O... ONEE-CHAN!! THERE'S SOME WEIRD NOISE IN THE—
ガチャッ
CLACK
...WHAT THE HECK ARE YOU DOING, ONEE-CHAN ...?
カリ
SCRITCH
カリ
SCRITCH
カリ
SCRITCH
カリ
SCRITCH
カリ
SCRITCH
カリ
SCRITCH
カリ
SCRITCH
カリカリ
SCRITCH
カリ
SCRITCH
うる
SOB
UUUU... IIIII...
WHAT? WHAT'S WRONG !?
うる
SOB
I'M SO WORRIED ABOUT POOR GUI-TA! I LEFT HIM AT SCHOOL OVERNIGHT, AND NOW I CAN'T SLEEP—!!
ONEE-CHAN ...
COME TO THINK OF IT, SHE HAS BEEN PRACTICING EVERY DAY EVER SINCE SHE BOUGHT THAT GUITAR.
I CAN'T TAKE IT ANY-MORE! I'M GONNA GO BACK AND GET HIM RIGHT NOW!
ONEE-CHAN! THIS IS THE SECOND FLOOR!! AND IT'S RAIN-ING!! AND YOU'RE IN YOUR PAJAMAS —!!

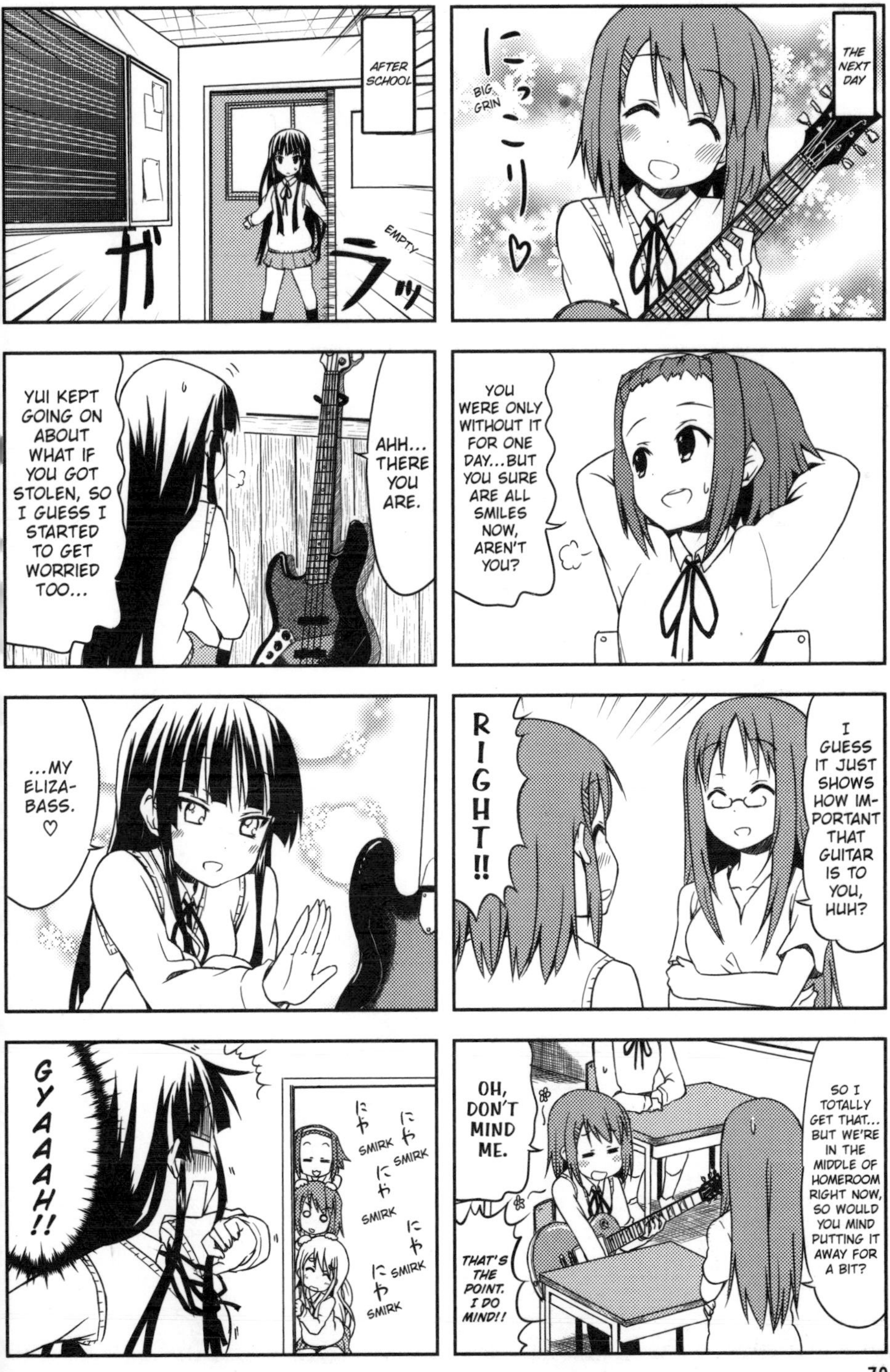
THE NEXT DAY
にっこりー♡
BIG GRIN
AFTER SCHOOL
ガラッ
EMPTY
YOU WERE ONLY WITHOUT IT FOR ONE DAY...BUT YOU SURE ARE ALL SMILES NOW, AREN'T YOU?
AHH... THERE YOU ARE.
YUI KEPT GOING ON ABOUT WHAT IF YOU GOT STOLEN, SO I GUESS I STARTED TO GET WORRIED TOO...
I GUESS IT JUST SHOWS HOW IM-PORTANT THAT GUITAR IS TO YOU, HUH?
RIGHT!!
...MY ELIZA-BASS. ♡
SO I TOTALLY GET THAT... BUT WE'RE IN THE MIDDLE OF HOMEROOM RIGHT NOW, SO WOULD YOU MIND PUTTING IT AWAY FOR A BIT?
OH, DON'T MIND ME.
THAT'S THE POINT. I DO MIND!!
にや SMIRK
にや SMIRK
にや SMIRK
にや SMIRK
にや SMIRK
GYAAAAH!!

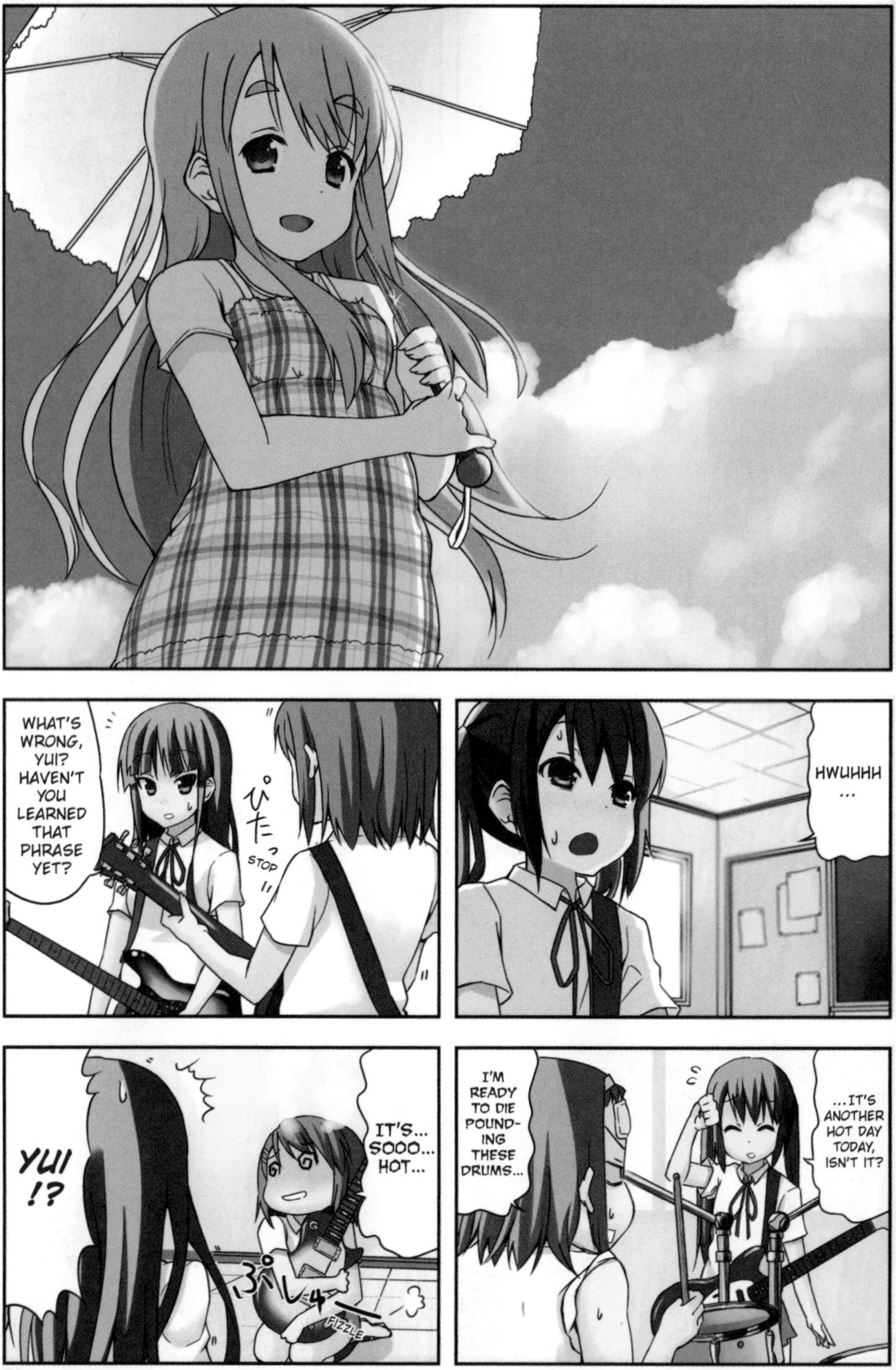
HWUHHH ...
WHAT'S WRONG, YUI? HAVEN'T YOU LEARNED THAT PHRASE YET?
ぴたっ
STOP
...IT'S ANOTHER HOT DAY TODAY, ISN'T IT?
I'M READY TO DIE POUNDING THESE DRUMS...
IT'S... SOOO... HOT...
YUI !?
ぷしー
FIZZLE

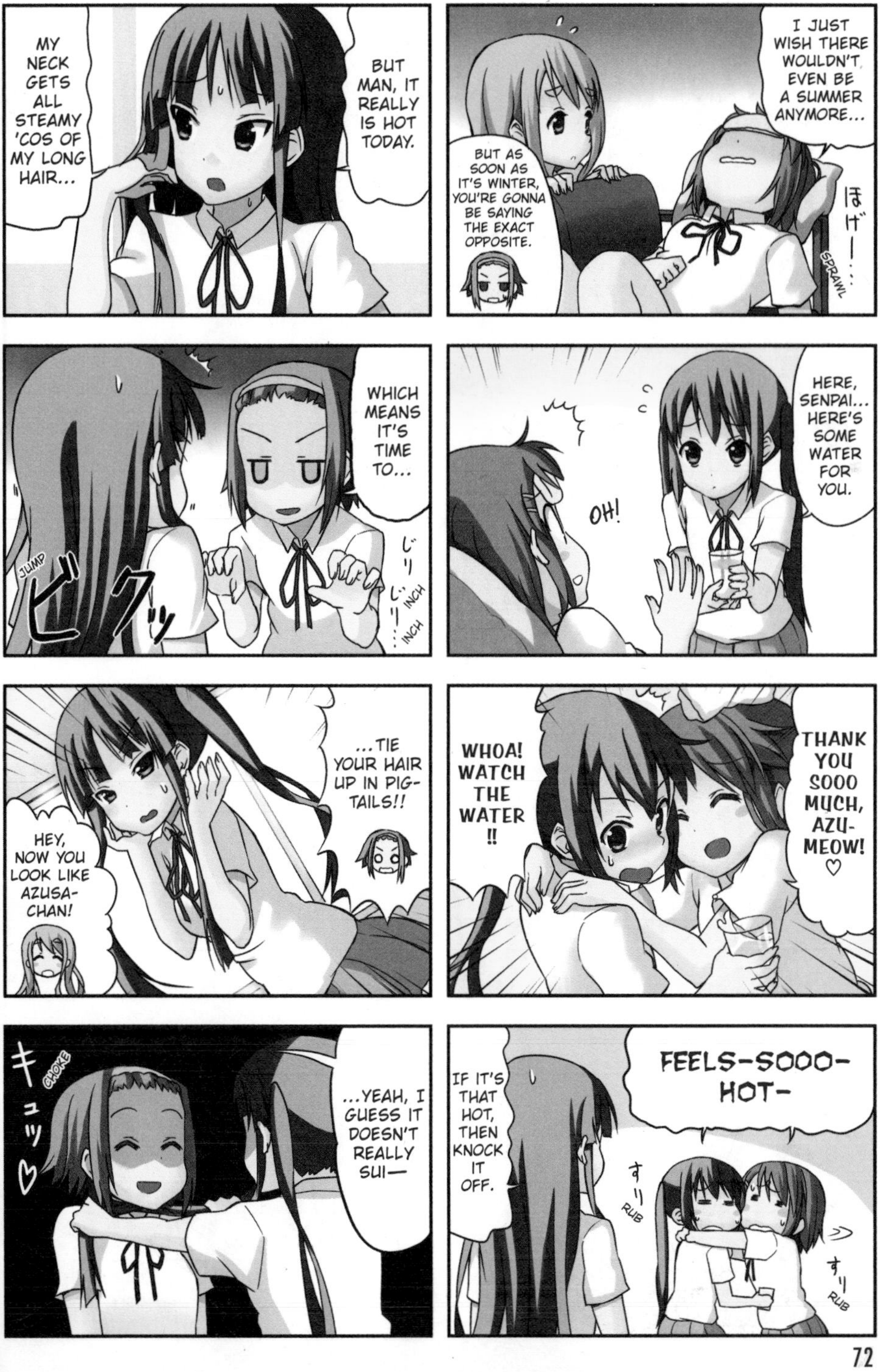
I JUST WISH THERE WOULDN'T EVEN BE A SUMMER ANYMORE...
ほげー...
SPRAWL
BUT AS SOON AS IT'S WINTER, YOU'RE GONNA BE SAYING THE EXACT OPPOSITE.
HERE, SENPAI... HERE'S SOME WATER FOR YOU.
OH!
THANK YOU SOOO MUCH, AZU-MEOW! ♡
WHOA! WATCH THE WATER !!
FEELS-SOOO-HOT-
IF IT'S THAT HOT, THEN KNOCK IT OFF.
すり
RUB
すり
RUB
BUT MAN, IT REALLY IS HOT TODAY.
MY NECK GETS ALL STEAMY 'COS OF MY LONG HAIR...
WHICH MEANS IT'S TIME TO...
じりじり...
INCH INCH
ビクッ
JUMP
...TIE YOUR HAIR UP IN PIG-TAILS!!
HEY, NOW YOU LOOK LIKE AZUSA-CHAN!
...YEAH, I GUESS IT DOESN'T REALLY SUI—
キュッ♡
CHOKE

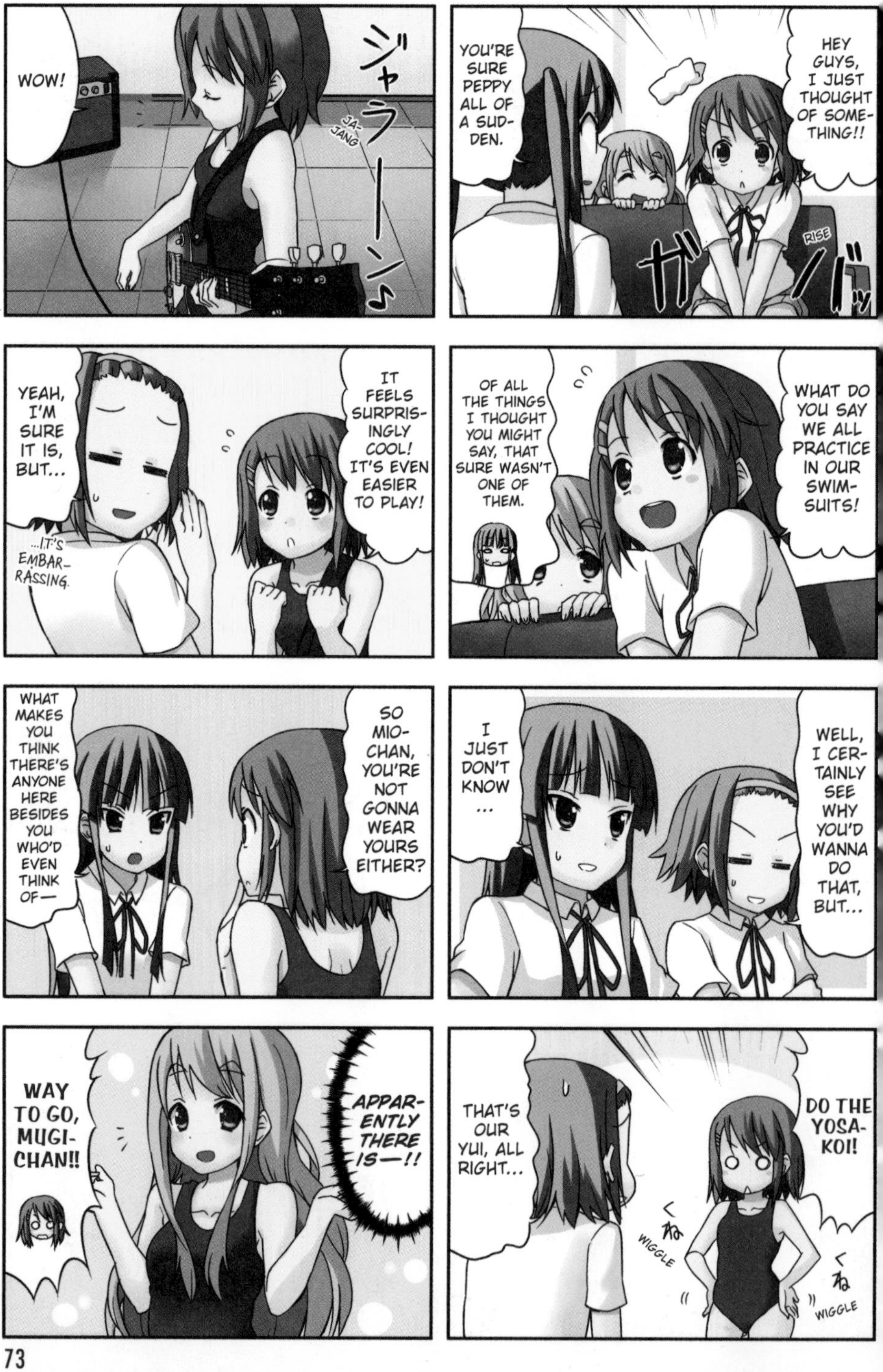
HEY GUYS, I JUST THOUGHT OF SOME-THING!!
RISE
ガバッ
YOU'RE SURE PEPPY ALL OF A SUD-DEN.
WHAT DO YOU SAY WE ALL PRACTICE IN OUR SWIM-SUITS!
OF ALL THE THINGS I THOUGHT YOU MIGHT SAY, THAT SURE WASN'T ONE OF THEM.
WELL, I CER-TAINLY SEE WHY YOU'D WANNA DO THAT, BUT...
I JUST DON'T KNOW ...
DO THE YOSA-KOI!
くね
WIGGLE
くね
WIGGLE
THAT'S OUR YUI, ALL RIGHT...
ジャラーン♪
JA-JANG
WOW!
IT FEELS SURPRIS-INGLY COOL! IT'S EVEN EASIER TO PLAY!
YEAH, I'M SURE IT IS, BUT...
...IT'S EMBAR-RASSING.
SO MIO-CHAN, YOU'RE NOT GONNA WEAR YOURS EITHER?
WHAT MAKES YOU THINK THERE'S ANYONE HERE BESIDES YOU WHO'D EVEN THINK OF—
WAY TO GO, MUGI-CHAN!!
APPAR-ENTLY THERE IS—!!

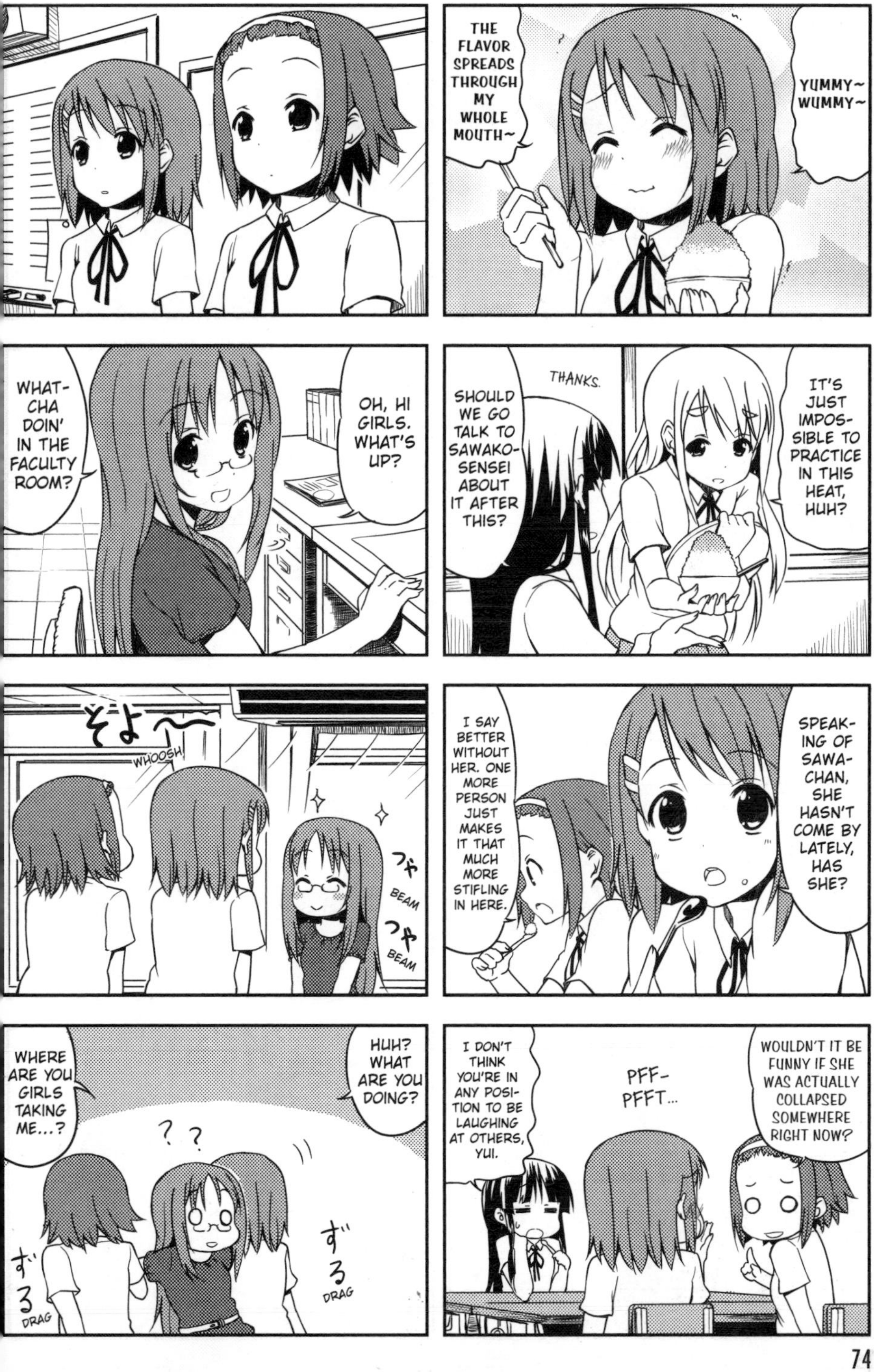
YUMMY~ WUMMY~
THE FLAVOR SPREADS THROUGH MY WHOLE MOUTH~
IT'S JUST IMPOSSIBLE TO PRACTICE IN THIS HEAT, HUH?
THANKS.
SHOULD WE GO TALK TO SAWAKO-SENSEI ABOUT IT AFTER THIS?
SPEAKING OF SAWA-CHAN, SHE HASN'T COME BY LATELY, HAS SHE?
I SAY BETTER WITHOUT HER. ONE MORE PERSON JUST MAKES IT THAT MUCH MORE STIFLING IN HERE.
WOULDN'T IT BE FUNNY IF SHE WAS ACTUALLY COLLAPSED SOMEWHERE RIGHT NOW?
PFF-PFFT...
I DON'T THINK YOU'RE IN ANY POSITION TO BE LAUGHING AT OTHERS, YUI.
OH, HI GIRLS. WHAT'S UP?
WHAT-CHA DOIN' IN THE FACULTY ROOM?
そよ〜
WHOOSH
つや
BEAM
つや
BEAM
HUH? WHAT ARE YOU DOING?
WHERE ARE YOU GIRLS TAKING ME...?
? ?
ずる
DRAG
ずる
DRAG

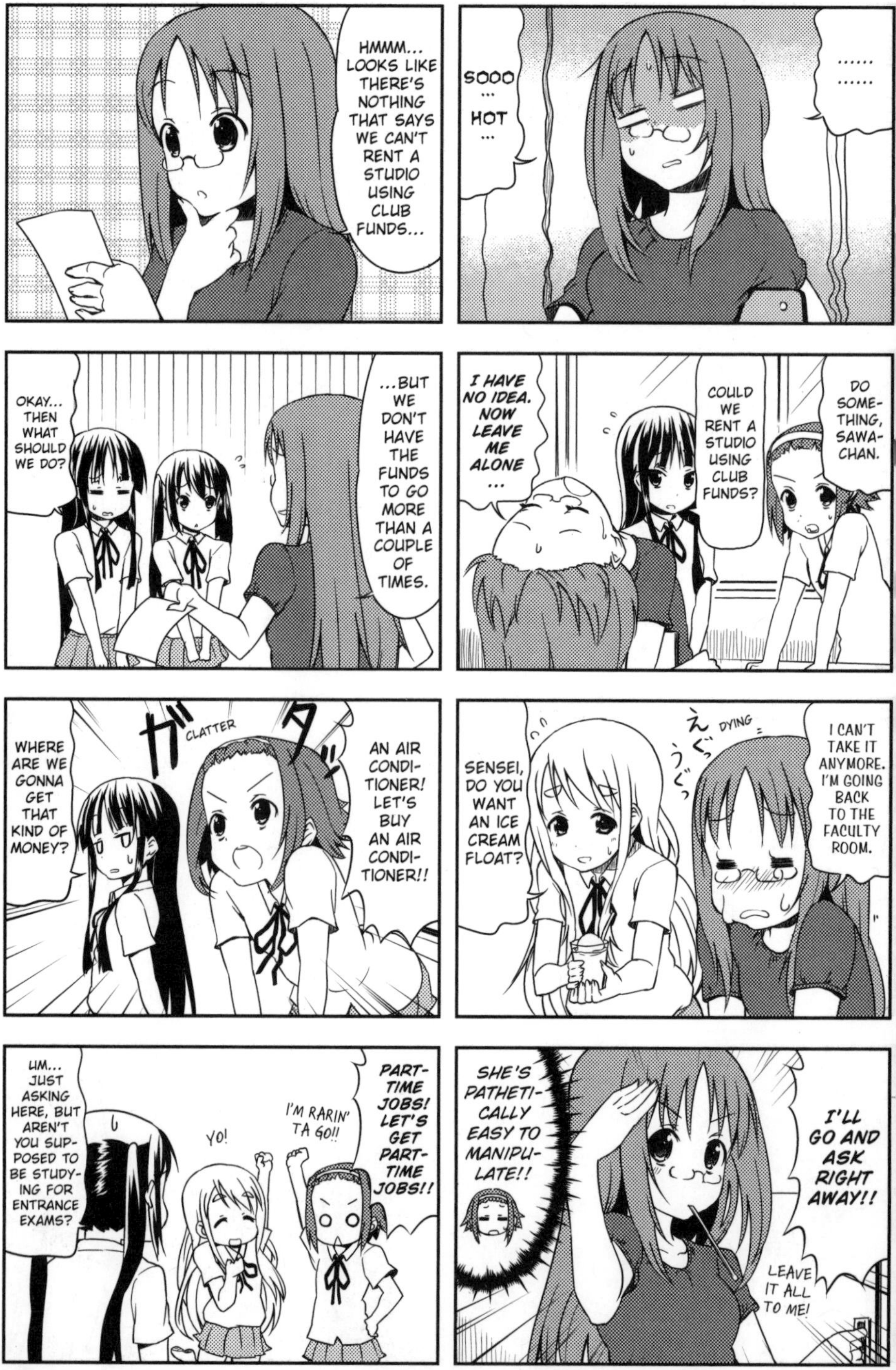
......
......
SOOO... HOT...
DO SOMETHING, SAWA-CHAN.
COULD WE RENT A STUDIO USING CLUB FUNDS?
I HAVE NO IDEA. NOW LEAVE ME ALONE...
I CAN'T TAKE IT ANYMORE. I'M GOING BACK TO THE FACULTY ROOM.
DYING
えぐっ うぐっ
SENSEI, DO YOU WANT AN ICE CREAM FLOAT?
I'LL GO AND ASK RIGHT AWAY!!
SHE'S PATHETICALLY EASY TO MANIPULATE!!
LEAVE IT ALL TO ME!
HMMM... LOOKS LIKE THERE'S NOTHING THAT SAYS WE CAN'T RENT A STUDIO USING CLUB FUNDS...
...BUT WE DON'T HAVE THE FUNDS TO GO MORE THAN A COUPLE OF TIMES.
OKAY... THEN WHAT SHOULD WE DO?
AN AIR CONDITIONER! LET'S BUY AN AIR CONDITIONER!!
ダッ
CLATTER
ガ
WHERE ARE WE GONNA GET THAT KIND OF MONEY?
PART-TIME JOBS! LET'S GET PART-TIME JOBS!!
I'M RARIN' TA GO!!
YO!
UM... JUST ASKING HERE, BUT AREN'T YOU SUPPOSED TO BE STUDYING FOR ENTRANCE EXAMS?

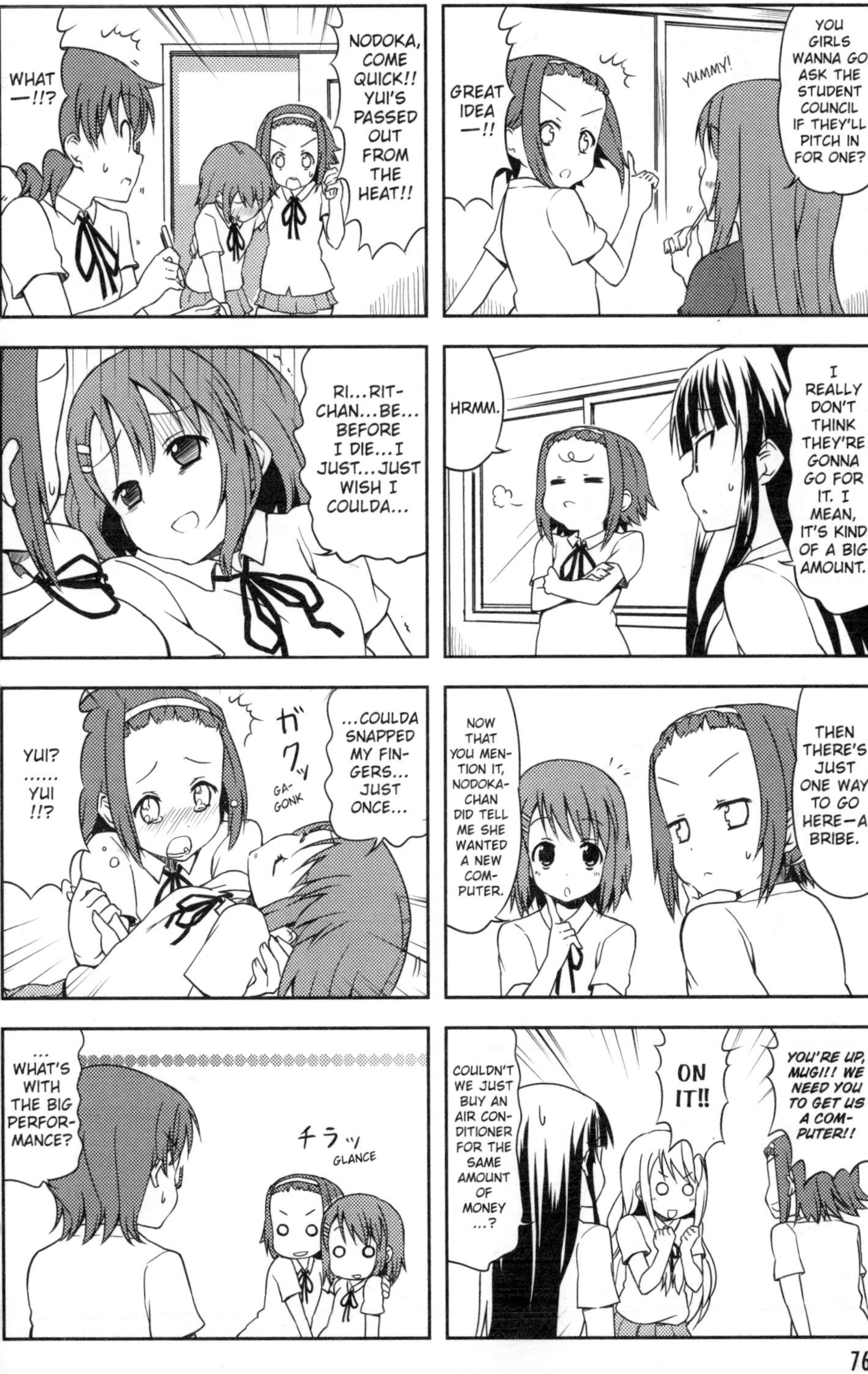
YOU GIRLS WANNA GO ASK THE STUDENT COUNCIL IF THEY'LL PITCH IN FOR ONE?
YUMMY!
GREAT IDEA—!!
I REALLY DON'T THINK THEY'RE GONNA GO FOR IT. I MEAN, IT'S KIND OF A BIG AMOUNT.
HRMM.
THEN THERE'S JUST ONE WAY TO GO HERE—A BRIBE.
NOW THAT YOU MENTION IT, NODOKA-CHAN DID TELL ME SHE WANTED A NEW COMPUTER.
YOU'RE UP, MUGI!! WE NEED YOU TO GET US A COMPUTER!!
ON IT!!
COULDN'T WE JUST BUY AN AIR CONDITIONER FOR THE SAME AMOUNT OF MONEY...?
NODOKA, COME QUICK!! YUI'S PASSED OUT FROM THE HEAT!!
WHAT—!!?
RI...RIT-CHAN...BE... BEFORE I DIE...I JUST...JUST WISH I COULDA...
...COULDA SNAPPED MY FINGERS... JUST ONCE...
ガクッ
GA-GONK
YUI? ...... YUI!!?
...WHAT'S WITH THE BIG PERFORMANCE?
チラッ
GLANCE

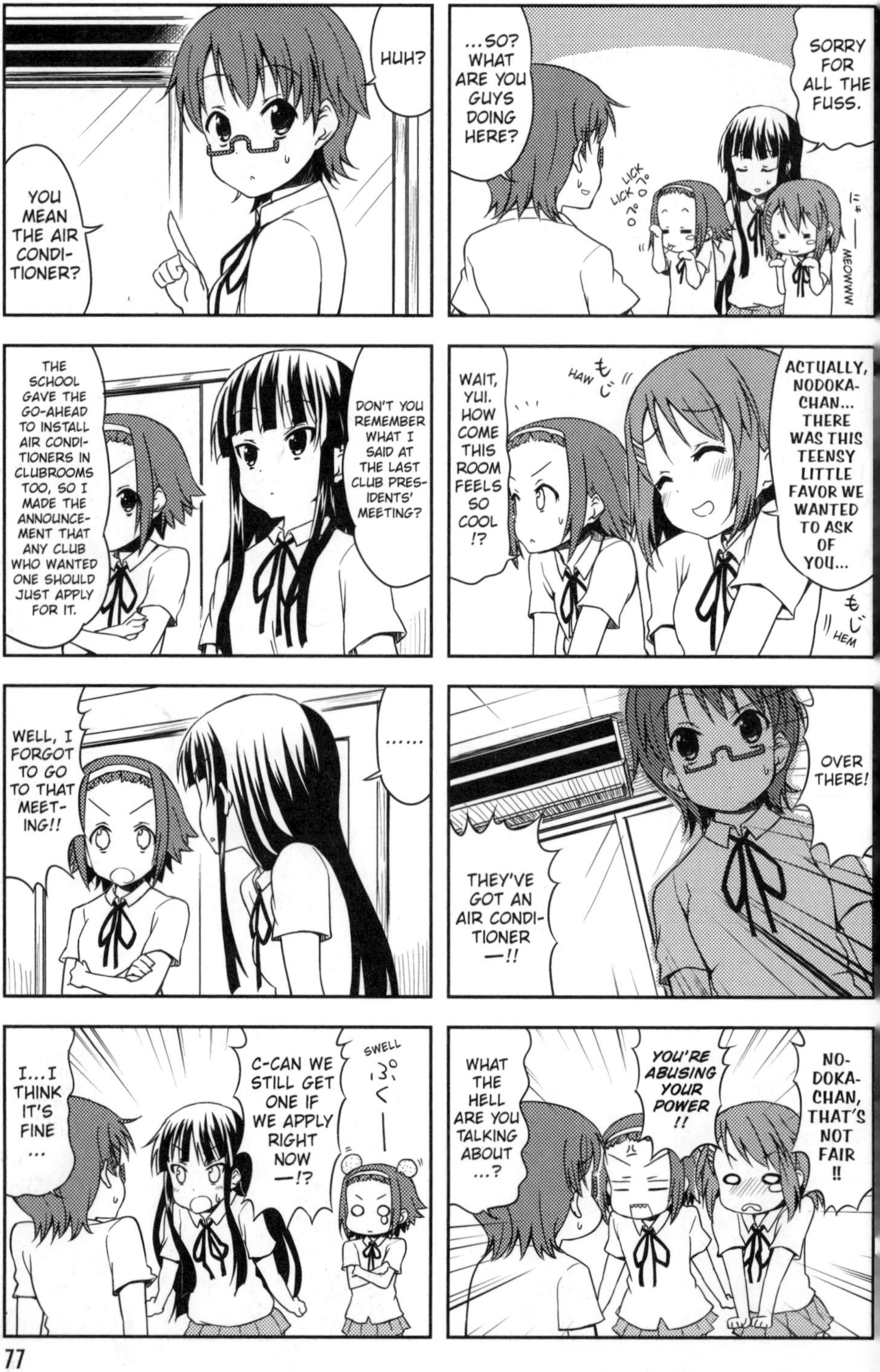
SORRY FOR ALL THE FUSS.
...SO? WHAT ARE YOU GUYS DOING HERE?
LICK LICK
にゃ—— MEOWWW
HUH?
YOU MEAN THE AIR CONDITIONER?
ACTUALLY, NODOKA-CHAN... THERE WAS THIS TEENSY LITTLE FAVOR WE WANTED TO ASK OF YOU...
もじ HEM
もじ HAW
WAIT, YUI. HOW COME THIS ROOM FEELS SO COOL!?
DON'T YOU REMEMBER WHAT I SAID AT THE LAST CLUB PRESIDENTS' MEETING?
THE SCHOOL GAVE THE GO-AHEAD TO INSTALL AIR CONDITIONERS IN CLUBROOMS TOO, SO I MADE THE ANNOUNCEMENT THAT ANY CLUB WHO WANTED ONE SHOULD JUST APPLY FOR IT.
OVER THERE!
THEY'VE GOT AN AIR CONDITIONER—!!
......
WELL, I FORGOT TO GO TO THAT MEETING!!
NODOKA-CHAN, THAT'S NOT FAIR!!
YOU'RE ABUSING YOUR POWER!!
WHAT THE HELL ARE YOU TALKING ABOUT...?
SWELL ぷく——
C-CAN WE STILL GET ONE IF WE APPLY RIGHT NOW—!?
I...I THINK IT'S FINE...

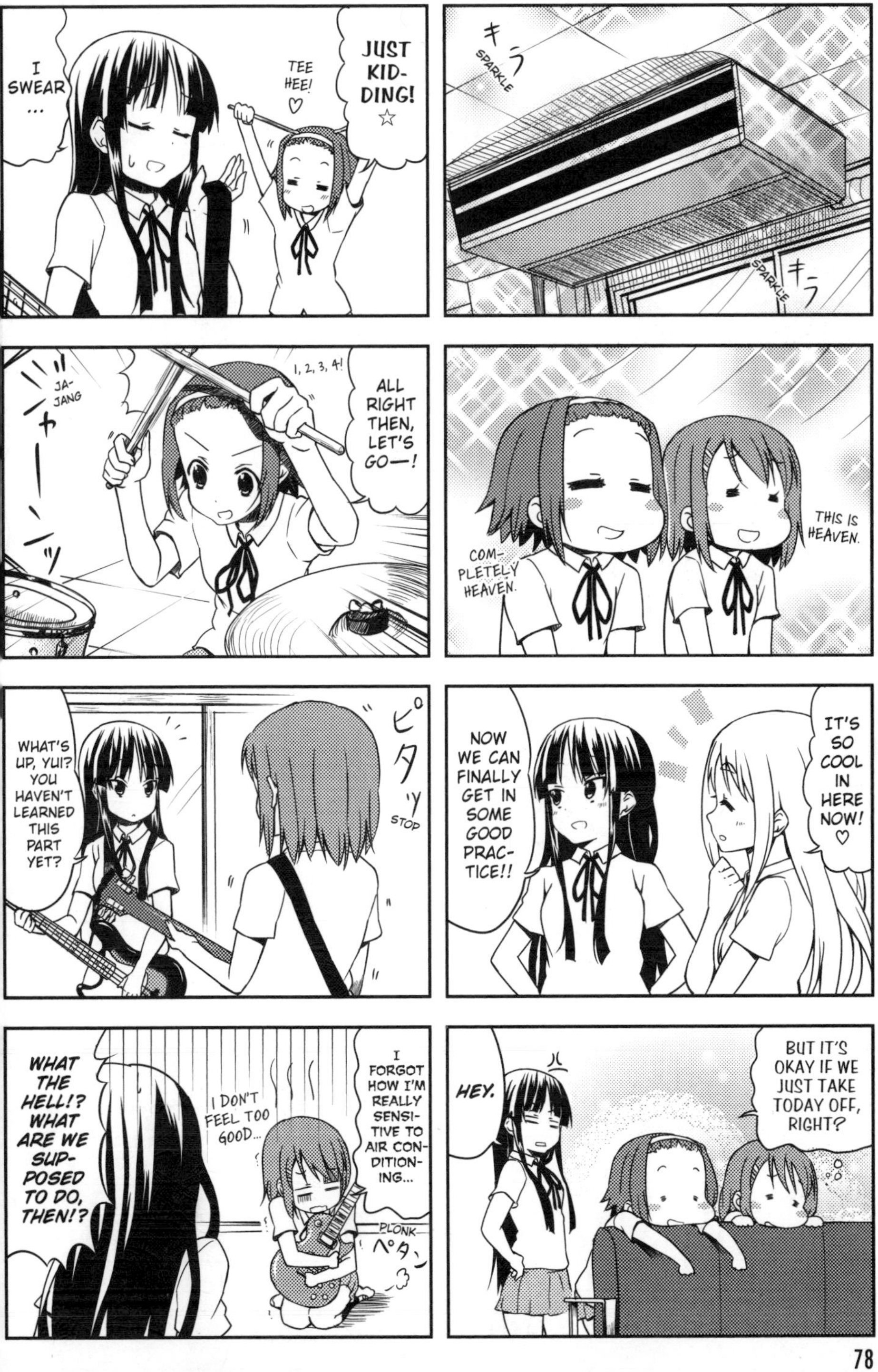

キラ
SPARKLE
キラ
SPARKLE
THIS IS HEAVEN.
COM-PLETELY HEAVEN.
IT'S SO COOL IN HERE NOW! ♡
NOW WE CAN FINALLY GET IN SOME GOOD PRAC-TICE!!
BUT IT'S OKAY IF WE JUST TAKE TODAY OFF, RIGHT?
HEY.
JUST KID-DING! ☆
TEE HEE! ♡
I SWEAR...
ALL RIGHT THEN, LET'S GO—!
1, 2, 3, 4!
ジャーーンッ
JA-JANG
ピタッ
STOP
WHAT'S UP, YUI? YOU HAVEN'T LEARNED THIS PART YET?
I FORGOT HOW I'M REALLY SENSI-TIVE TO AIR CON-DITION-ING...
I DON'T FEEL TOO GOOD...
ペタン
PLONK
WHAT THE HELL!? WHAT ARE WE SUP-POSED TO DO, THEN!?

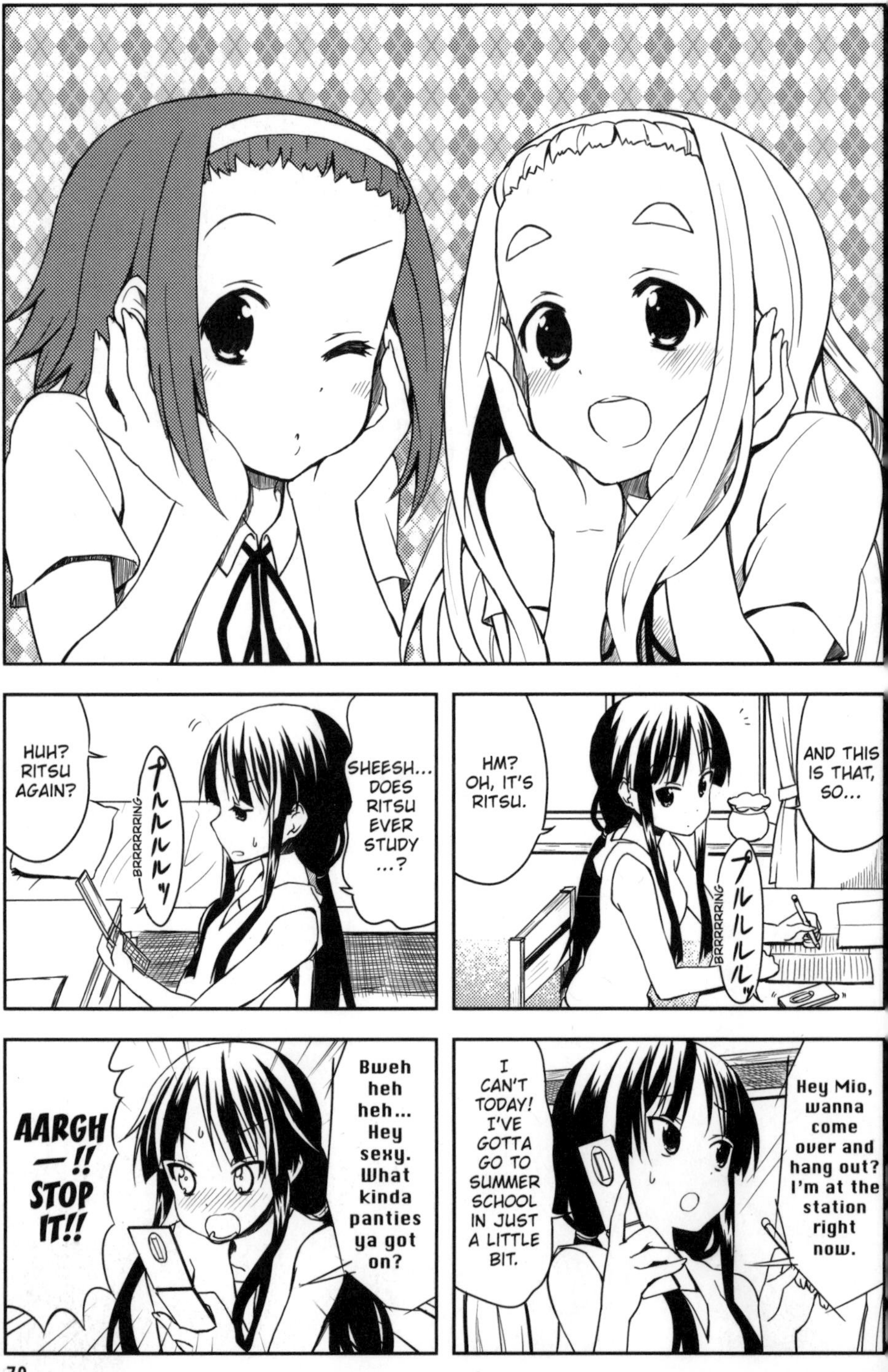
AND THIS IS THAT, SO...
HM? OH, IT'S RITSU.
プルルルッ
BRRRRRRING
SHEESH... DOES RITSU EVER STUDY ...?
プルルルッ
BRRRRRRING
HUH? RITSU AGAIN?
Hey Mio, wanna come over and hang out? I'm at the station right now.
I CAN'T TODAY! I'VE GOTTA GO TO SUMMER SCHOOL IN JUST A LITTLE BIT.
Bweh heh heh... Hey sexy. What kinda panties ya got on?
AARGH—!! STOP IT!!

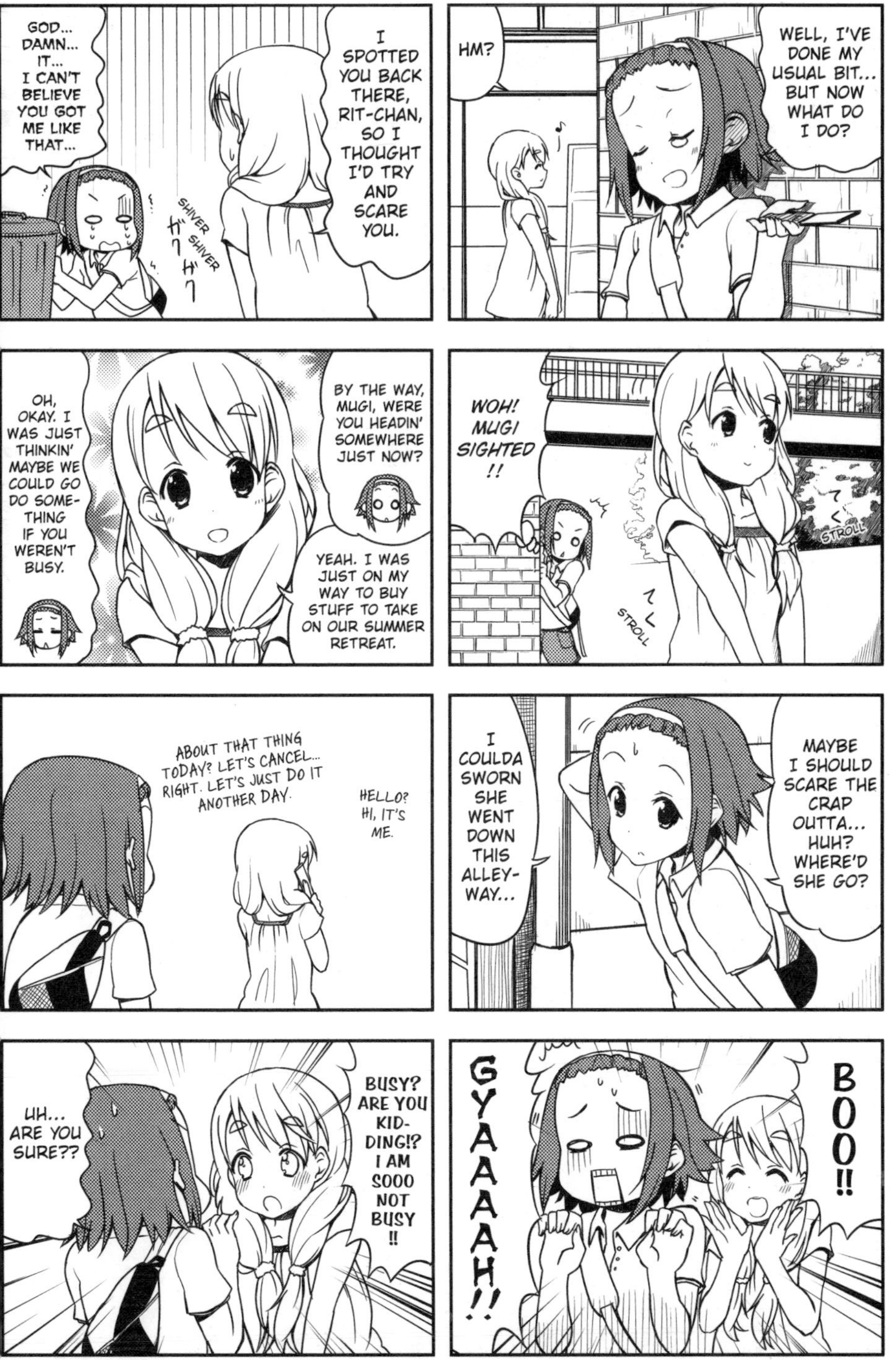
WELL, I'VE DONE MY USUAL BIT... BUT NOW WHAT DO I DO?
HM?
WOH! MUGI SIGHTED!!
STROLL
STROLL
MAYBE I SHOULD SCARE THE CRAP OUTTA... HUH? WHERE'D SHE GO?
I COULDA SWORN SHE WENT DOWN THIS ALLEY-WAY...
BOOO!!
GYAAAAH!!
I SPOTTED YOU BACK THERE, RIT-CHAN, SO I THOUGHT I'D TRY AND SCARE YOU.
GOD... DAMN... IT... I CAN'T BELIEVE YOU GOT ME LIKE THAT...
SHIVER SHIVER
BY THE WAY, MUGI, WERE YOU HEADIN' SOMEWHERE JUST NOW?
YEAH. I WAS JUST ON MY WAY TO BUY STUFF TO TAKE ON OUR SUMMER RETREAT.
OH, OKAY. I WAS JUST THINKIN' MAYBE WE COULD GO DO SOME-THING IF YOU WEREN'T BUSY.
HELLO? HI, IT'S ME.
ABOUT THAT THING TODAY? LET'S CANCEL... RIGHT. LET'S JUST DO IT ANOTHER DAY.
BUSY? ARE YOU KID-DING!? I AM SOOO NOT BUSY!!
UH... ARE YOU SURE??

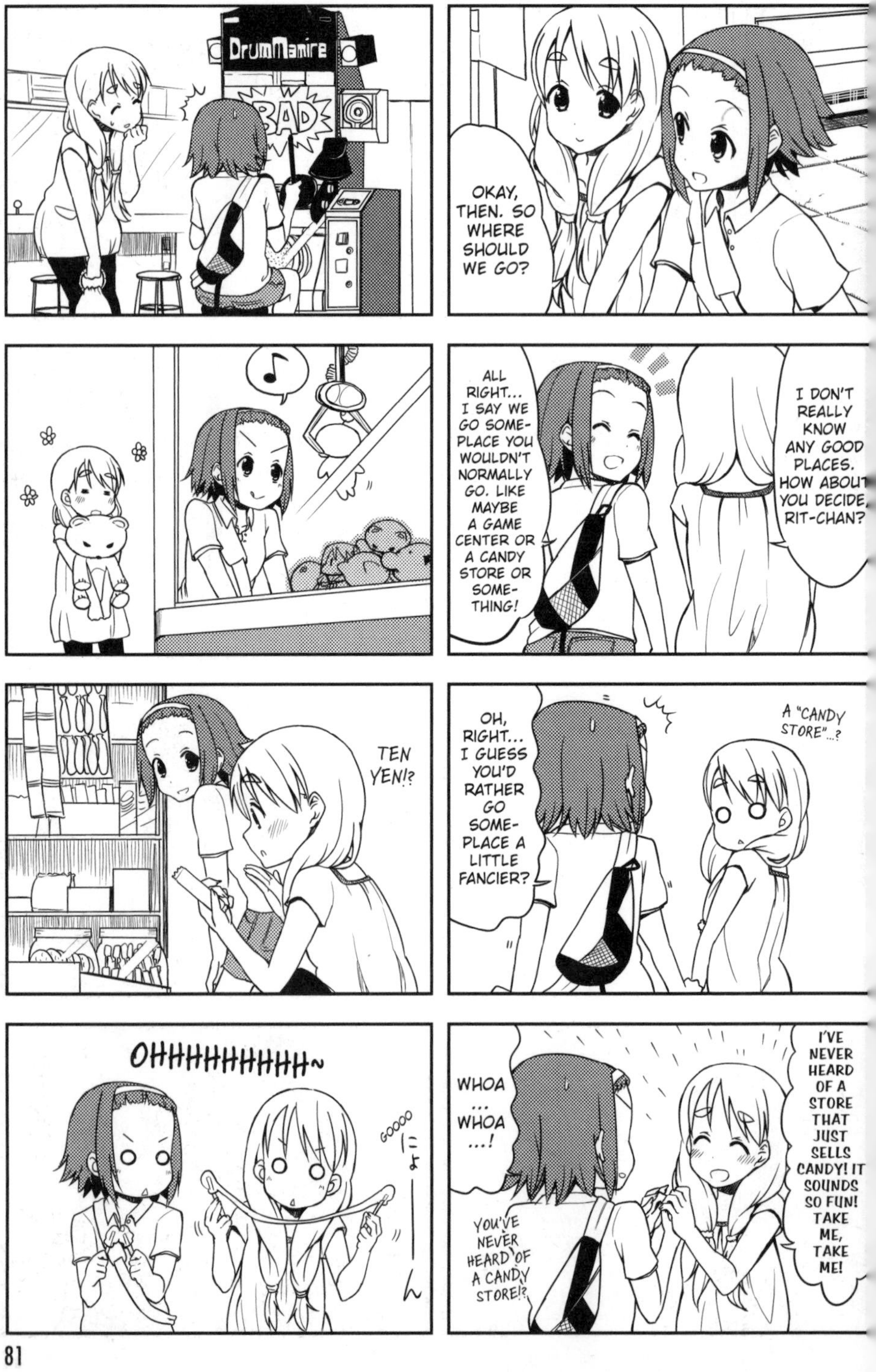
OKAY, THEN. SO WHERE SHOULD WE GO?
DrumMamire
BAD
I DON'T REALLY KNOW ANY GOOD PLACES. HOW ABOUT YOU DECIDE, RIT-CHAN?
ALL RIGHT... I SAY WE GO SOME-PLACE YOU WOULDN'T NORMALLY GO. LIKE MAYBE A GAME CENTER OR A CANDY STORE OR SOME-THING!
A "CANDY STORE"...?
OH, RIGHT... I GUESS YOU'D RATHER GO SOME-PLACE A LITTLE FANCIER?
TEN YEN!?
I'VE NEVER HEARD OF A STORE THAT JUST SELLS CANDY! IT SOUNDS SO FUN! TAKE ME, TAKE ME!
WHOA ... WHOA ...!
YOU'VE NEVER HEARD OF A CANDY STORE!?
OHHHHHHHHHH~
GOOOO
にょーーーん

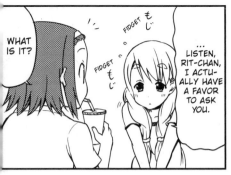

......
HWWWWOWWW!!
...LISTEN, RIT-CHAN, I ACTUALLY HAVE A FAVOR TO ASK YOU.
FIDGET もじ
FIDGET もじ
WHAT IS IT?
THAT WAS SO. MUCH. FUN! ♡
GLAD YOU LIKED IT.
I...I WANT...
...I WANT YOU TO HIT ME!!
RIT-CHAN, YOU KNOW ALL KINDS OF PLACES I'VE NEVER EVEN HEARD OF! IT'S SO COOL!
HEE-HEE-HEE... JUST KEEP THE COMPLIMENTS COMIN'.
...HUH?
RIT-CHAN—YOU'RE A TOTAL EXPERT AT HAVING FUN USING HARDLY ANY MONEY!
WE GOT THIS THING FOR, LIKE, 500 YEN!
WELL, FOR NORMAL PEOPLE, EVEN WHAT LITTLE WE SPENT TODAY STILL FEELS LIKE A LOT...
...WOULD YOU MIND?
WOW... I NEVER KNEW MUGI WAS INTO THAT KINDA THING.

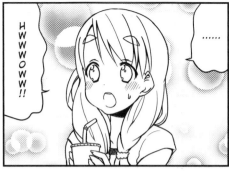

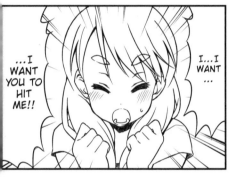

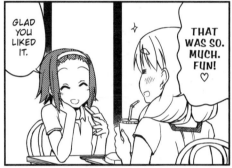

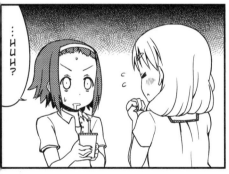

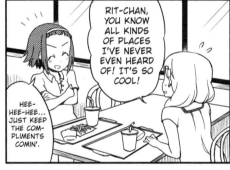

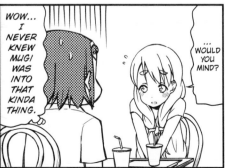

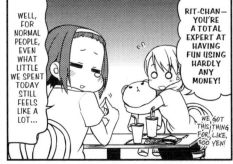

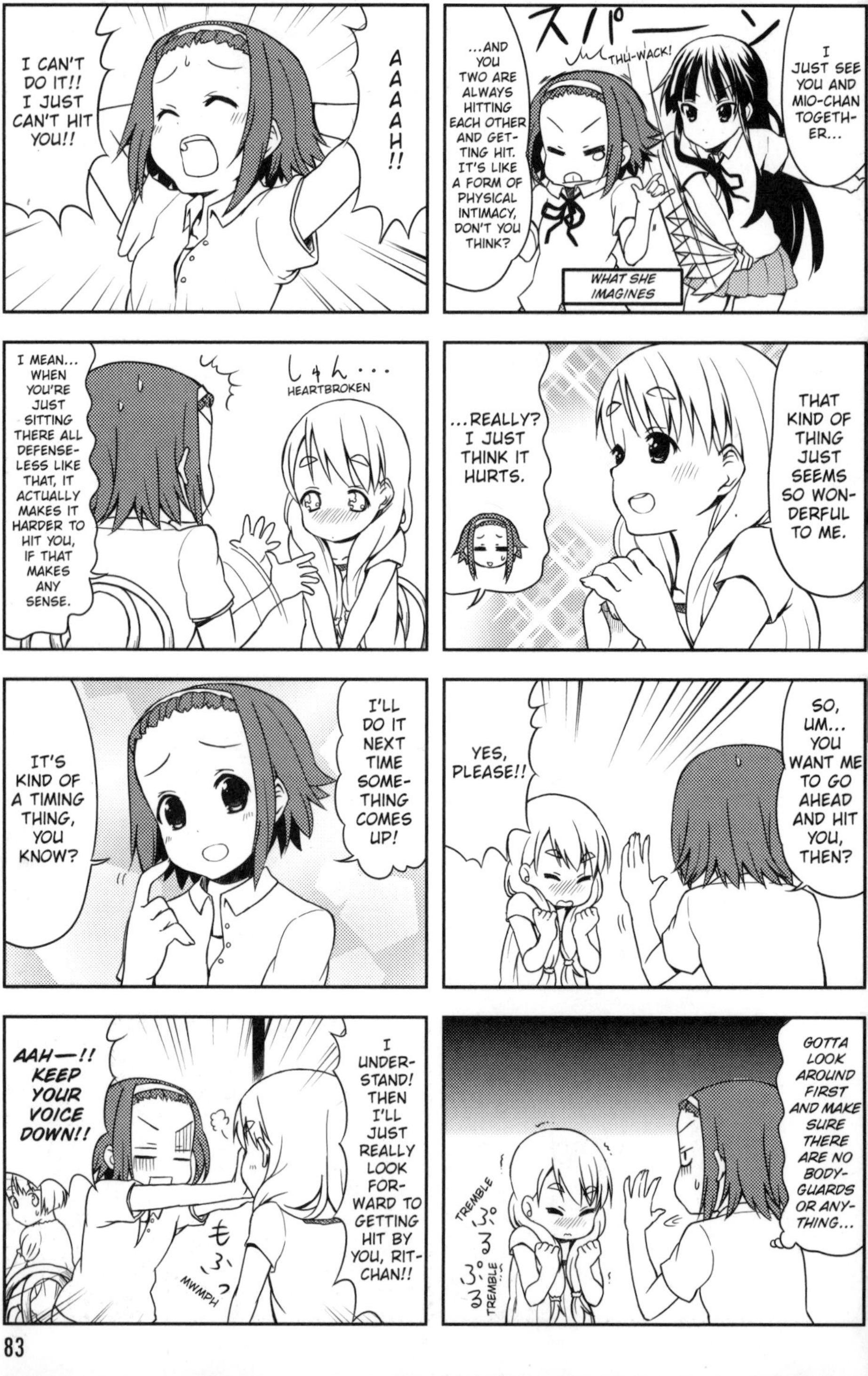
I JUST SEE YOU AND MIO-CHAN TOGETHER...
スパーン
THU-WACK!
...AND YOU TWO ARE ALWAYS HITTING EACH OTHER AND GETTING HIT. IT'S LIKE A FORM OF PHYSICAL INTIMACY, DON'T YOU THINK?
WHAT SHE IMAGINES
AAAAAH!!
I CAN'T DO IT!! I JUST CAN'T HIT YOU!!
THAT KIND OF THING JUST SEEMS SO WONDERFUL TO ME.
...REALLY? I JUST THINK IT HURTS.
しゅん...
HEARTBROKEN
I MEAN... WHEN YOU'RE JUST SITTING THERE ALL DEFENSELESS LIKE THAT, IT ACTUALLY MAKES IT HARDER TO HIT YOU, IF THAT MAKES ANY SENSE.
SO, UM... YOU WANT ME TO GO AHEAD AND HIT YOU, THEN?
YES, PLEASE!!
I'LL DO IT NEXT TIME SOMETHING COMES UP!
IT'S KIND OF A TIMING THING, YOU KNOW?
GOTTA LOOK AROUND FIRST AND MAKE SURE THERE ARE NO BODYGUARDS OR ANYTHING...
ぷるぷる
TREMBLE TREMBLE
I UNDERSTAND! THEN I'LL JUST REALLY LOOK FORWARD TO GETTING HIT BY YOU, RIT-CHAN!!
AAH—!! KEEP YOUR VOICE DOWN!!
もふっ
MWMPH

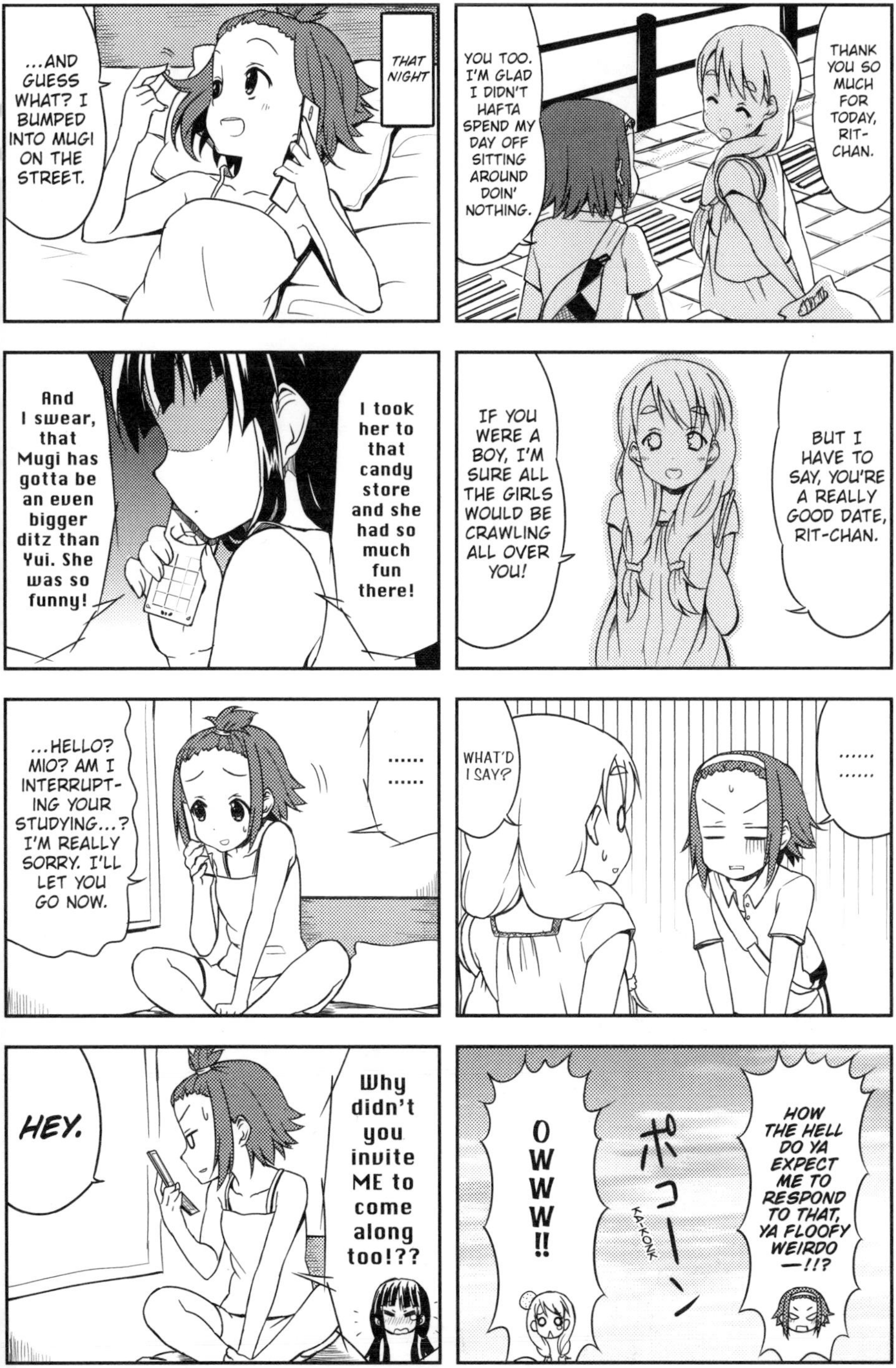
THANK YOU SO MUCH FOR TODAY, RIT-CHAN.
YOU TOO. I'M GLAD I DIDN'T HAFTA SPEND MY DAY OFF SITTING AROUND DOIN' NOTHING.
THAT NIGHT
...AND GUESS WHAT? I BUMPED INTO MUGI ON THE STREET.
BUT I HAVE TO SAY, YOU'RE A REALLY GOOD DATE, RIT-CHAN.
IF YOU WERE A BOY, I'M SURE ALL THE GIRLS WOULD BE CRAWLING ALL OVER YOU!
I took her to that candy store and she had so much fun there!
And I swear, that Mugi has gotta be an even bigger ditz than Yui. She was so funny!
....
WHAT'D I SAY?
....
...HELLO? MIO? AM I INTERRUPTING YOUR STUDYING...? I'M REALLY SORRY. I'LL LET YOU GO NOW.
HOW THE HELL DO YA EXPECT ME TO RESPOND TO THAT, YA FLOOFY WEIRDO—!!?
ポコーン
KA-KONK
OWWW!!
Why didn't you invite ME to come along too!??
HEY.

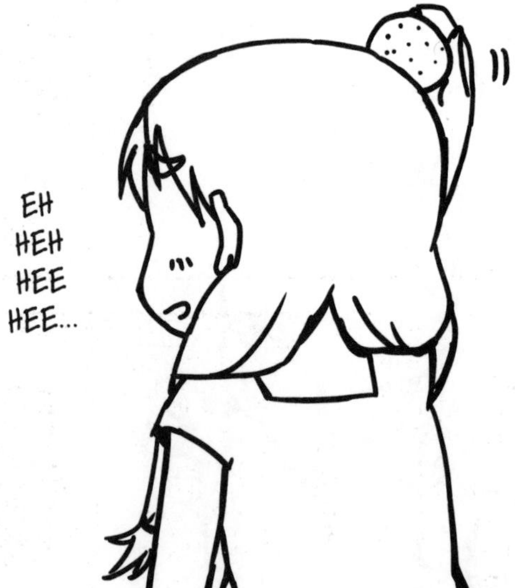
EH HEH HEE HEE...

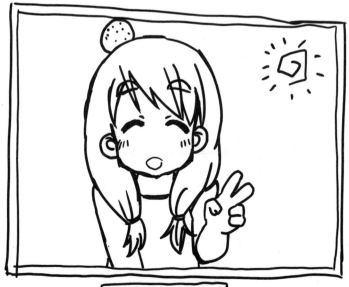

ME AND MY LUMP

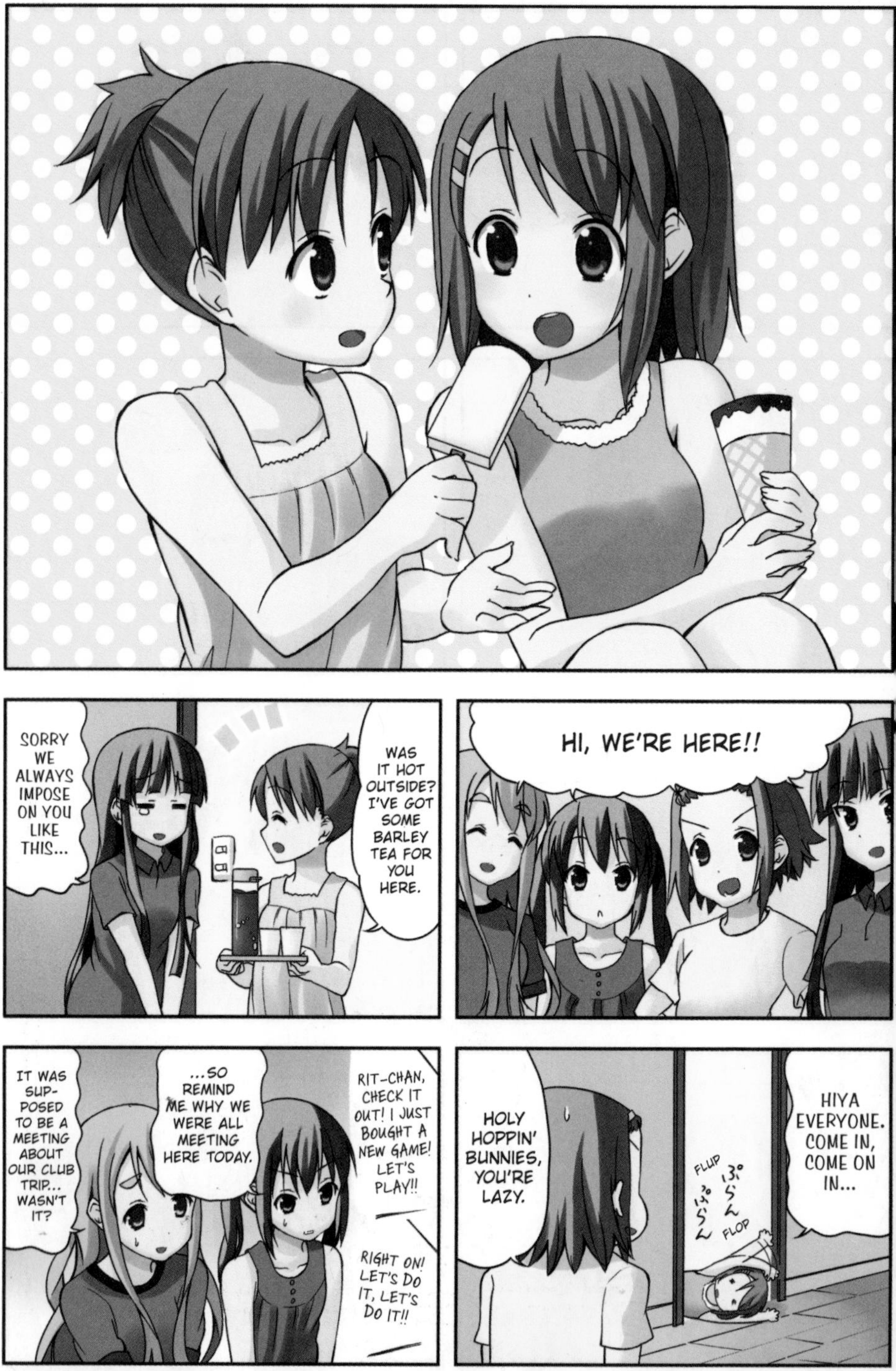
HI, WE'RE HERE!!
WAS IT HOT OUTSIDE? I'VE GOT SOME BARLEY TEA FOR YOU HERE.
SORRY WE ALWAYS IMPOSE ON YOU LIKE THIS...
HIYA EVERYONE. COME IN, COME ON IN...
ぷらん ぷらん
FLUP FLOP
HOLY HOPPIN' BUNNIES, YOU'RE LAZY.
RIT-CHAN, CHECK IT OUT! I JUST BOUGHT A NEW GAME! LET'S PLAY!!
RIGHT ON! LET'S DO IT, LET'S DO IT!!
...SO REMIND ME WHY WE WERE ALL MEETING HERE TODAY.
IT WAS SUP-POSED TO BE A MEETING ABOUT OUR CLUB TRIP... WASN'T IT?

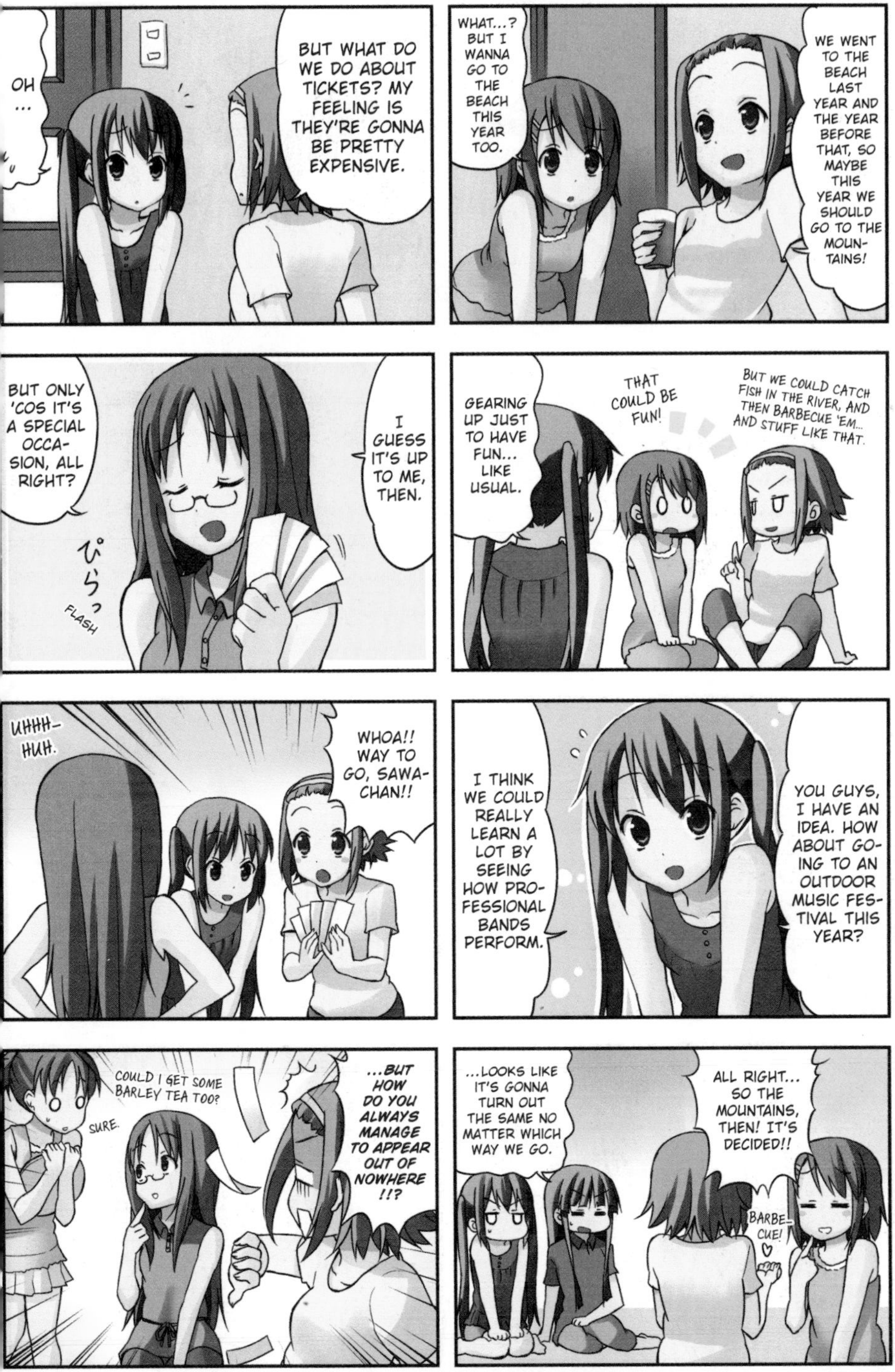
WE WENT TO THE BEACH LAST YEAR AND THE YEAR BEFORE THAT, SO MAYBE THIS YEAR WE SHOULD GO TO THE MOUNTAINS!
WHAT...? BUT I WANNA GO TO THE BEACH THIS YEAR TOO.
BUT WE COULD CATCH FISH IN THE RIVER, AND THEN BARBECUE 'EM... AND STUFF LIKE THAT.
THAT COULD BE FUN!
GEARING UP JUST TO HAVE FUN... LIKE USUAL.
YOU GUYS, I HAVE AN IDEA. HOW ABOUT GO-ING TO AN OUTDOOR MUSIC FES-TIVAL THIS YEAR?
I THINK WE COULD REALLY LEARN A LOT BY SEEING HOW PRO-FESSIONAL BANDS PERFORM.
ALL RIGHT... SO THE MOUNTAINS, THEN! IT'S DECIDED!!
BARBE-CUE! ♡
...LOOKS LIKE IT'S GONNA TURN OUT THE SAME NO MATTER WHICH WAY WE GO.
BUT WHAT DO WE DO ABOUT TICKETS? MY FEELING IS THEY'RE GONNA BE PRETTY EXPENSIVE.
OH ...
I GUESS IT'S UP TO ME, THEN.
BUT ONLY 'COS IT'S A SPECIAL OCCA-SION, ALL RIGHT?
ぴらっ
FLASH
WHOA!! WAY TO GO, SAWA-CHAN!!
UHHH-HUH.
...BUT HOW DO YOU ALWAYS MANAGE TO APPEAR OUT OF NOWHERE !!?
COULD I GET SOME BARLEY TEA TOO?
SURE.

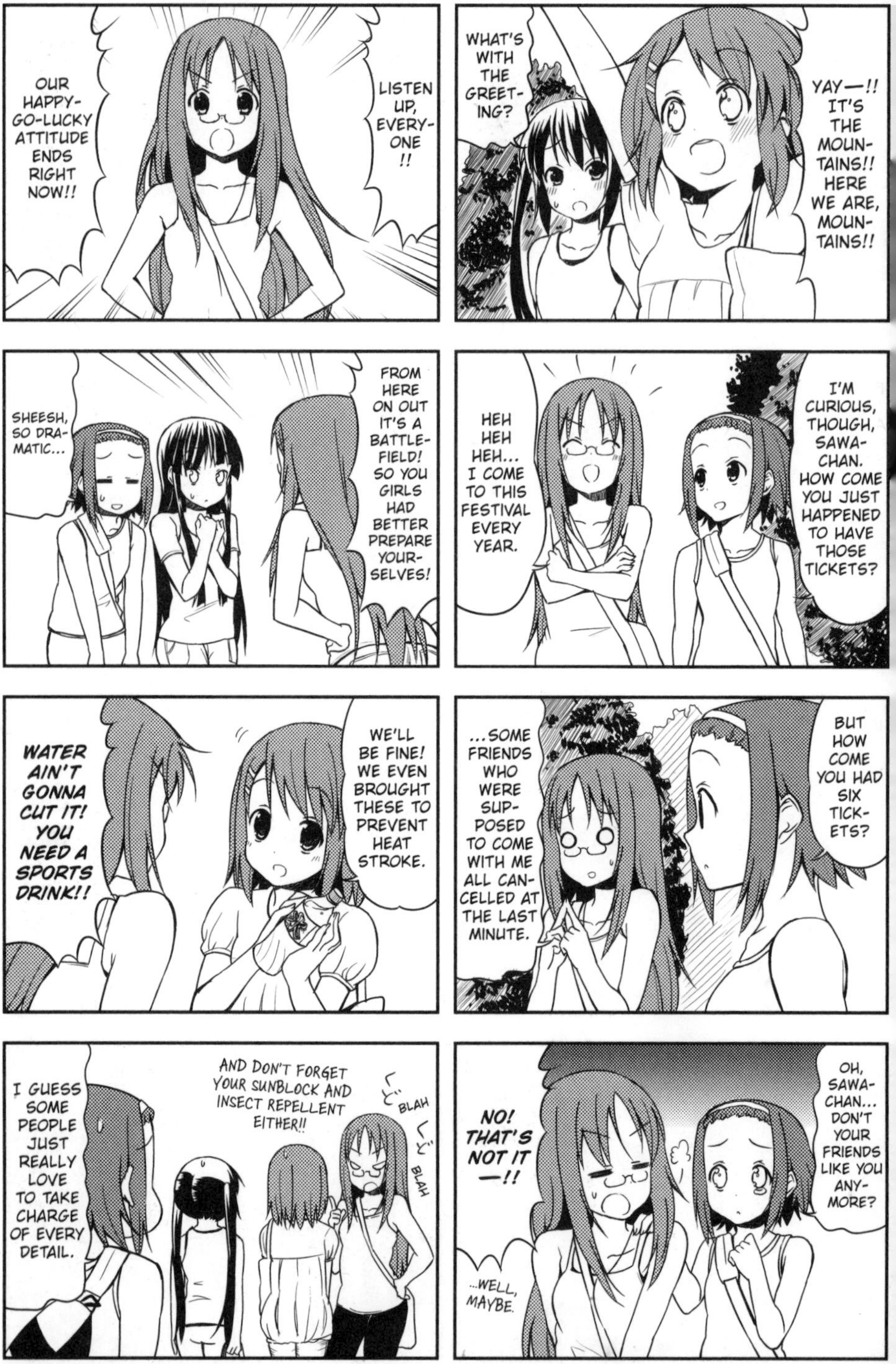
YAY—!! IT'S THE MOUNTAINS!! HERE WE ARE, MOUNTAINS!!
WHAT'S WITH THE GREETING?
LISTEN UP, EVERYONE!!
OUR HAPPY-GO-LUCKY ATTITUDE ENDS RIGHT NOW!!
I'M CURIOUS, THOUGH, SAWA-CHAN. HOW COME YOU JUST HAPPENED TO HAVE THOSE TICKETS?
HEH HEH HEH... I COME TO THIS FESTIVAL EVERY YEAR.
FROM HERE ON OUT IT'S A BATTLEFIELD! SO YOU GIRLS HAD BETTER PREPARE YOURSELVES!
SHEESH, SO DRAMATIC...
BUT HOW COME YOU HAD SIX TICKETS?
...SOME FRIENDS WHO WERE SUPPOSED TO COME WITH ME ALL CANCELLED AT THE LAST MINUTE.
WE'LL BE FINE! WE EVEN BROUGHT THESE TO PREVENT HEAT STROKE.
WATER AIN'T GONNA CUT IT! YOU NEED A SPORTS DRINK!!
OH, SAWA-CHAN... DON'T YOUR FRIENDS LIKE YOU ANYMORE?
NO! THAT'S NOT IT—!!
...WELL, MAYBE.
BLAH
BLAH
AND DON'T FORGET YOUR SUNBLOCK AND INSECT REPELLENT EITHER!!
I GUESS SOME PEOPLE JUST REALLY LOVE TO TAKE CHARGE OF EVERY DETAIL.

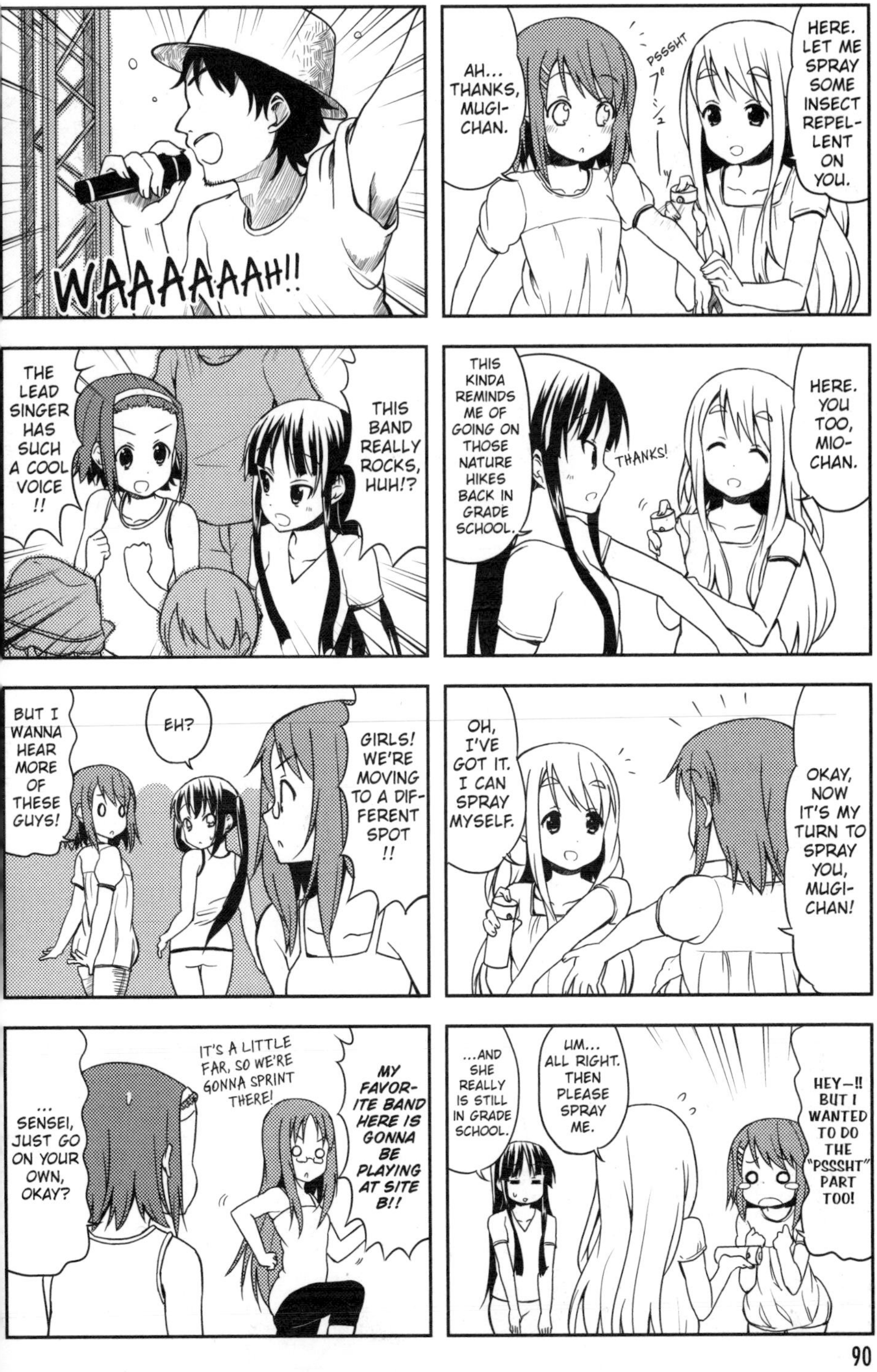
HERE. LET ME SPRAY SOME INSECT REPEL-LENT ON YOU.
PSSSHT
AH... THANKS, MUGI-CHAN.
WAAAAAAH!!
HERE. YOU TOO, MIO-CHAN.
THANKS!
THIS KINDA REMINDS ME OF GOING ON THOSE NATURE HIKES BACK IN GRADE SCHOOL.
THIS BAND REALLY ROCKS, HUH!?
THE LEAD SINGER HAS SUCH A COOL VOICE!!
OKAY, NOW IT'S MY TURN TO SPRAY YOU, MUGI-CHAN!
OH, I'VE GOT IT. I CAN SPRAY MYSELF.
GIRLS! WE'RE MOVING TO A DIF-FERENT SPOT!!
EH?
BUT I WANNA HEAR MORE OF THESE GUYS!
HEY—!! BUT I WANTED TO DO THE "PSSSHT" PART TOO!
UM... ALL RIGHT. THEN PLEASE SPRAY ME.
...AND SHE REALLY IS STILL IN GRADE SCHOOL.
MY FAVOR-ITE BAND HERE IS GONNA BE PLAYING AT SITE B!!
IT'S A LITTLE FAR, SO WE'RE GONNA SPRINT THERE!
...SENSEI, JUST GO ON YOUR OWN, OKAY?

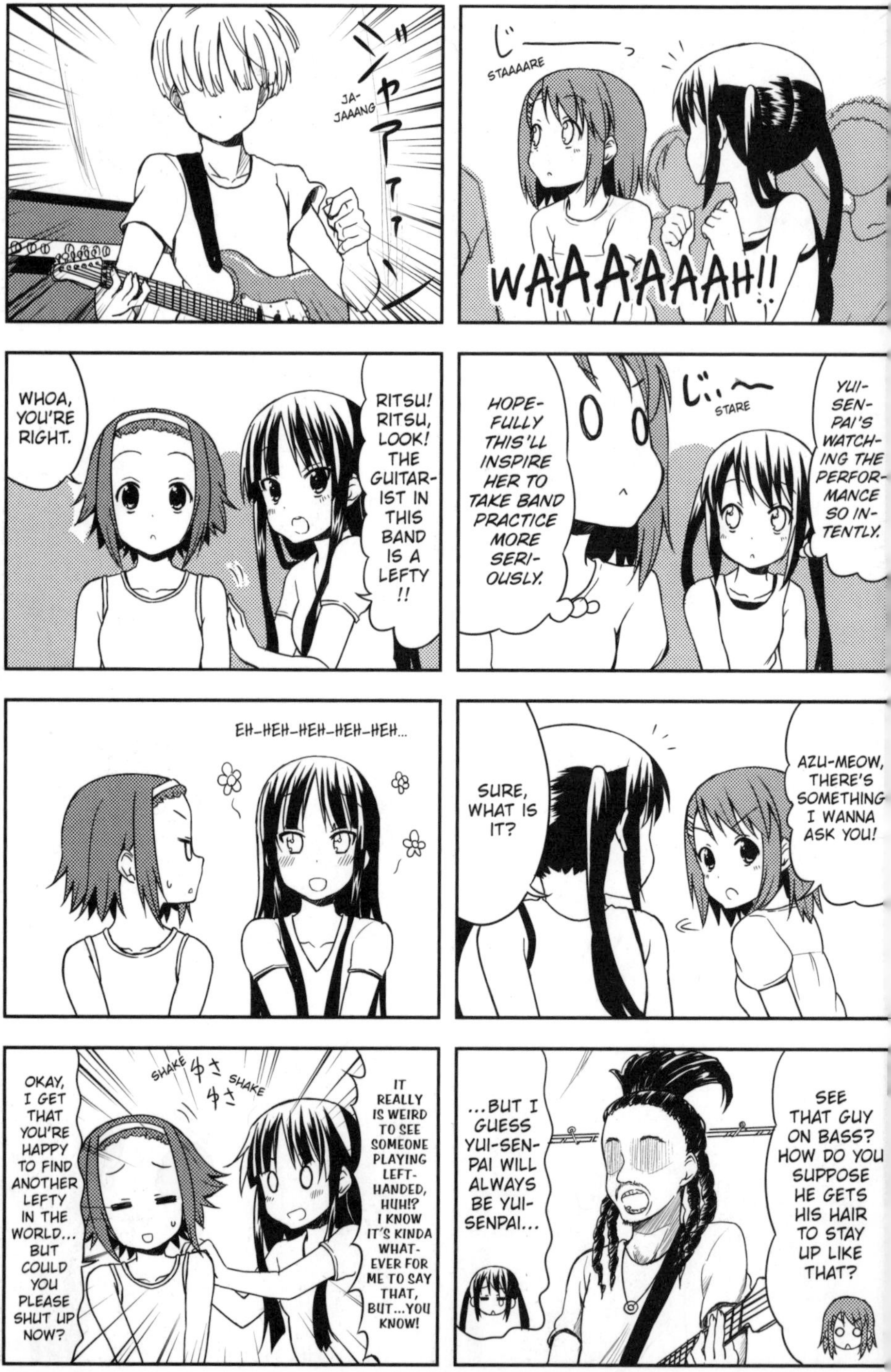
じーーーっ
STAAAARE
WAAAAAAH!!
ジャアァァ
JA-JAAANG
YUI-SENPAI'S WATCHING THE PERFORMANCE SO INTENTLY.
じぃ〜
STARE
HOPEFULLY THIS'LL INSPIRE HER TO TAKE BAND PRACTICE MORE SERIOUSLY.
RITSU! RITSU, LOOK! THE GUITARIST IN THIS BAND IS A LEFTY!!
WHOA, YOU'RE RIGHT.
AZU-MEOW, THERE'S SOMETHING I WANNA ASK YOU!
SURE, WHAT IS IT?
EH-HEH-HEH-HEH-HEH...
SEE THAT GUY ON BASS? HOW DO YOU SUPPOSE HE GETS HIS HAIR TO STAY UP LIKE THAT?
...BUT I GUESS YUI-SENPAI WILL ALWAYS BE YUI-SENPAI...
IT REALLY IS WEIRD TO SEE SOMEONE PLAYING LEFT-HANDED, HUH!? I KNOW IT'S KINDA WHATEVER FOR ME TO SAY THAT, BUT...YOU KNOW!
ゆさゆさ
SHAKE SHAKE
OKAY, I GET THAT YOU'RE HAPPY TO FIND ANOTHER LEFTY IN THE WORLD... BUT COULD YOU PLEASE SHUT UP NOW?

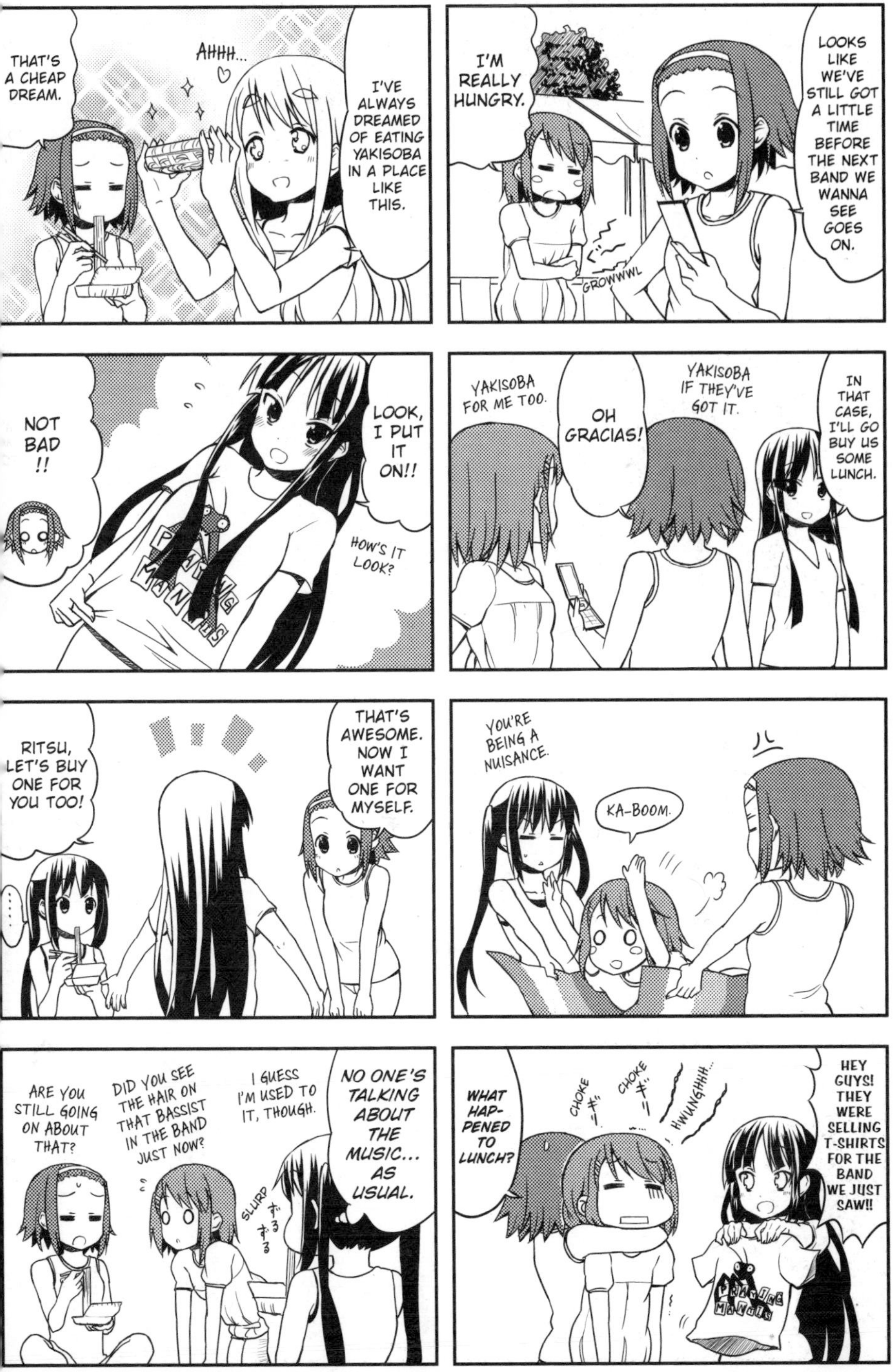
LOOKS LIKE WE'VE STILL GOT A LITTLE TIME BEFORE THE NEXT BAND WE WANNA SEE GOES ON.
GROWWWL
I'M REALLY HUNGRY.
IN THAT CASE, I'LL GO BUY US SOME LUNCH.
YAKISOBA IF THEY'VE GOT IT.
OH GRACIAS!
YAKISOBA FOR ME TOO.
YOU'RE BEING A NUISANCE.
KA-BOOM.
HEY GUYS! THEY WERE SELLING T-SHIRTS FOR THE BAND WE JUST SAW!!
HWUNGHHH...
CHOKE ギリ
CHOKE ギリ
WHAT HAPPENED TO LUNCH?
I'VE ALWAYS DREAMED OF EATING YAKISOBA IN A PLACE LIKE THIS.
AHHH...
THAT'S A CHEAP DREAM.
LOOK, I PUT IT ON!!
HOW'S IT LOOK?
NOT BAD!!
THAT'S AWESOME. NOW I WANT ONE FOR MYSELF.
RITSU, LET'S BUY ONE FOR YOU TOO!
NO ONE'S TALKING ABOUT THE MUSIC... AS USUAL.
I GUESS I'M USED TO IT, THOUGH.
SLURP ずるずる
DID YOU SEE THE HAIR ON THAT BASSIST IN THE BAND JUST NOW?
ARE YOU STILL GOING ON ABOUT THAT?

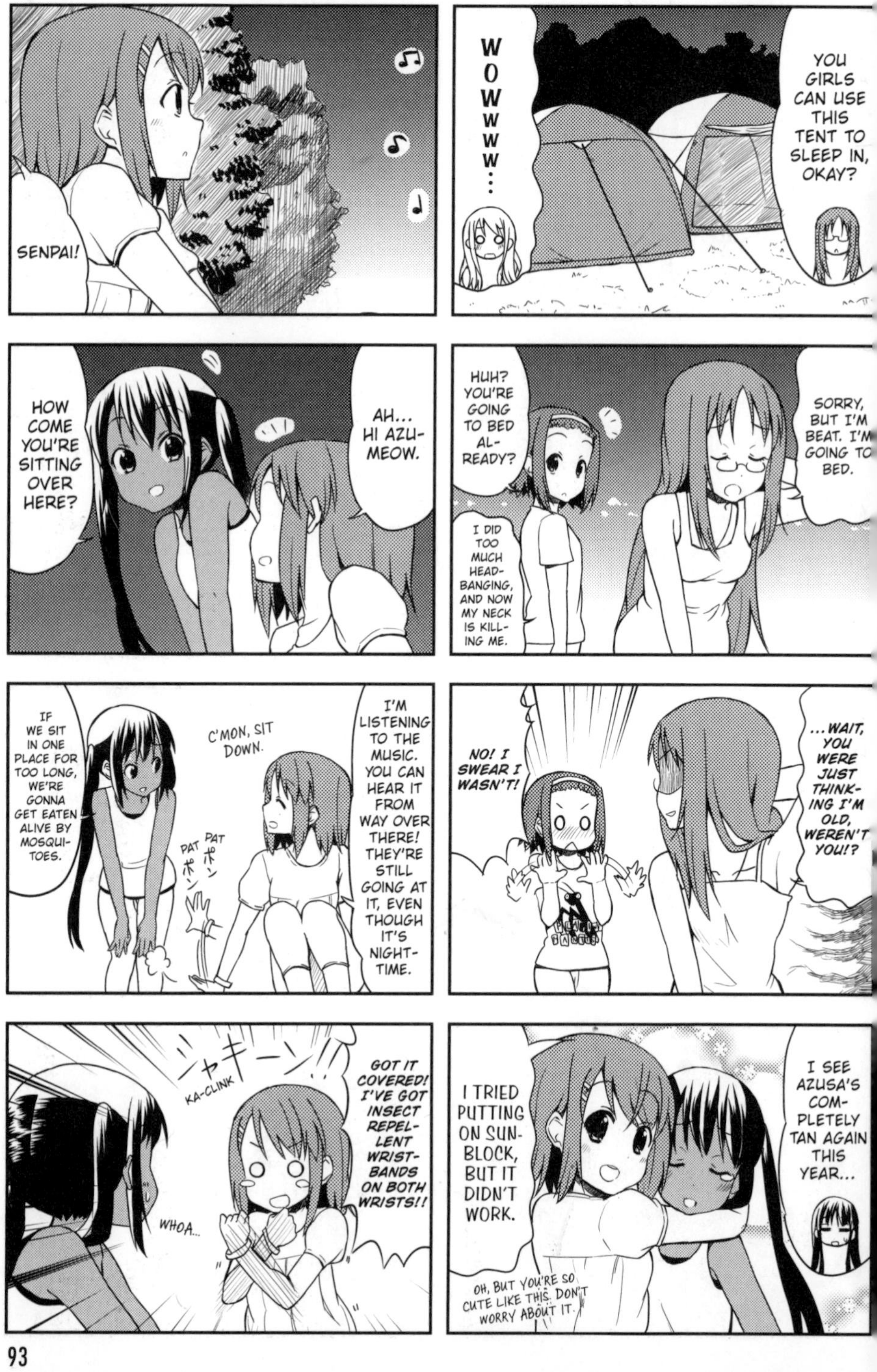
YOU GIRLS CAN USE THIS TENT TO SLEEP IN, OKAY?
WOWWWWW...
SENPAI!
SORRY, BUT I'M BEAT. I'M GOING TO BED.
HUH? YOU'RE GOING TO BED AL-READY?
I DID TOO MUCH HEAD-BANGING, AND NOW MY NECK IS KILL-ING ME.
AH... HI AZU-MEOW.
HOW COME YOU'RE SITTING OVER HERE?
...WAIT, YOU WERE JUST THINK-ING I'M OLD, WEREN'T YOU!?
NO! I SWEAR I WASN'T!
I'M LISTENING TO THE MUSIC. YOU CAN HEAR IT FROM WAY OVER THERE! THEY'RE STILL GOING AT IT, EVEN THOUGH IT'S NIGHT-TIME.
C'MON, SIT DOWN.
PAT PAT
ポン ポン
IF WE SIT IN ONE PLACE FOR TOO LONG, WE'RE GONNA GET EATEN ALIVE BY MOSQUI-TOES.
I SEE AZUSA'S COM-PLETELY TAN AGAIN THIS YEAR...
I TRIED PUTTING ON SUN-BLOCK, BUT IT DIDN'T WORK.
OH, BUT YOU'RE SO CUTE LIKE THIS. DON'T WORRY ABOUT IT.
GOT IT COVERED! I'VE GOT INSECT REPEL-LENT WRIST-BANDS ON BOTH WRISTS!!
シャキーン!!
KA-CLINK
WHOA...

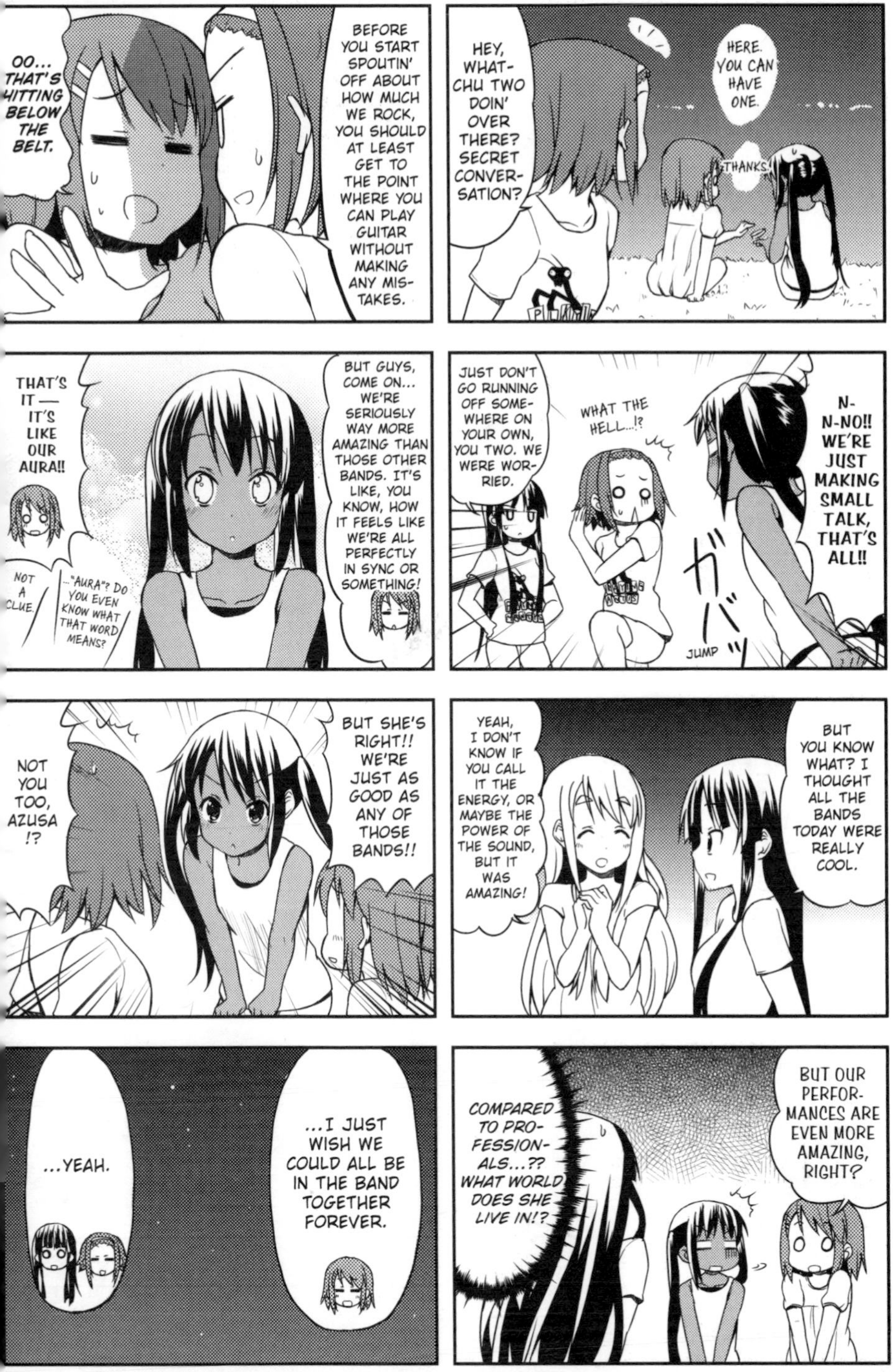

HERE. YOU CAN HAVE ONE.
THANKS.
HEY, WHATCHU TWO DOIN' OVER THERE? SECRET CONVERSATION?
BEFORE YOU START SPOUTIN' OFF ABOUT HOW MUCH WE ROCK, YOU SHOULD AT LEAST GET TO THE POINT WHERE YOU CAN PLAY GUITAR WITHOUT MAKING ANY MISTAKES.
OO... THAT'S HITTING BELOW THE BELT.
N-N-NO!! WE'RE JUST MAKING SMALL TALK, THAT'S ALL!!
WHAT THE HELL...!?
JUST DON'T GO RUNNING OFF SOMEWHERE ON YOUR OWN, YOU TWO. WE WERE WORRIED.
JUMP
BUT GUYS, COME ON... WE'RE SERIOUSLY WAY MORE AMAZING THAN THOSE OTHER BANDS. IT'S LIKE, YOU KNOW, HOW IT FEELS LIKE WE'RE ALL PERFECTLY IN SYNC OR SOMETHING!
THAT'S IT — IT'S LIKE OUR AURA!!
..."AURA"? DO YOU EVEN KNOW WHAT THAT WORD MEANS?
NOT A CLUE.
BUT YOU KNOW WHAT? I THOUGHT ALL THE BANDS TODAY WERE REALLY COOL.
YEAH, I DON'T KNOW IF YOU CALL IT THE ENERGY, OR MAYBE THE POWER OF THE SOUND, BUT IT WAS AMAZING!
BUT SHE'S RIGHT!! WE'RE JUST AS GOOD AS ANY OF THOSE BANDS!!
NOT YOU TOO, AZUSA!?
BUT OUR PERFORMANCES ARE EVEN MORE AMAZING, RIGHT?
COMPARED TO PROFESSIONALS...?? WHAT WORLD DOES SHE LIVE IN!?
...I JUST WISH WE COULD ALL BE IN THE BAND TOGETHER FOREVER.
...YEAH.

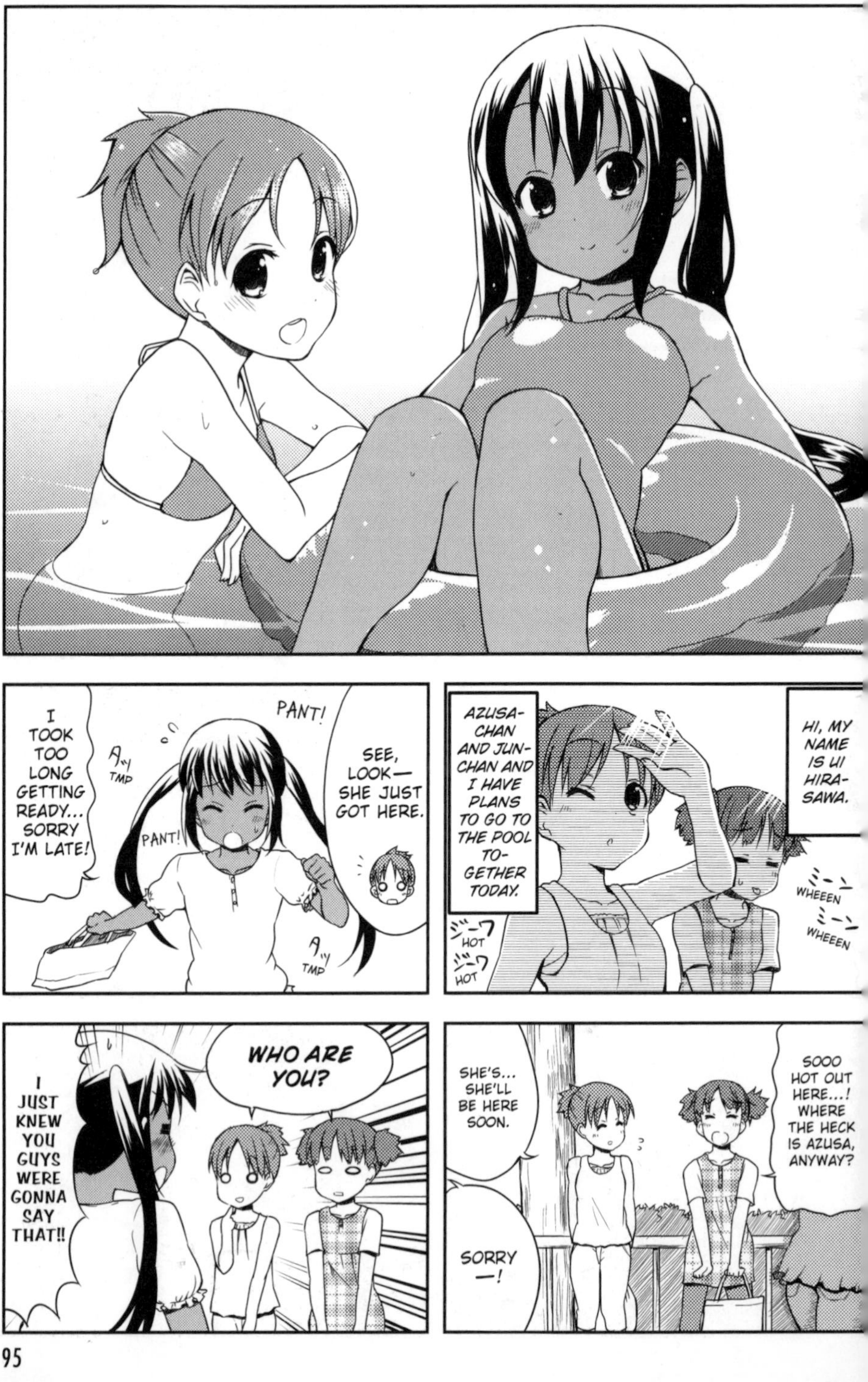

HI, MY NAME IS UI HIRA-SAWA.
AZUSA-CHAN AND JUN-CHAN AND I HAVE PLANS TO GO TO THE POOL TO-GETHER TODAY.
WHEEEN
WHEEEN
HOT
HOT
SOOO HOT OUT HERE...! WHERE THE HECK IS AZUSA, ANYWAY?
SHE'S... SHE'LL BE HERE SOON.
SORRY—!
PANT!
SEE, LOOK— SHE JUST GOT HERE.
TMP
PANT!
I TOOK TOO LONG GETTING READY... SORRY I'M LATE!
TMP
WHO ARE YOU?
I JUST KNEW YOU GUYS WERE GONNA SAY THAT!!

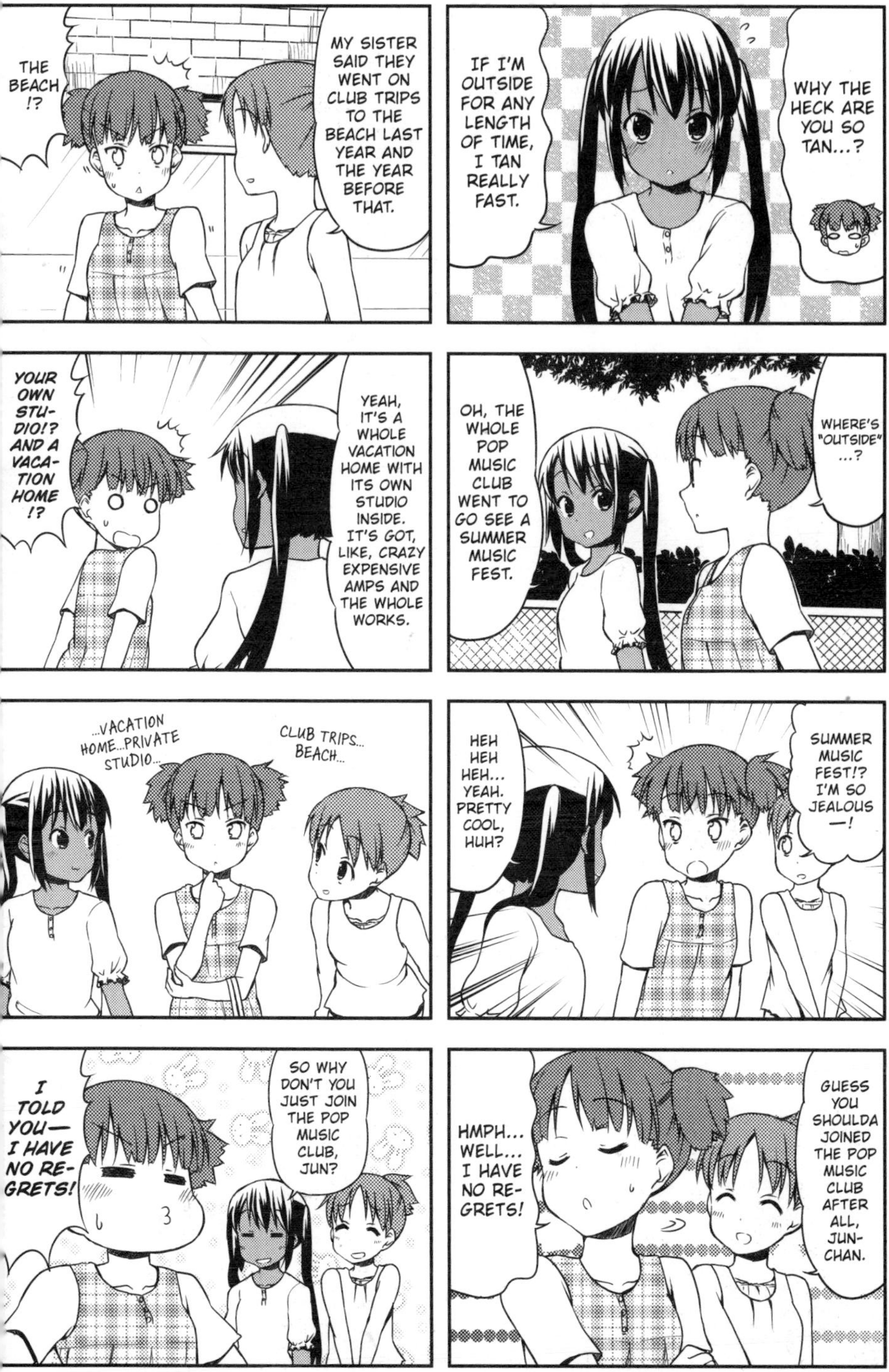
WHY THE HECK ARE YOU SO TAN...?
IF I'M OUTSIDE FOR ANY LENGTH OF TIME, I TAN REALLY FAST.
MY SISTER SAID THEY WENT ON CLUB TRIPS TO THE BEACH LAST YEAR AND THE YEAR BEFORE THAT.
THE BEACH!?
WHERE'S "OUTSIDE"...?
OH, THE WHOLE POP MUSIC CLUB WENT TO GO SEE A SUMMER MUSIC FEST.
YEAH, IT'S A WHOLE VACATION HOME WITH ITS OWN STUDIO INSIDE. IT'S GOT, LIKE, CRAZY EXPENSIVE AMPS AND THE WHOLE WORKS.
YOUR OWN STUDIO!? AND A VACATION HOME!?
SUMMER MUSIC FEST!? I'M SO JEALOUS—!
HEH HEH HEH... YEAH. PRETTY COOL, HUH?
CLUB TRIPS... BEACH...
...VACATION HOME...PRIVATE STUDIO...
GUESS YOU SHOULDA JOINED THE POP MUSIC CLUB AFTER ALL, JUN-CHAN.
HMPH... WELL... I HAVE NO REGRETS!
SO WHY DON'T YOU JUST JOIN THE POP MUSIC CLUB, JUN?
I TOLD YOU— I HAVE NO REGRETS!

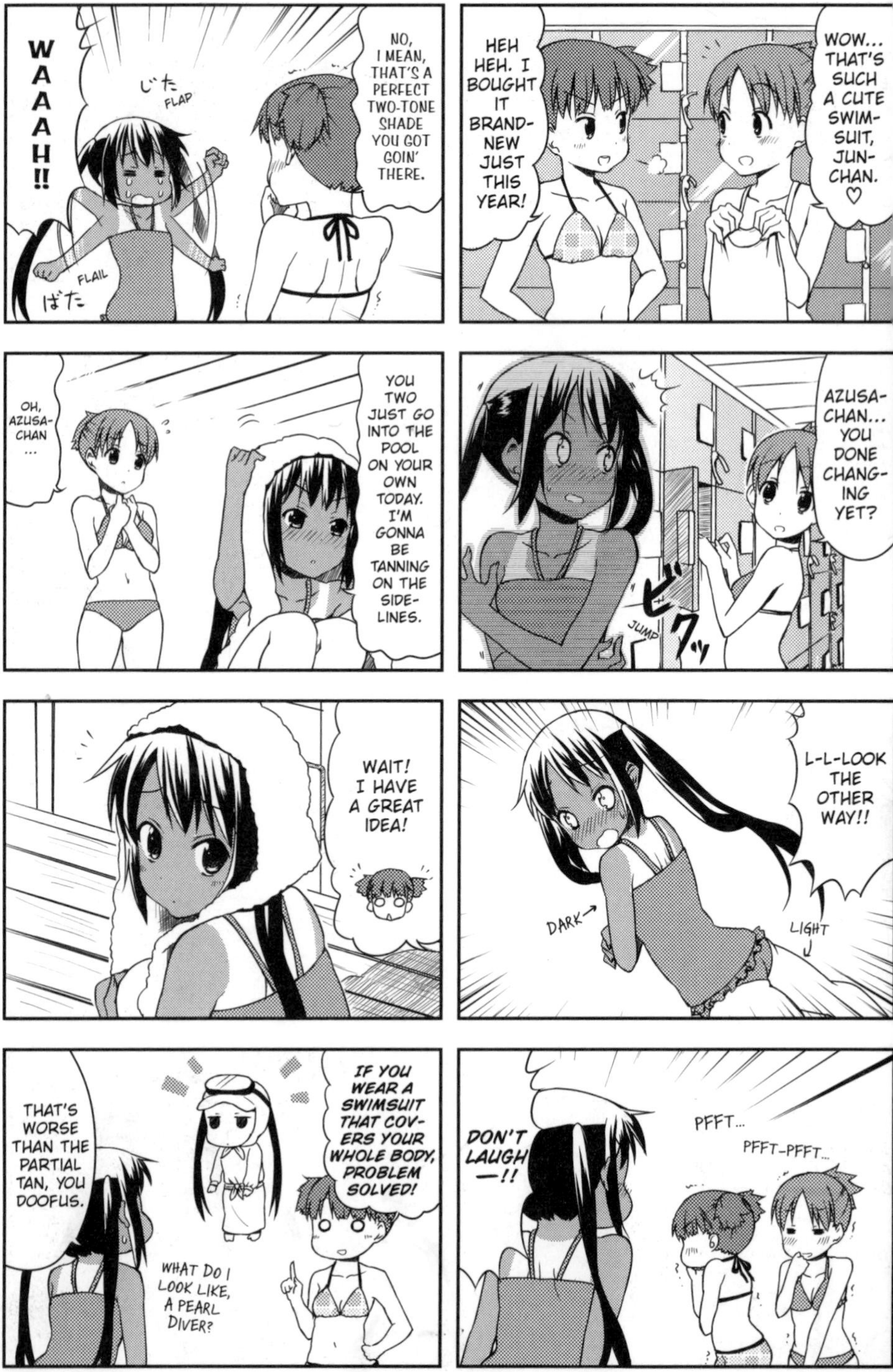
WOW... THAT'S SUCH A CUTE SWIMSUIT, JUN-CHAN. ♡
HEH HEH. I BOUGHT IT BRAND-NEW JUST THIS YEAR!
NO, I MEAN, THAT'S A PERFECT TWO-TONE SHADE YOU GOT GOIN' THERE.
WAAAAH!!
じた FLAP
ばた FLAIL
AZUSA-CHAN... YOU DONE CHANGING YET?
ビクッ JUMP
YOU TWO JUST GO INTO THE POOL ON YOUR OWN TODAY. I'M GONNA BE TANNING ON THE SIDELINES.
OH, AZUSA-CHAN...
L-L-LOOK THE OTHER WAY!!
DARK
LIGHT
WAIT! I HAVE A GREAT IDEA!
PFFT...
PFFT-PFFT...
DON'T LAUGH—!!
IF YOU WEAR A SWIMSUIT THAT COVERS YOUR WHOLE BODY, PROBLEM SOLVED!
WHAT DO I LOOK LIKE, A PEARL DIVER?
THAT'S WORSE THAN THE PARTIAL TAN, YOU DOOFUS.

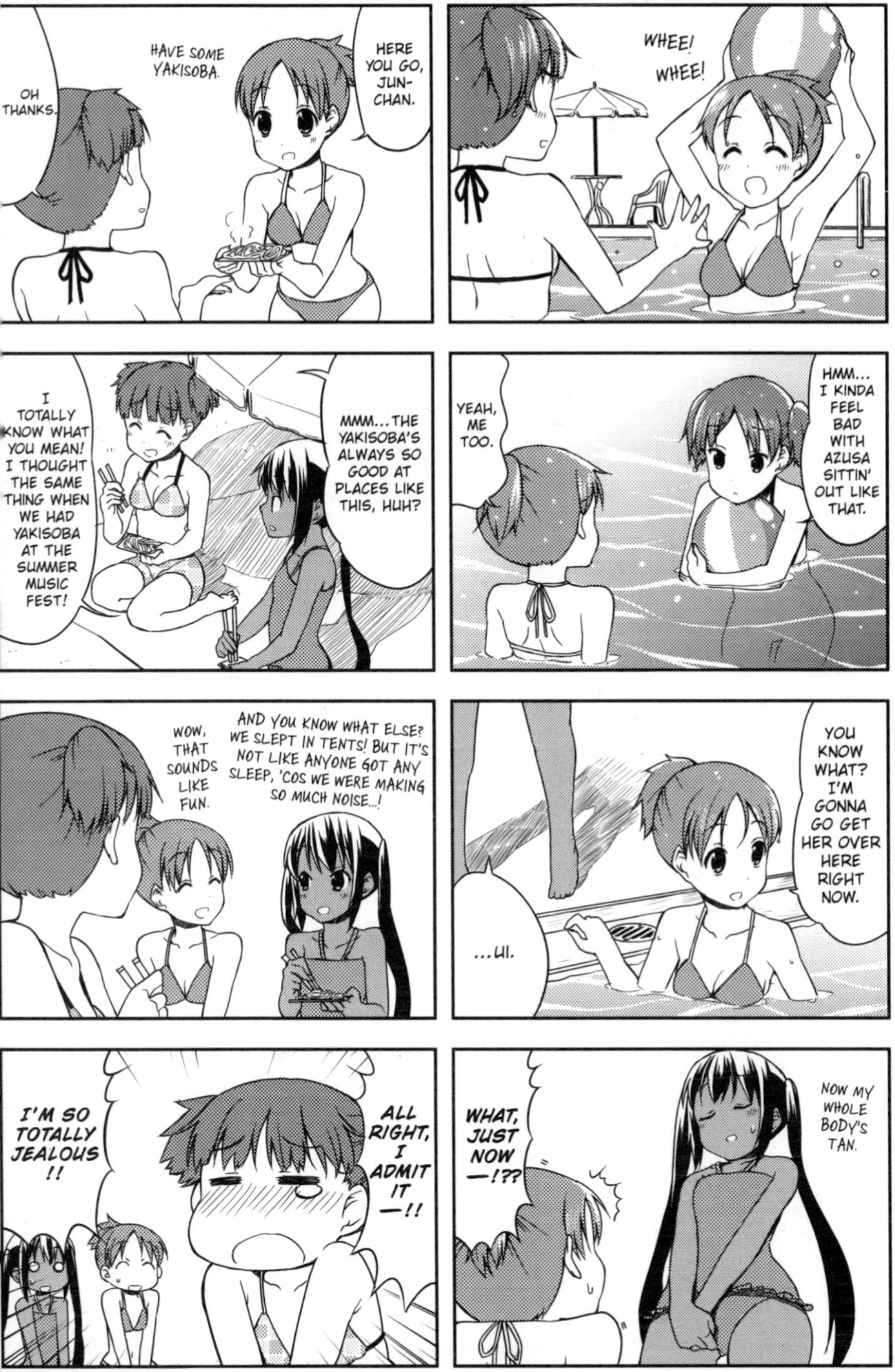
WHEE!
WHEE!
HMM... I KINDA FEEL BAD WITH AZUSA SITTIN' OUT LIKE THAT.
YEAH, ME TOO.
YOU KNOW WHAT? I'M GONNA GO GET HER OVER HERE RIGHT NOW.
...UI.
NOW MY WHOLE BODY'S TAN.
WHAT, JUST NOW —!??
HERE YOU GO, JUN-CHAN.
HAVE SOME YAKISOBA.
OH THANKS.
MMM... THE YAKISOBA'S ALWAYS SO GOOD AT PLACES LIKE THIS, HUH?
I TOTALLY KNOW WHAT YOU MEAN! I THOUGHT THE SAME THING WHEN WE HAD YAKISOBA AT THE SUMMER MUSIC FEST!
AND YOU KNOW WHAT ELSE? WE SLEPT IN TENTS! BUT IT'S NOT LIKE ANYONE GOT ANY SLEEP, 'COS WE WERE MAKING SO MUCH NOISE...!
WOW, THAT SOUNDS LIKE FUN.
ALL RIGHT, I ADMIT IT —!!
I'M SO TOTALLY JEALOUS !!

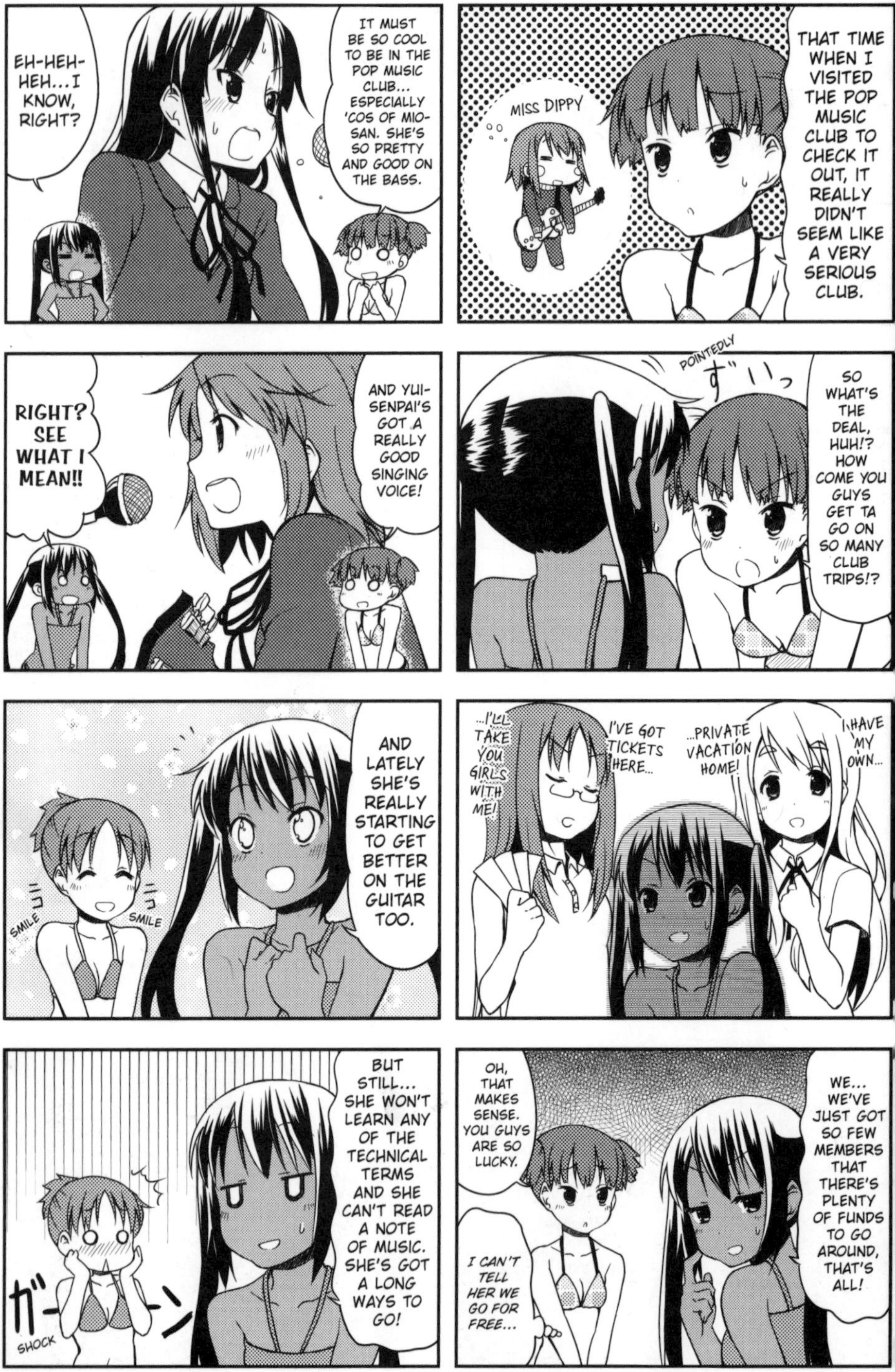
THAT TIME WHEN I VISITED THE POP MUSIC CLUB TO CHECK IT OUT, IT REALLY DIDN'T SEEM LIKE A VERY SERIOUS CLUB.
MISS DIPPY
IT MUST BE SO COOL TO BE IN THE POP MUSIC CLUB... ESPECIALLY 'COS OF MIO-SAN. SHE'S SO PRETTY AND GOOD ON THE BASS.
EH-HEH-HEH...I KNOW, RIGHT?
SO WHAT'S THE DEAL, HUH!? HOW COME YOU GUYS GET TA GO ON SO MANY CLUB TRIPS!?
ずいっ
POINTEDLY
AND YUI-SENPAI'S GOT A REALLY GOOD SINGING VOICE!
RIGHT? SEE WHAT I MEAN!!
I HAVE MY OWN...
...PRIVATE VACATION HOME!
I'VE GOT TICKETS HERE...
...I'LL TAKE YOU GIRLS WITH ME!
AND LATELY SHE'S REALLY STARTING TO GET BETTER ON THE GUITAR TOO.
SMILE
SMILE
WE... WE'VE JUST GOT SO FEW MEMBERS THAT THERE'S PLENTY OF FUNDS TO GO AROUND, THAT'S ALL!
OH, THAT MAKES SENSE. YOU GUYS ARE SO LUCKY.
I CAN'T TELL HER WE GO FOR FREE...
BUT STILL... SHE WON'T LEARN ANY OF THE TECHNICAL TERMS AND SHE CAN'T READ A NOTE OF MUSIC. SHE'S GOT A LONG WAYS TO GO!
ガーン
SHOCK

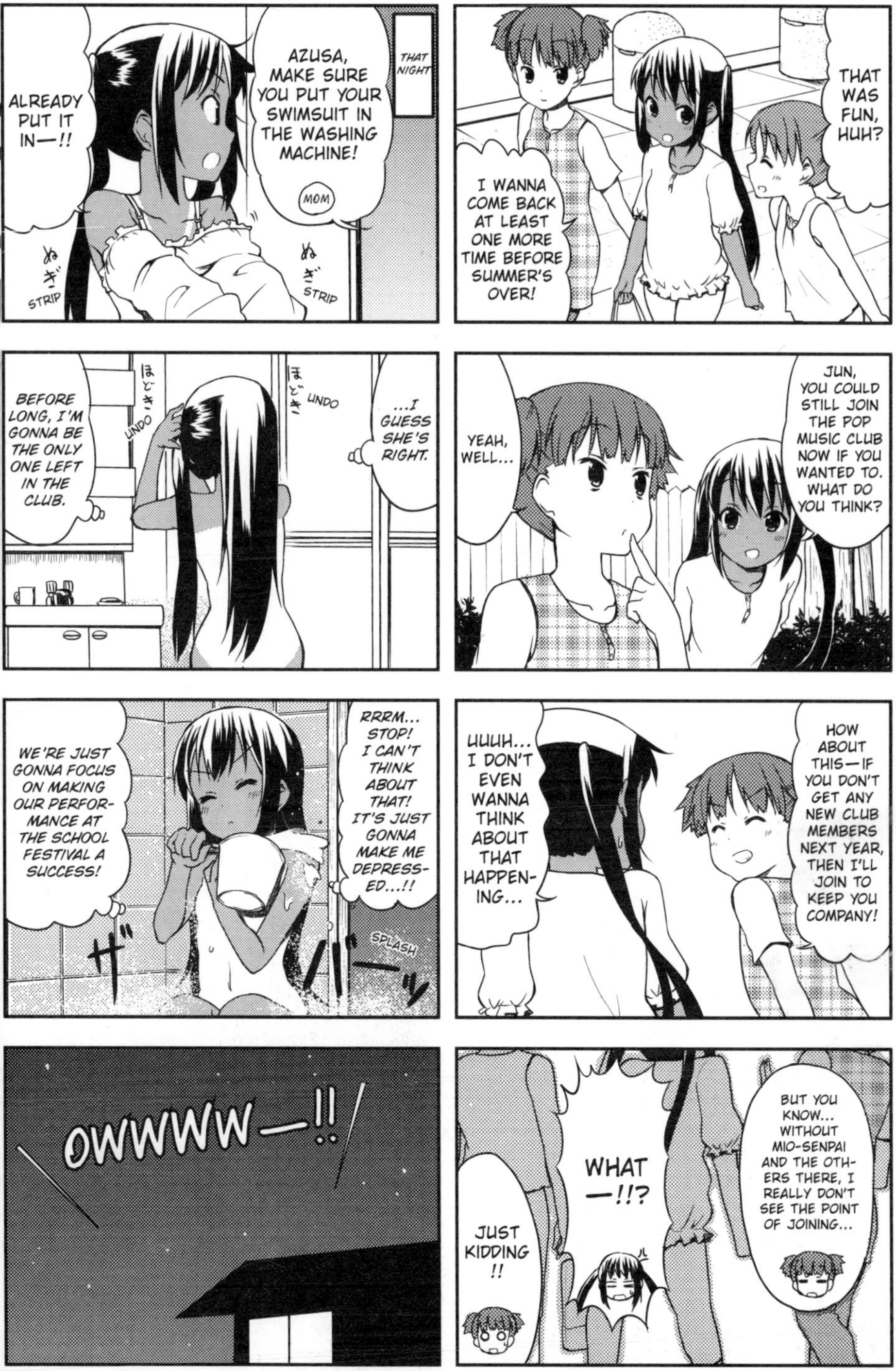
THAT WAS FUN, HUH?
I WANNA COME BACK AT LEAST ONE MORE TIME BEFORE SUMMER'S OVER!
JUN, YOU COULD STILL JOIN THE POP MUSIC CLUB NOW IF YOU WANTED TO. WHAT DO YOU THINK?
YEAH, WELL...
HOW ABOUT THIS—IF YOU DON'T GET ANY NEW CLUB MEMBERS NEXT YEAR, THEN I'LL JOIN TO KEEP YOU COMPANY!
UUUH... I DON'T EVEN WANNA THINK ABOUT THAT HAPPEN-ING...
BUT YOU KNOW... WITHOUT MIO-SENPAI AND THE OTH-ERS THERE, I REALLY DON'T SEE THE POINT OF JOINING...
WHAT—!!?
JUST KIDDING!!
THAT NIGHT
AZUSA, MAKE SURE YOU PUT YOUR SWIMSUIT IN THE WASHING MACHINE!
MOM
ALREADY PUT IT IN—!!
ぬぎ STRIP
ぬぎ STRIP
...I GUESS SHE'S RIGHT.
ほどき UNDO
ほどき UNDO
BEFORE LONG, I'M GONNA BE THE ONLY ONE LEFT IN THE CLUB.
RRRM... STOP! I CAN'T THINK ABOUT THAT! IT'S JUST GONNA MAKE ME DEPRESS-ED...!!
WE'RE JUST GONNA FOCUS ON MAKING OUR PERFOR-MANCE AT THE SCHOOL FESTIVAL A SUCCESS!
ザバーッ SPLASH
OWWWW—!!

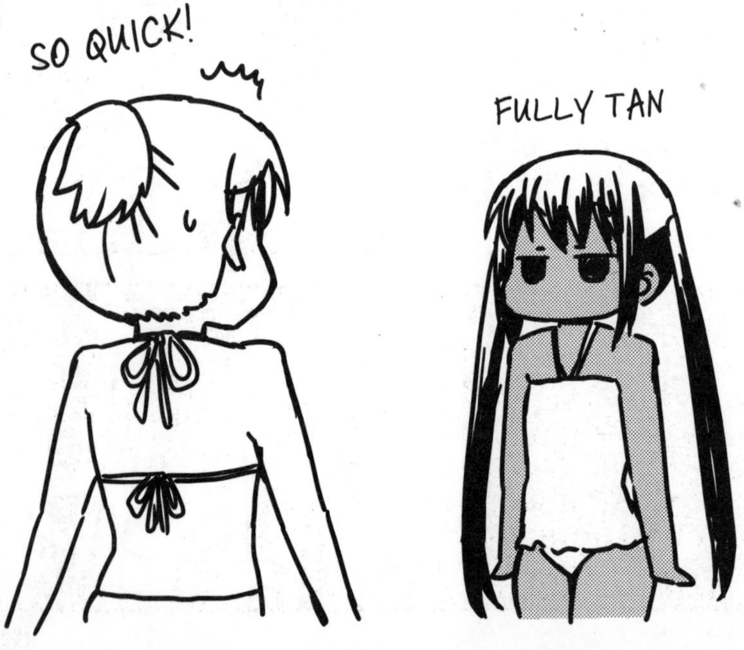

SO QUICK!

FULLY TAN

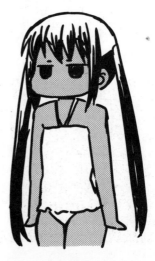

TOO QUICK!!

FULLY PALE

NEXT DAY

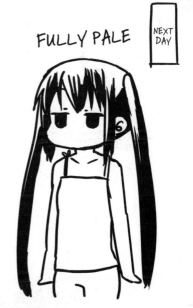

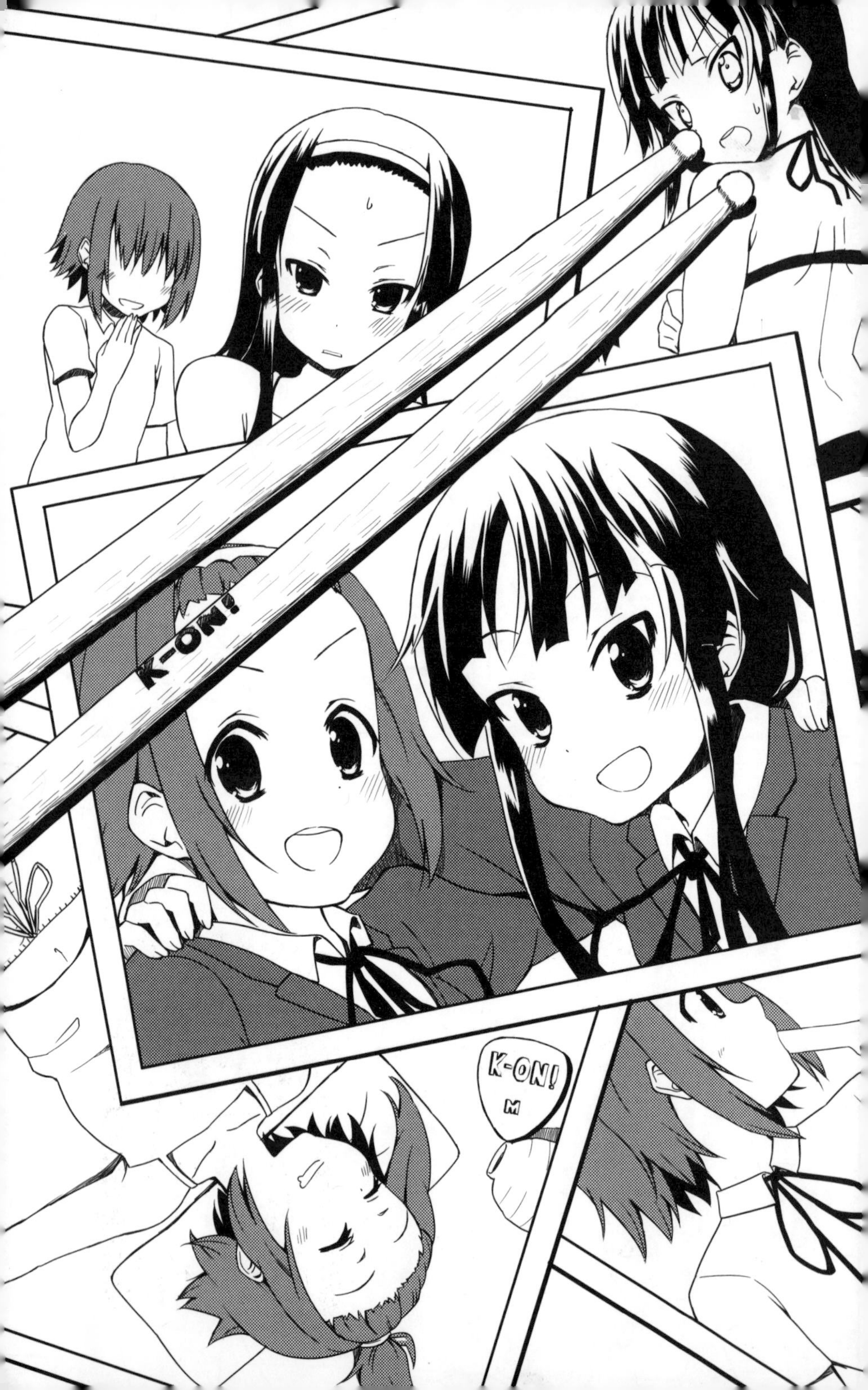
K-ON!
K-ON!
M

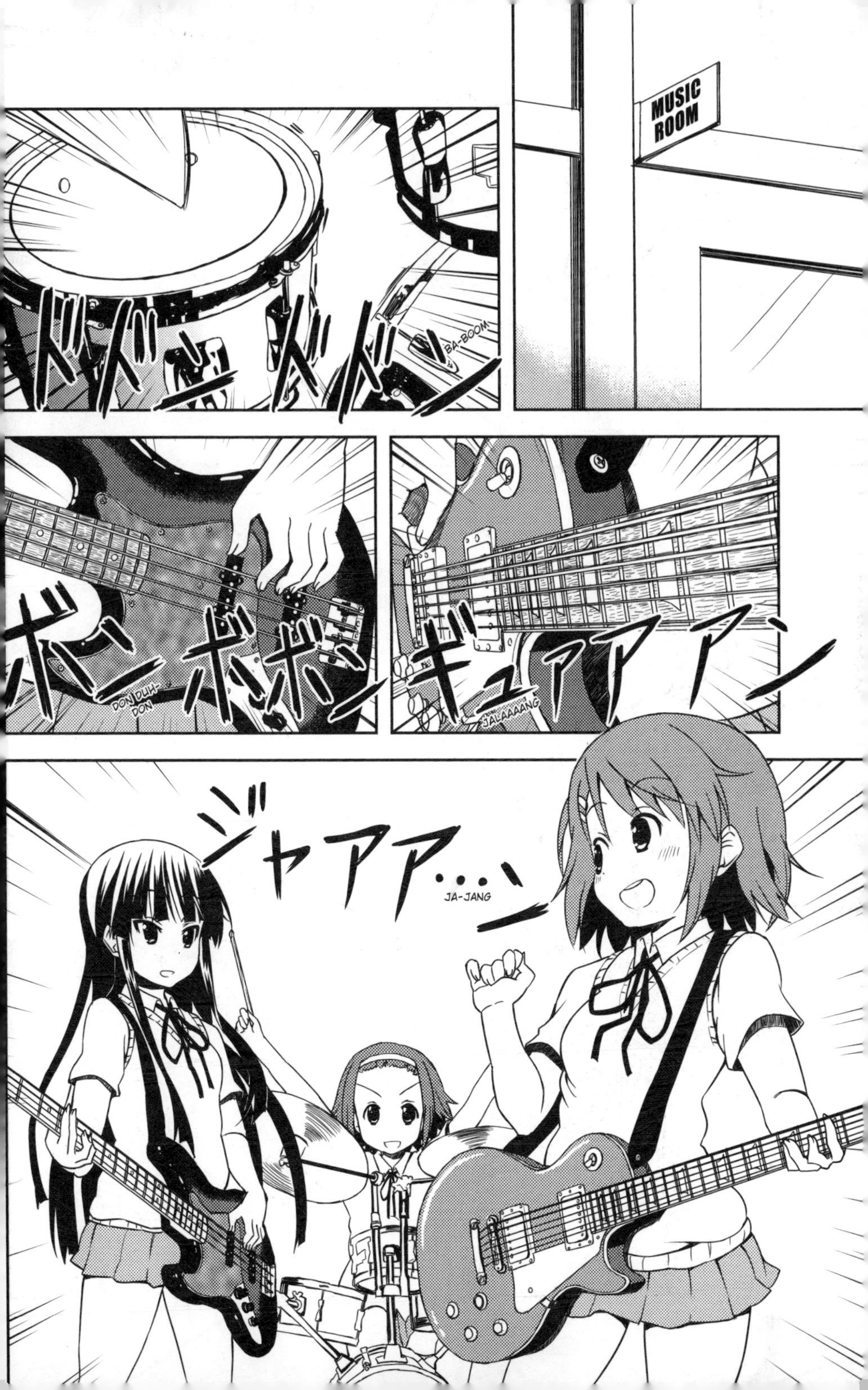

MUSIC ROOM
BA-BOOM
ギュアアアン
JALAAAANG
DON DUH-DON
ジャアア…ン
JA-JANG

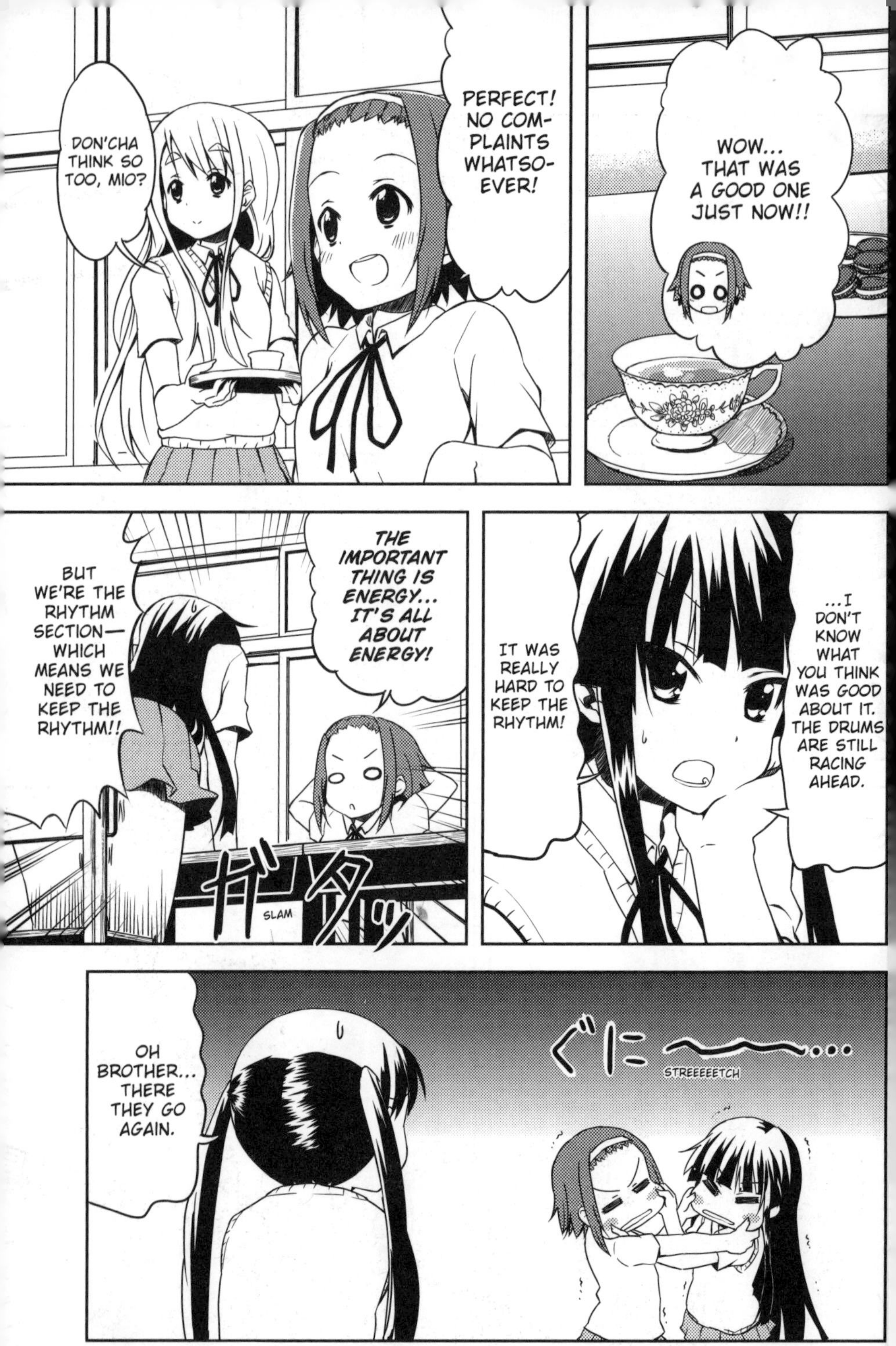
WOW... THAT WAS A GOOD ONE JUST NOW!!
PERFECT! NO COM-PLAINTS WHATSO-EVER!
DON'CHA THINK SO TOO, MIO?
...I DON'T KNOW WHAT YOU THINK WAS GOOD ABOUT IT. THE DRUMS ARE STILL RACING AHEAD.
IT WAS REALLY HARD TO KEEP THE RHYTHM!
THE IMPORTANT THING IS ENERGY... IT'S ALL ABOUT ENERGY!
BUT WE'RE THE RHYTHM SECTION—WHICH MEANS WE NEED TO KEEP THE RHYTHM!!
ガタッ
SLAM
ぐに〜〜〜…
STREEEEETCH
OH BROTHER... THERE THEY GO AGAIN.

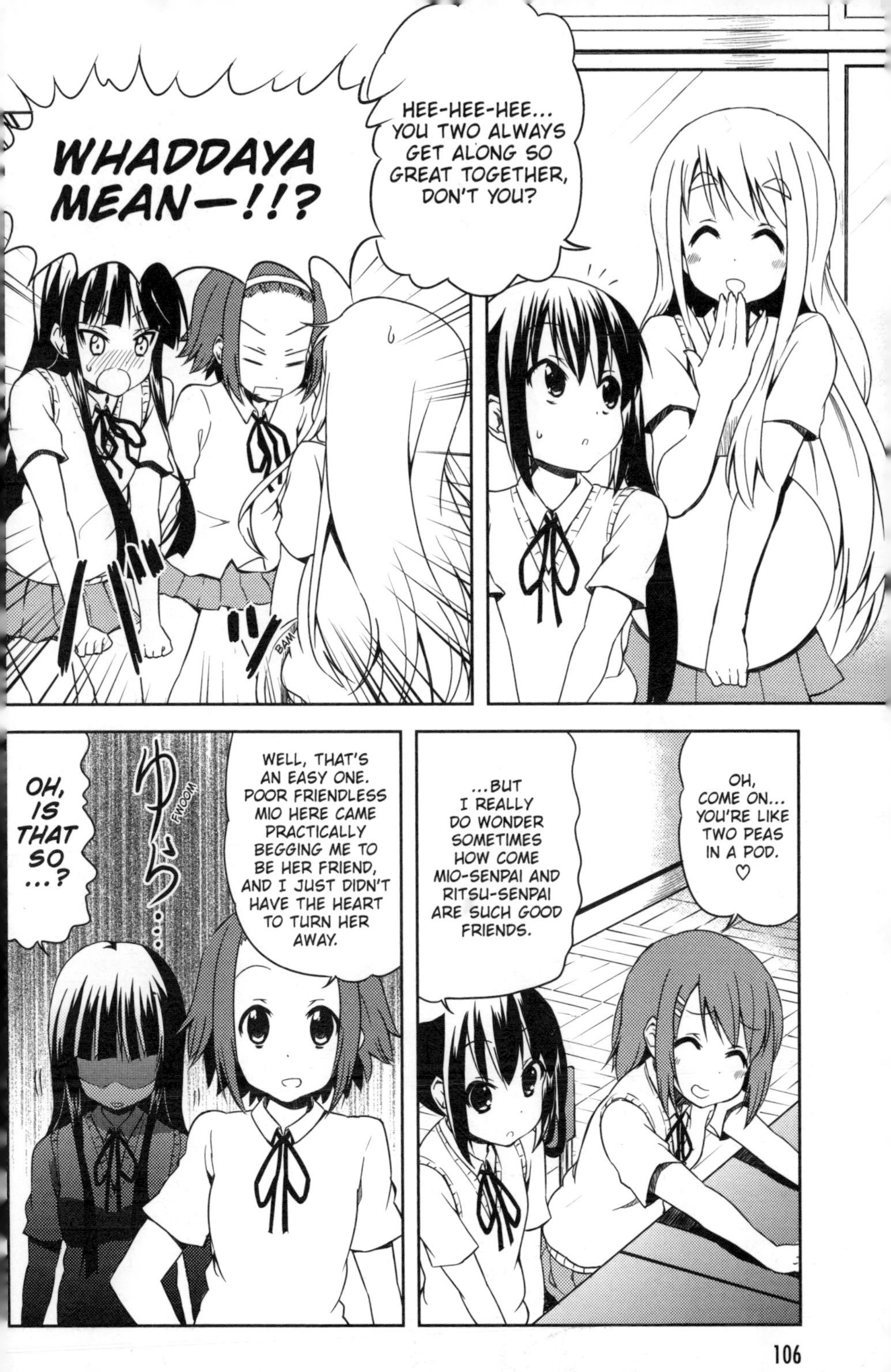
HEE-HEE-HEE... YOU TWO ALWAYS GET ALONG SO GREAT TOGETHER, DON'T YOU?
WHADDAYA MEAN—!!?
BAM
OH, COME ON... YOU'RE LIKE TWO PEAS IN A POD. ♡
...BUT I REALLY DO WONDER SOMETIMES HOW COME MIO-SENPAI AND RITSU-SENPAI ARE SUCH GOOD FRIENDS.
WELL, THAT'S AN EASY ONE. POOR FRIENDLESS MIO HERE CAME PRACTICALLY BEGGING ME TO BE HER FRIEND, AND I JUST DIDN'T HAVE THE HEART TO TURN HER AWAY.
ゆら…
FWOOM
OH, IS THAT SO...?

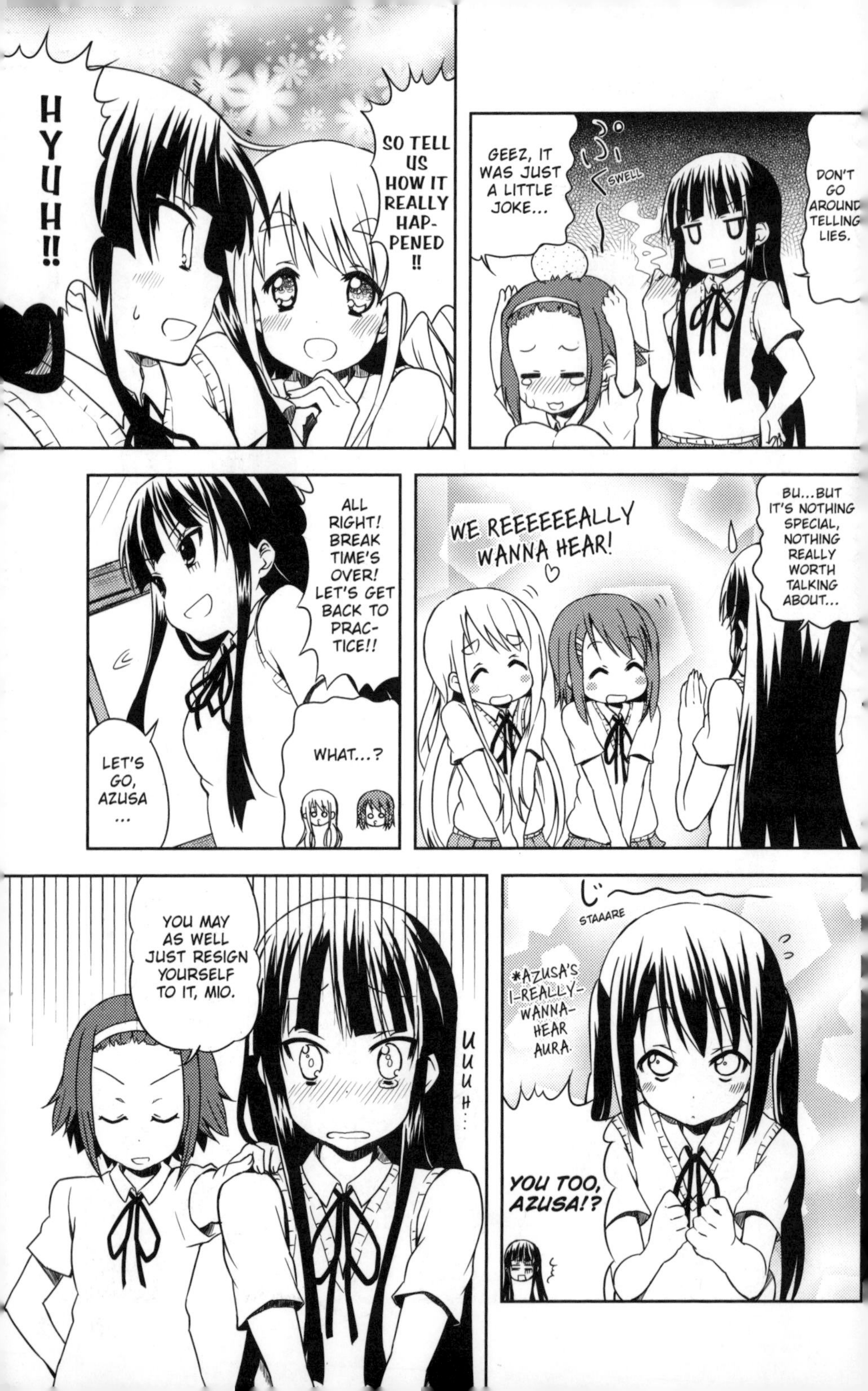
DON'T GO AROUND TELLING LIES.
SWELL
GEEZ, IT WAS JUST A LITTLE JOKE...
SO TELL US HOW IT REALLY HAPPENED !!
HYUH!!
BU...BUT IT'S NOTHING SPECIAL, NOTHING REALLY WORTH TALKING ABOUT...
WE REEEEEEALLY WANNA HEAR!
ALL RIGHT! BREAK TIME'S OVER! LET'S GET BACK TO PRACTICE!!
WHAT...?
LET'S GO, AZUSA ...
STAAARE
*AZUSA'S I-REALLY-WANNA-HEAR AURA.
YOU TOO, AZUSA!?
UUUH...
YOU MAY AS WELL JUST RESIGN YOURSELF TO IT, MIO.

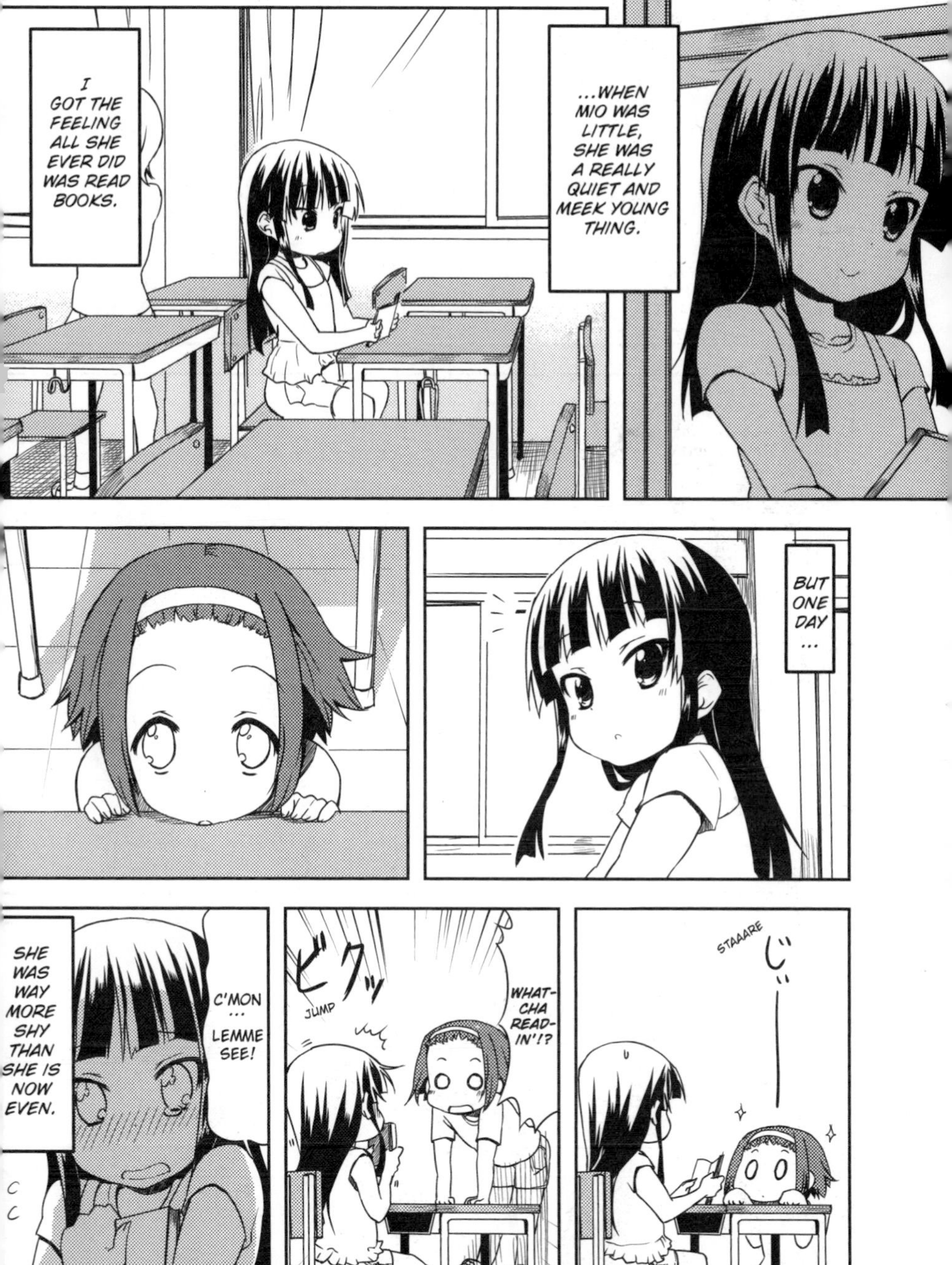

...WHEN MIO WAS LITTLE, SHE WAS A REALLY QUIET AND MEEK YOUNG THING.
I GOT THE FEELING ALL SHE EVER DID WAS READ BOOKS.
BUT ONE DAY ...
じー
STAAARE
WHAT-CHA READ-IN'!?
ビクッ
JUMP
C'MON ... LEMME SEE!
SHE WAS WAY MORE SHY THAN SHE IS NOW EVEN.

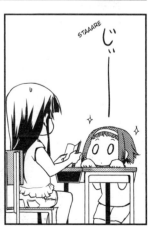

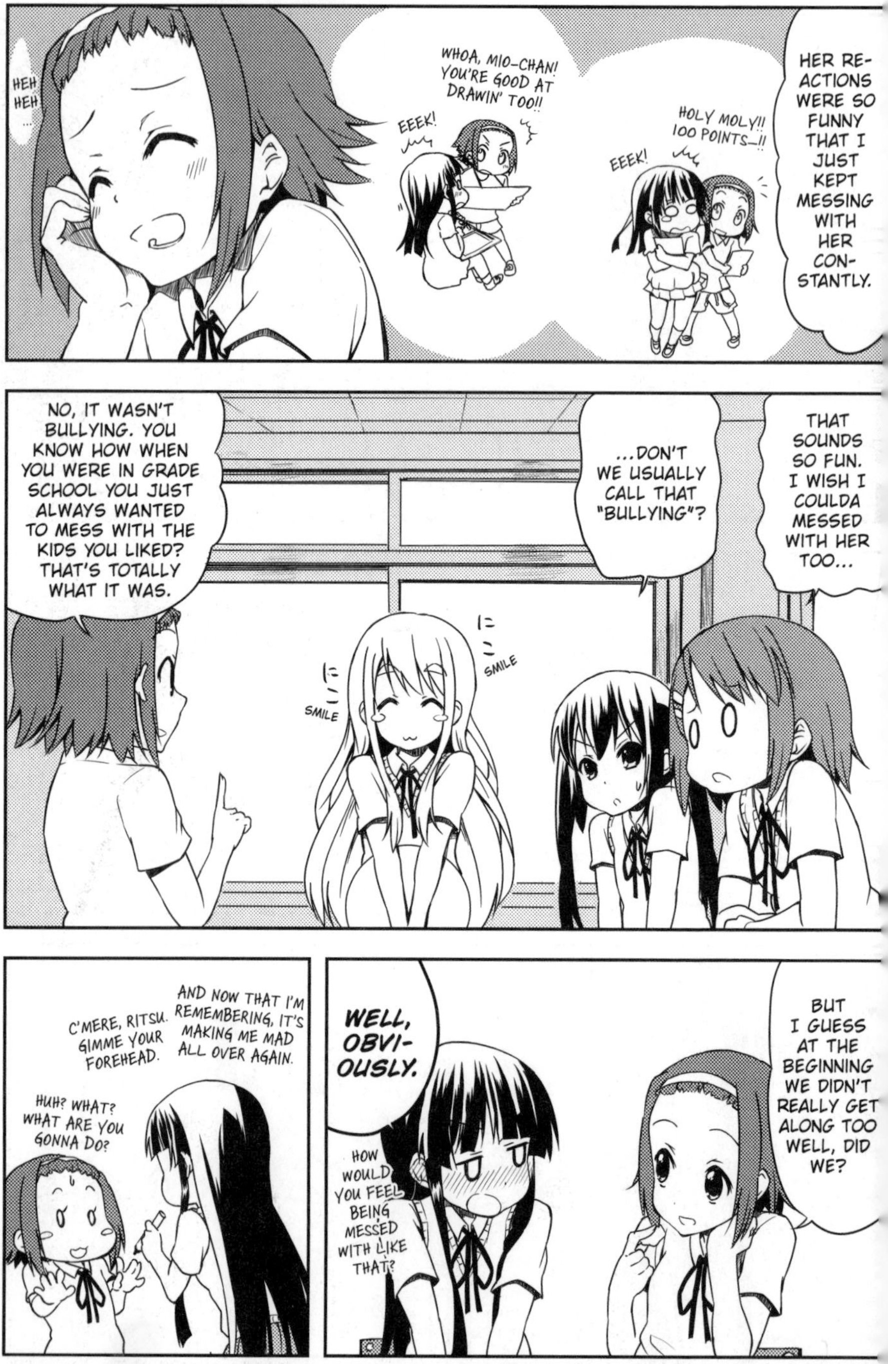
HER REACTIONS WERE SO FUNNY THAT I JUST KEPT MESSING WITH HER CONSTANTLY.
HOLY MOLY!! 100 POINTS—!!
EEEK!
WHOA, MIO-CHAN! YOU'RE GOOD AT DRAWIN' TOO!!
EEEK!
HEH HEH ...
THAT SOUNDS SO FUN. I WISH I COULDA MESSED WITH HER TOO...
...DON'T WE USUALLY CALL THAT "BULLYING"?
にこ SMILE
にこ SMILE
NO, IT WASN'T BULLYING. YOU KNOW HOW WHEN YOU WERE IN GRADE SCHOOL YOU JUST ALWAYS WANTED TO MESS WITH THE KIDS YOU LIKED? THAT'S TOTALLY WHAT IT WAS.
BUT I GUESS AT THE BEGINNING WE DIDN'T REALLY GET ALONG TOO WELL, DID WE?
WELL, OBVIOUSLY.
HOW WOULD YOU FEEL BEING MESSED WITH LIKE THAT?
AND NOW THAT I'M REMEMBERING, IT'S MAKING ME MAD ALL OVER AGAIN.
C'MERE, RITSU. GIMME YOUR FOREHEAD.
HUH? WHAT? WHAT ARE YOU GONNA DO?

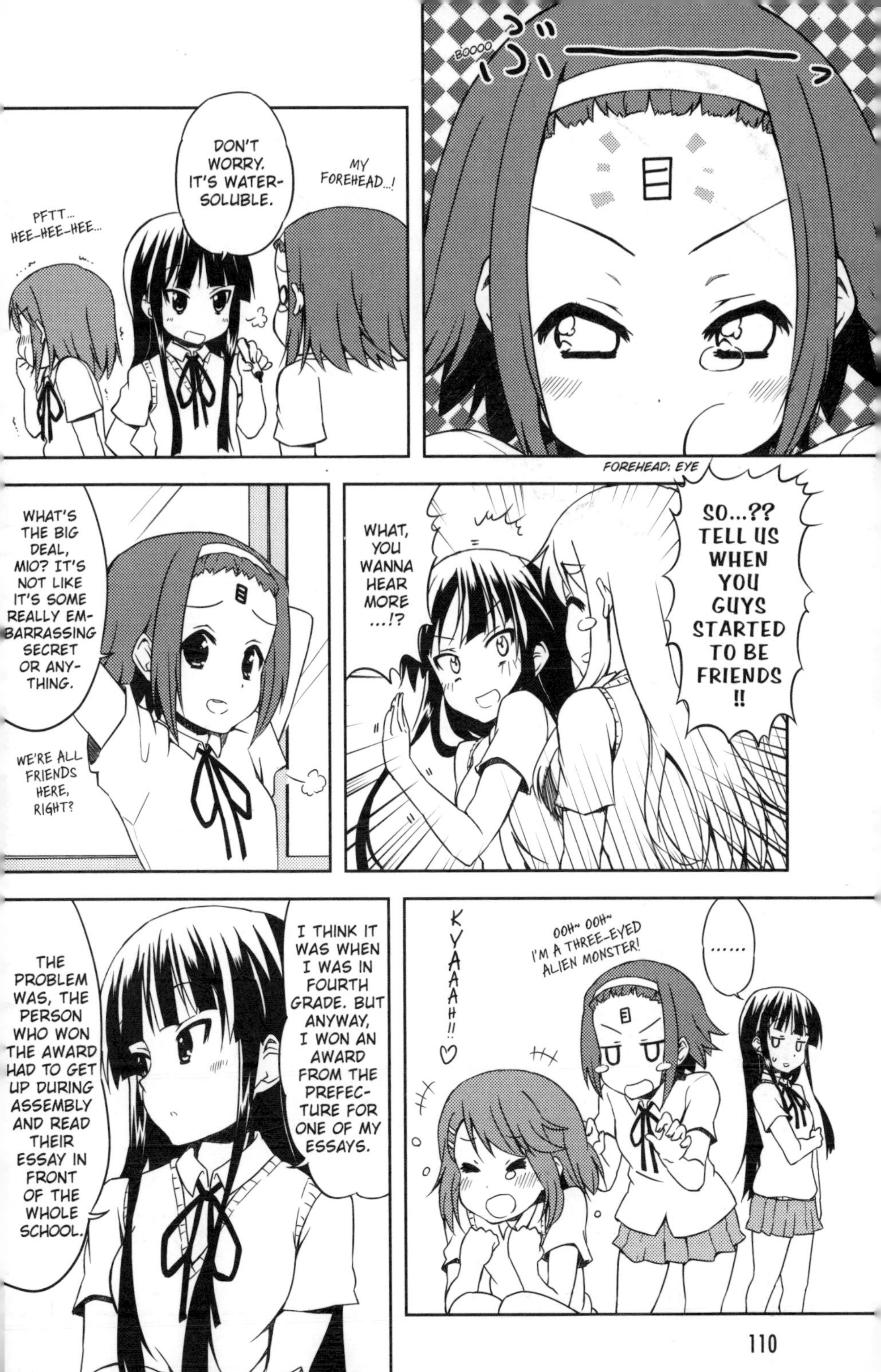
BOOOO
FOREHEAD: EYE
MY FOREHEAD...!
DON'T WORRY. IT'S WATER-SOLUBLE.
PFTT... HEE-HEE-HEE...
SO...?? TELL US WHEN YOU GUYS STARTED TO BE FRIENDS !!
WHAT, YOU WANNA HEAR MORE ...!?
WHAT'S THE BIG DEAL, MIO? IT'S NOT LIKE IT'S SOME REALLY EM-BARRASSING SECRET OR ANY-THING.
WE'RE ALL FRIENDS HERE, RIGHT?
......
OOH~ OOH~ I'M A THREE-EYED ALIEN MONSTER!
KYAAAAH!! ♡
I THINK IT WAS WHEN I WAS IN FOURTH GRADE. BUT ANYWAY, I WON AN AWARD FROM THE PREFEC-TURE FOR ONE OF MY ESSAYS.
THE PROBLEM WAS, THE PERSON WHO WON THE AWARD HAD TO GET UP DURING ASSEMBLY AND READ THEIR ESSAY IN FRONT OF THE WHOLE SCHOOL.

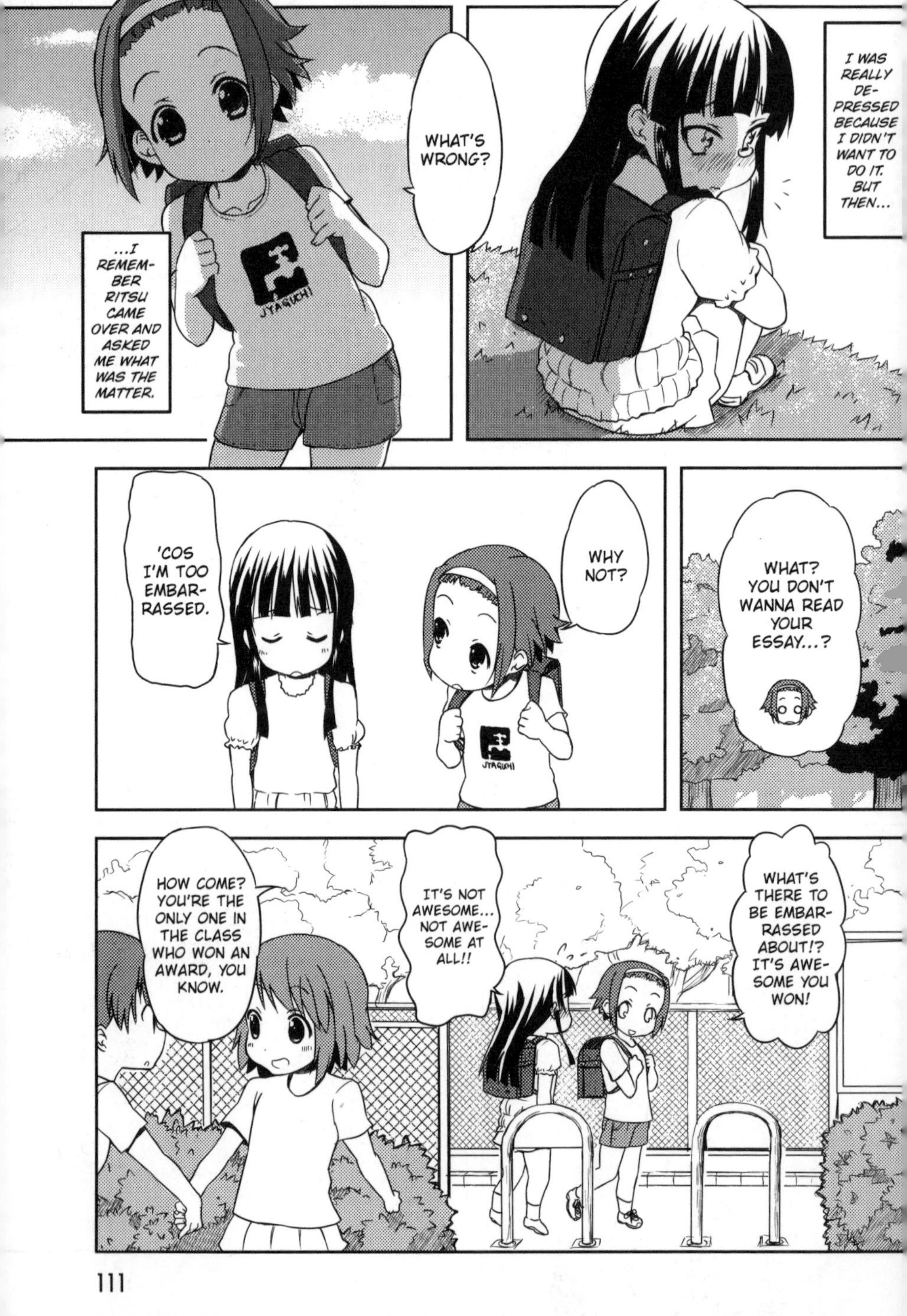
I WAS REALLY DEPRESSED BECAUSE I DIDN'T WANT TO DO IT. BUT THEN...
WHAT'S WRONG?
...I REMEMBER RITSU CAME OVER AND ASKED ME WHAT WAS THE MATTER.
JYAGUCHI
WHAT? YOU DON'T WANNA READ YOUR ESSAY...?
WHY NOT?
'COS I'M TOO EMBARRASSED.
JYAGUCHI
WHAT'S THERE TO BE EMBARRASSED ABOUT!? IT'S AWESOME YOU WON!
IT'S NOT AWESOME... NOT AWESOME AT ALL!!
HOW COME? YOU'RE THE ONLY ONE IN THE CLASS WHO WON AN AWARD, YOU KNOW.

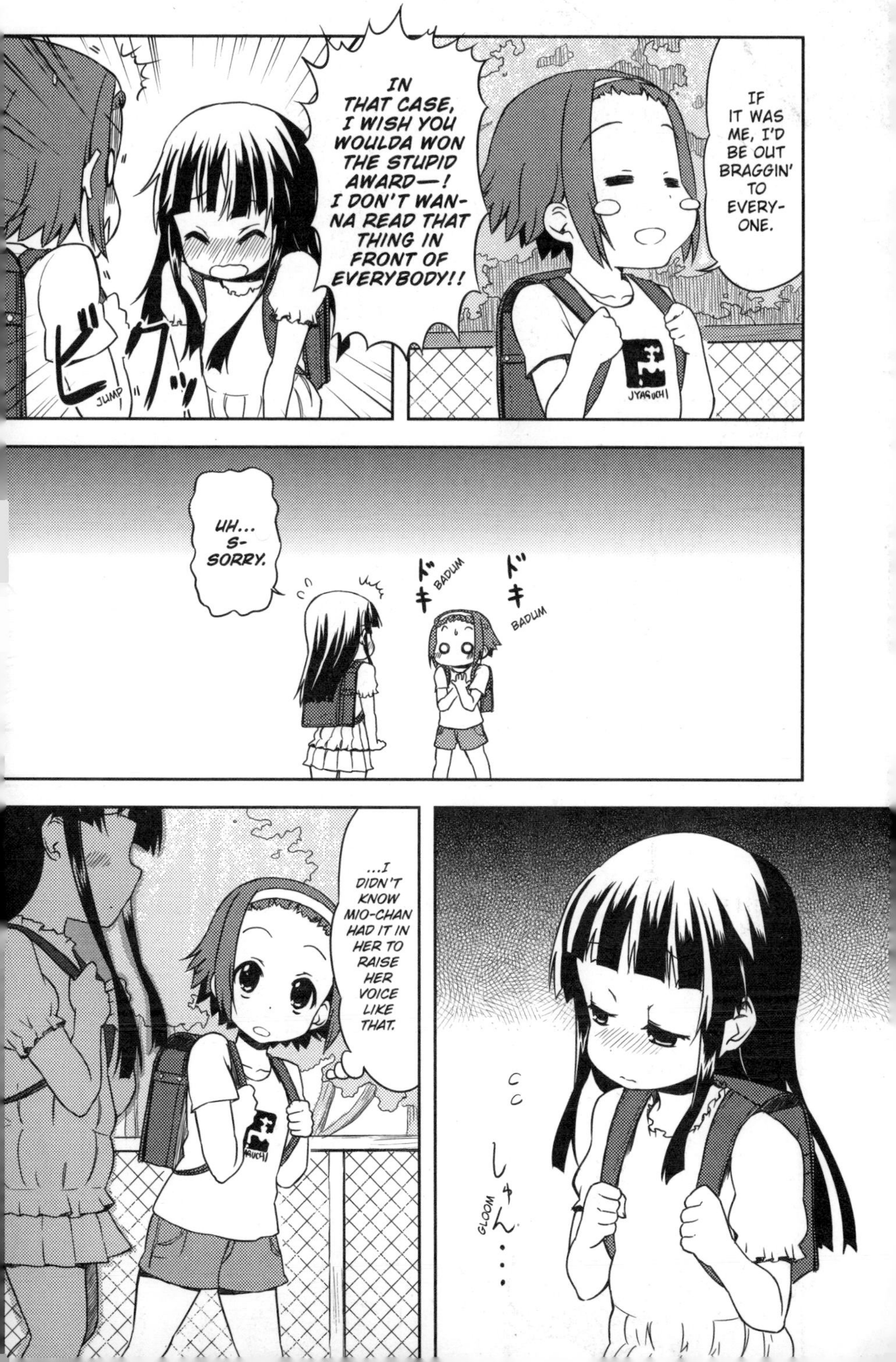
IF IT WAS ME, I'D BE OUT BRAGGIN' TO EVERY-ONE.
JYAGUCHI
IN THAT CASE, I WISH YOU WOULDA WON THE STUPID AWARD—! I DON'T WAN-NA READ THAT THING IN FRONT OF EVERYBODY!!
ビクッ
JUMP
ドキ
BADUM
ドキ
BADUM
UH... S-SORRY.
しゅん…
GLOOM
...I DIDN'T KNOW MIO-CHAN HAD IT IN HER TO RAISE HER VOICE LIKE THAT.

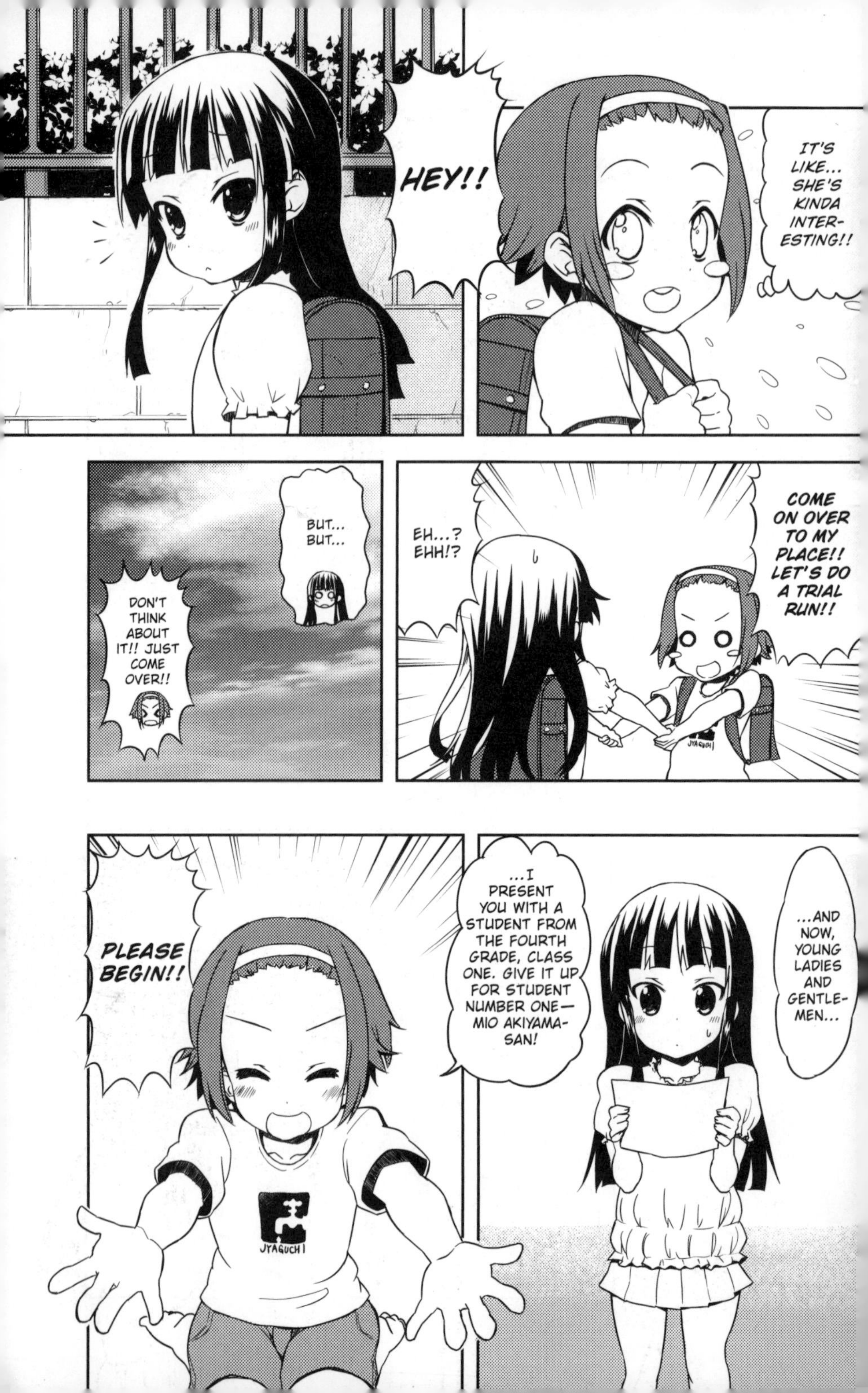
IT'S LIKE... SHE'S KINDA INTERESTING!!
HEY!!
COME ON OVER TO MY PLACE!! LET'S DO A TRIAL RUN!!
EH...? EHH!?
BUT... BUT...
DON'T THINK ABOUT IT!! JUST COME OVER!!
...AND NOW, YOUNG LADIES AND GENTLEMEN...
...I PRESENT YOU WITH A STUDENT FROM THE FOURTH GRADE, CLASS ONE. GIVE IT UP FOR STUDENT NUMBER ONE—MIO AKIYAMA-SAN!
PLEASE BEGIN!!
JYAGUCHI

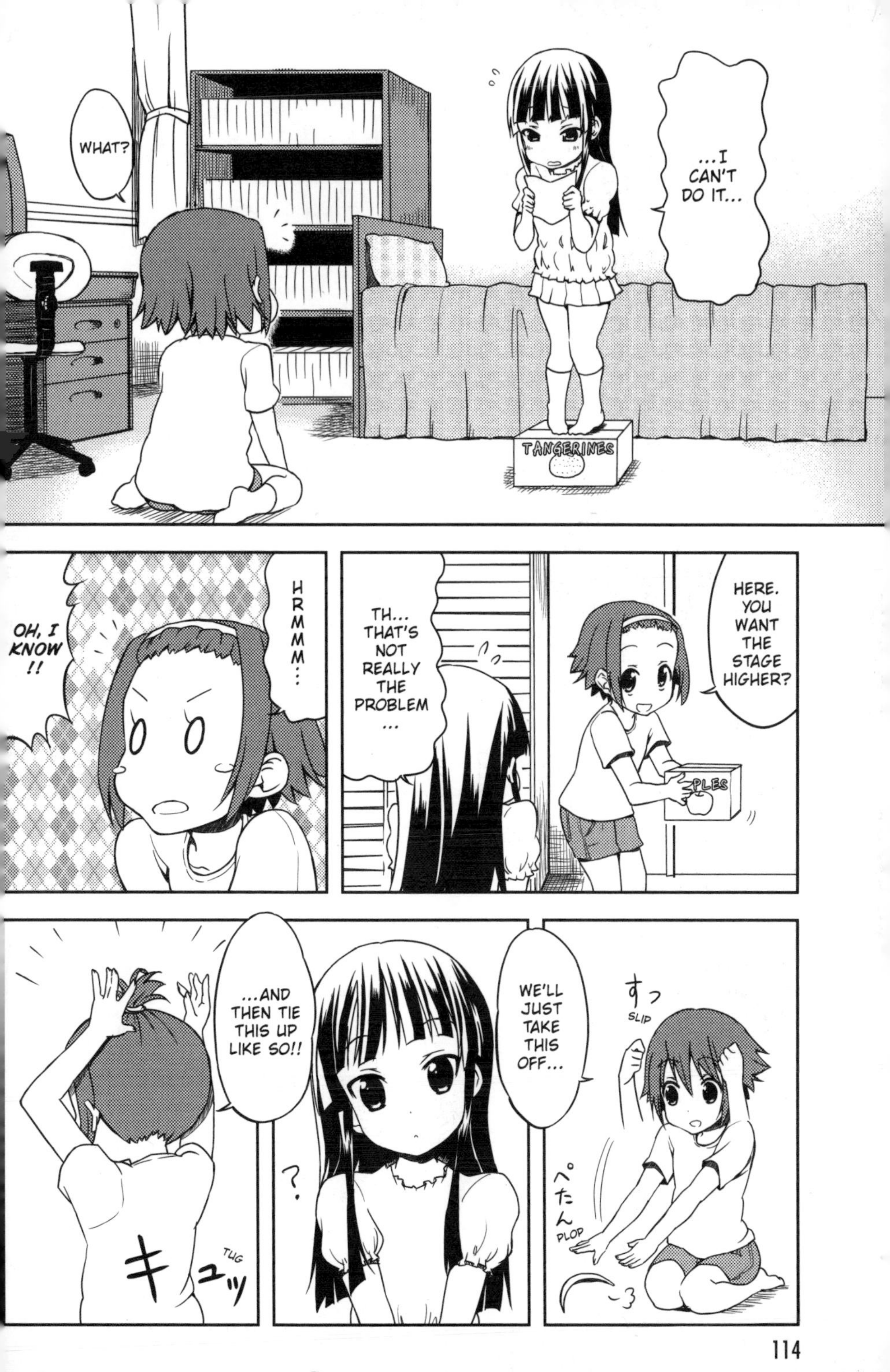

...I CAN'T DO IT...
WHAT?
TANGERINES
HERE. YOU WANT THE STAGE HIGHER?
PLES
TH... THAT'S NOT REALLY THE PROBLEM ...
HRMMM...
OH, I KNOW!!
すっ
SLIP
WE'LL JUST TAKE THIS OFF...
ぺたん
PLOP
...AND THEN TIE THIS UP LIKE SO!!
?
キュッ
TUG

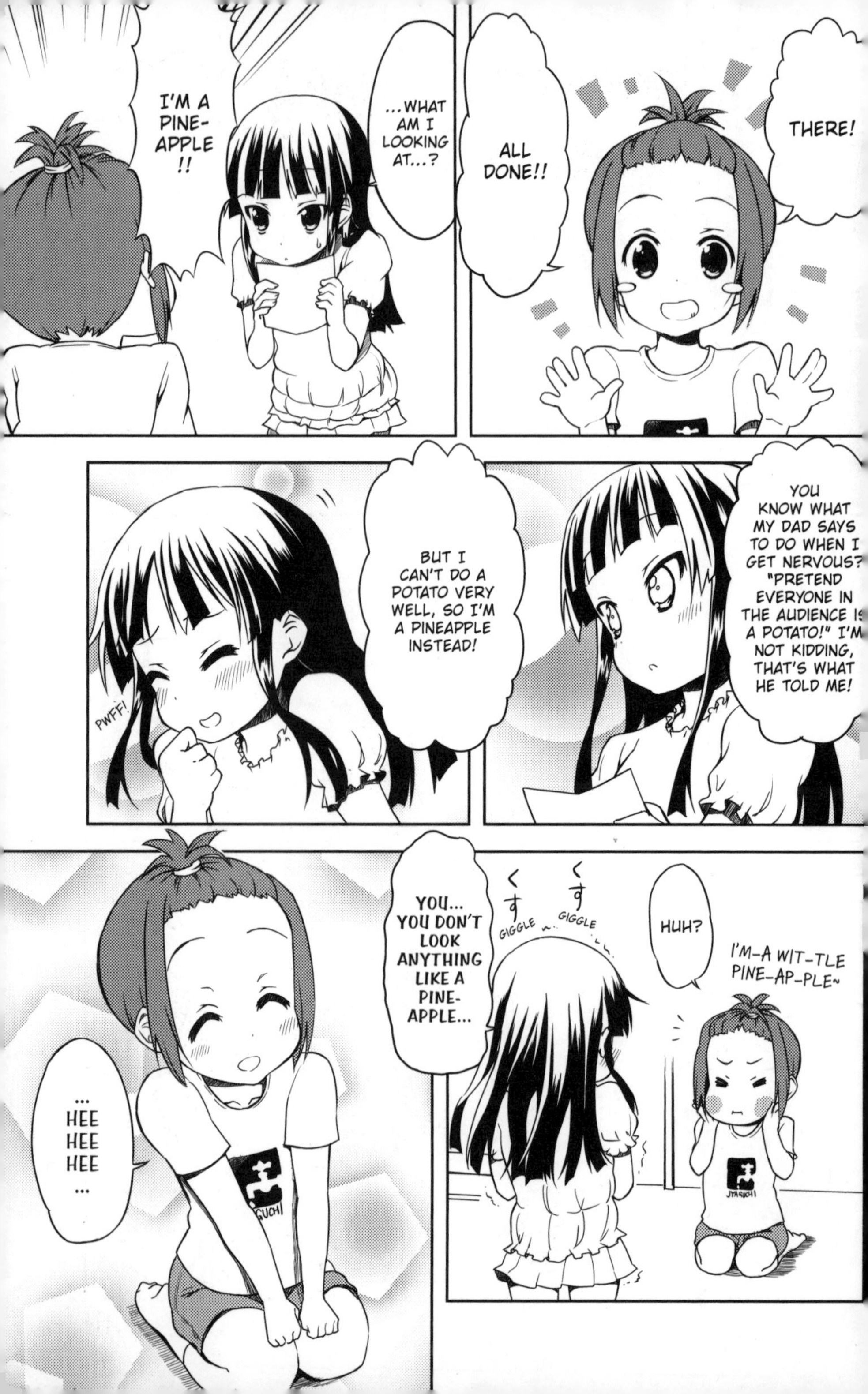
THERE!
ALL DONE!!
...WHAT AM I LOOKING AT...?
I'M A PINE-APPLE!!
YOU KNOW WHAT MY DAD SAYS TO DO WHEN I GET NERVOUS? "PRETEND EVERYONE IN THE AUDIENCE IS A POTATO!" I'M NOT KIDDING, THAT'S WHAT HE TOLD ME!
BUT I CAN'T DO A POTATO VERY WELL, SO I'M A PINEAPPLE INSTEAD!
PWFF!
I'M-A WIT-TLE PINE-AP-PLE~
HUH?
くす GIGGLE
くす GIGGLE
YOU... YOU DON'T LOOK ANYTHING LIKE A PINE-APPLE...
...HEE HEE HEE...

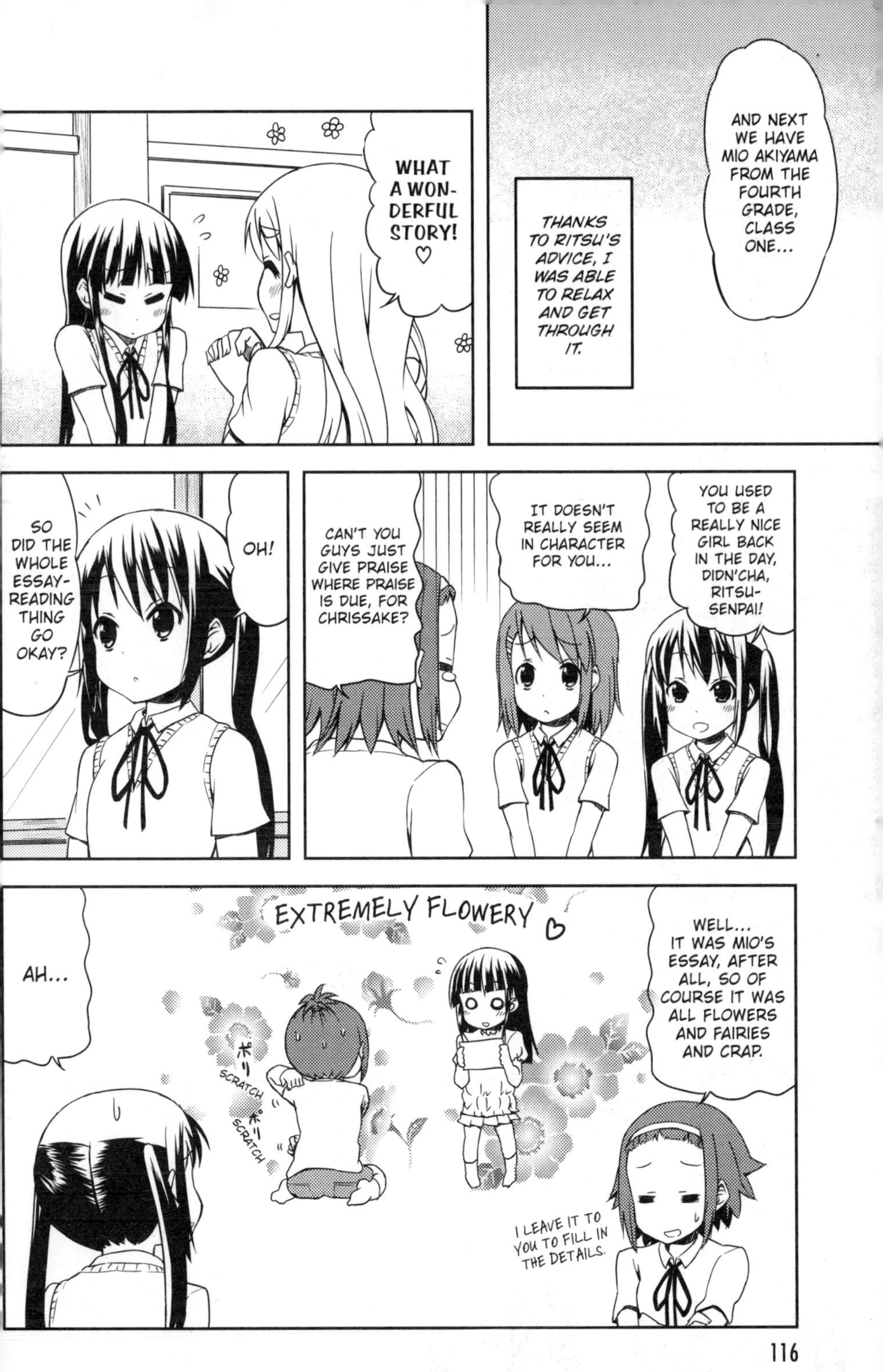

AND NEXT WE HAVE MIO AKIYAMA FROM THE FOURTH GRADE, CLASS ONE...
THANKS TO RITSU'S ADVICE, I WAS ABLE TO RELAX AND GET THROUGH IT.
WHAT A WON-DERFUL STORY! ♡
YOU USED TO BE A REALLY NICE GIRL BACK IN THE DAY, DIDN'CHA, RITSU-SENPAI!
IT DOESN'T REALLY SEEM IN CHARACTER FOR YOU...
CAN'T YOU GUYS JUST GIVE PRAISE WHERE PRAISE IS DUE, FOR CHRISSAKE?
OH!
SO DID THE WHOLE ESSAY-READING THING GO OKAY?
WELL... IT WAS MIO'S ESSAY, AFTER ALL, SO OF COURSE IT WAS ALL FLOWERS AND FAIRIES AND CRAP.
EXTREMELY FLOWERY ♡
ポリ SCRATCH
ポリ SCRATCH
I LEAVE IT TO YOU TO FILL IN THE DETAILS.
AH...

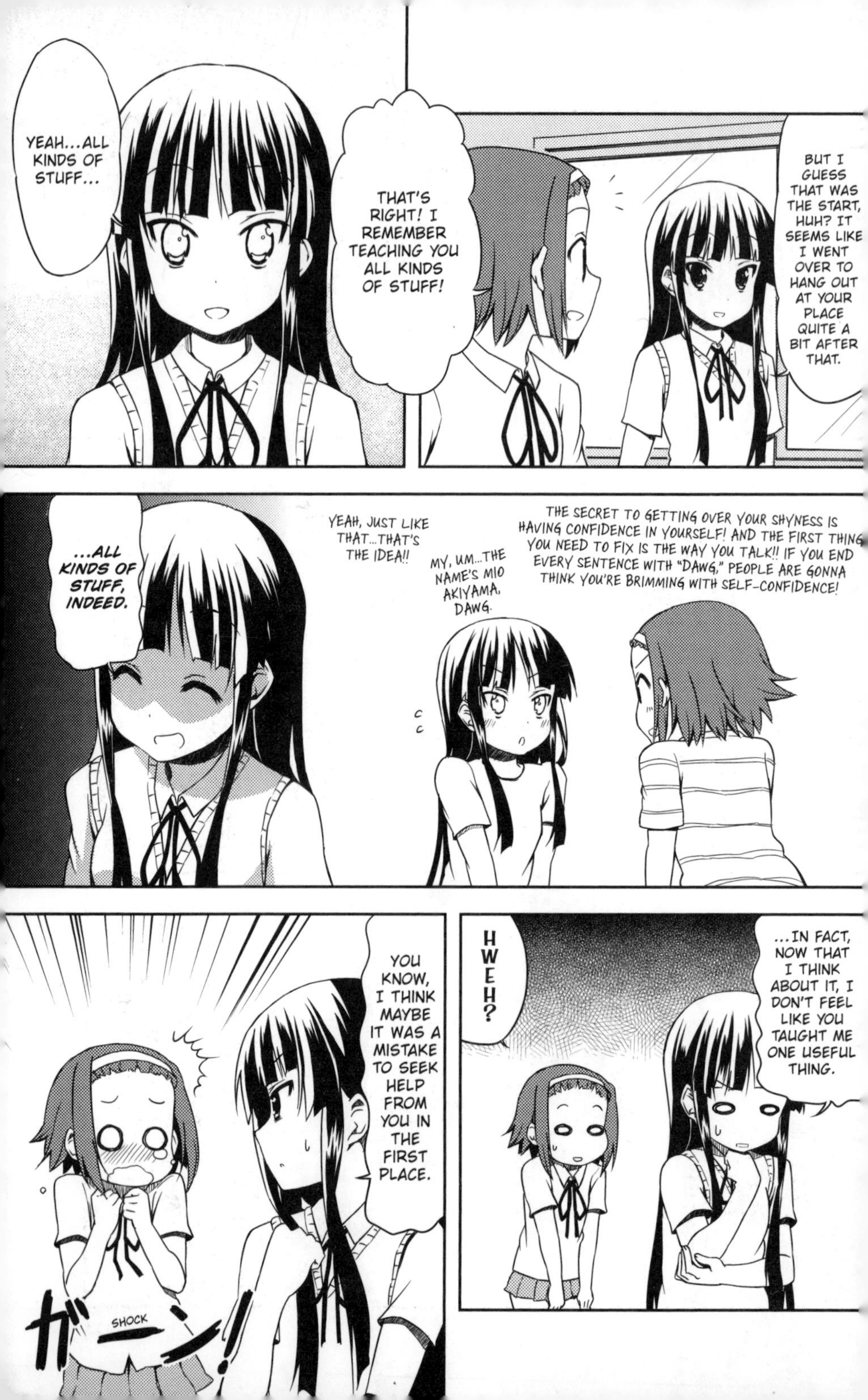
BUT I GUESS THAT WAS THE START, HUH? IT SEEMS LIKE I WENT OVER TO HANG OUT AT YOUR PLACE QUITE A BIT AFTER THAT.
THAT'S RIGHT! I REMEMBER TEACHING YOU ALL KINDS OF STUFF!
YEAH...ALL KINDS OF STUFF...
THE SECRET TO GETTING OVER YOUR SHYNESS IS HAVING CONFIDENCE IN YOURSELF! AND THE FIRST THING YOU NEED TO FIX IS THE WAY YOU TALK!! IF YOU END EVERY SENTENCE WITH "DAWG," PEOPLE ARE GONNA THINK YOU'RE BRIMMING WITH SELF-CONFIDENCE!
MY, UM...THE NAME'S MIO AKIYAMA, DAWG.
YEAH, JUST LIKE THAT...THAT'S THE IDEA!!
...ALL KINDS OF STUFF, INDEED.
...IN FACT, NOW THAT I THINK ABOUT IT, I DON'T FEEL LIKE YOU TAUGHT ME ONE USEFUL THING.
HWEH?
YOU KNOW, I THINK MAYBE IT WAS A MISTAKE TO SEEK HELP FROM YOU IN THE FIRST PLACE.
SHOCK

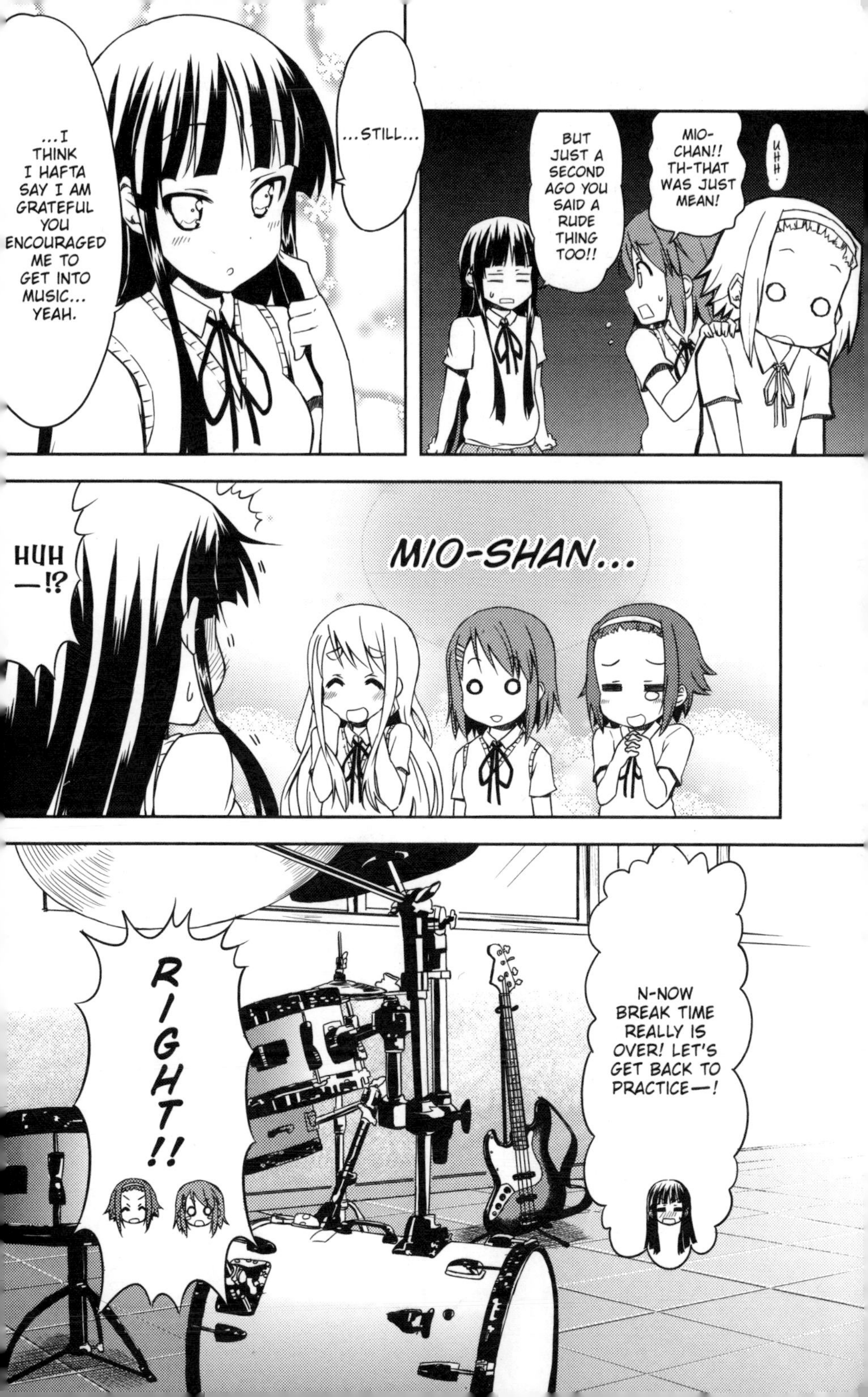
UHH
MIO-CHAN!! TH-THAT WAS JUST MEAN!
BUT JUST A SECOND AGO YOU SAID A RUDE THING TOO!!
...STILL...
...I THINK I HAFTA SAY I AM GRATEFUL YOU ENCOURAGED ME TO GET INTO MUSIC... YEAH.
MIO-SHAN...
HUH—!?
N-NOW BREAK TIME REALLY IS OVER! LET'S GET BACK TO PRACTICE—!
RIGHT!!

HELLO, THIS IS KAKIFLY.
THE ONLY REASON I WAS ABLE TO GET THIS THIRD VOLUME OUT AT ALL WAS BECAUSE OF THE SUPPORT FROM YOU, THE PEOPLE WHO'VE BEEN SO KINDLY READING THIS SERIES, AND I WANT TO THANK YOU FROM THE BOTTOM OF MY HEART! IT FEELS LIKE MY WHOLE LIFE THIS YEAR HAS BEEN *K-ON!* IN THE MORNING TO *K-ON!* IN THE EVENING. SO THIS THIRD VOLUME IS TRULY THE CULMINATION OF MY YEAR. I HOPE THAT YOU ALL ENJOY IT, BECAUSE NOTHING WOULD MAKE ME HAPPIER. I PLAN TO CONTINUE TO DEVOTE MYSELF UTTERLY TO THIS SERIES, SO I BEG YOUR CONTINUED SUPPORT.
THANKS VERY MUCH, EVERYONE.

I'D ALSO LIKE TO APOLOGIZE TO MY EDITOR "S-HARA" FOR BEING SUCH A ROYAL PAIN IN THE NECK ALL THE TIME!!

KAKIFLY

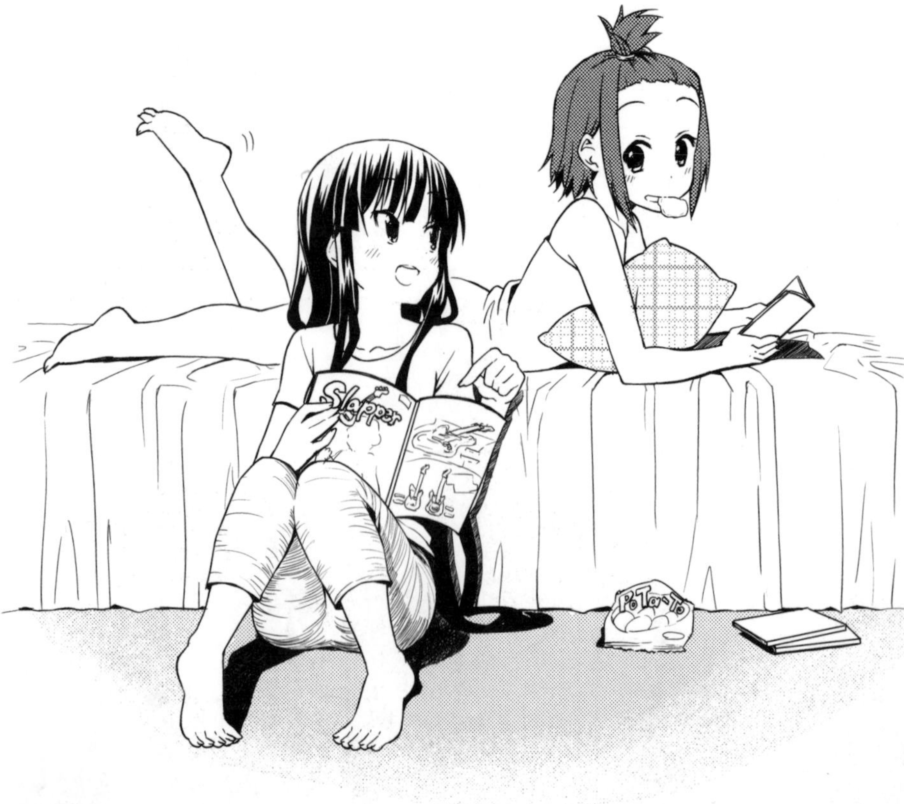
Slapper

BONUS COMICS

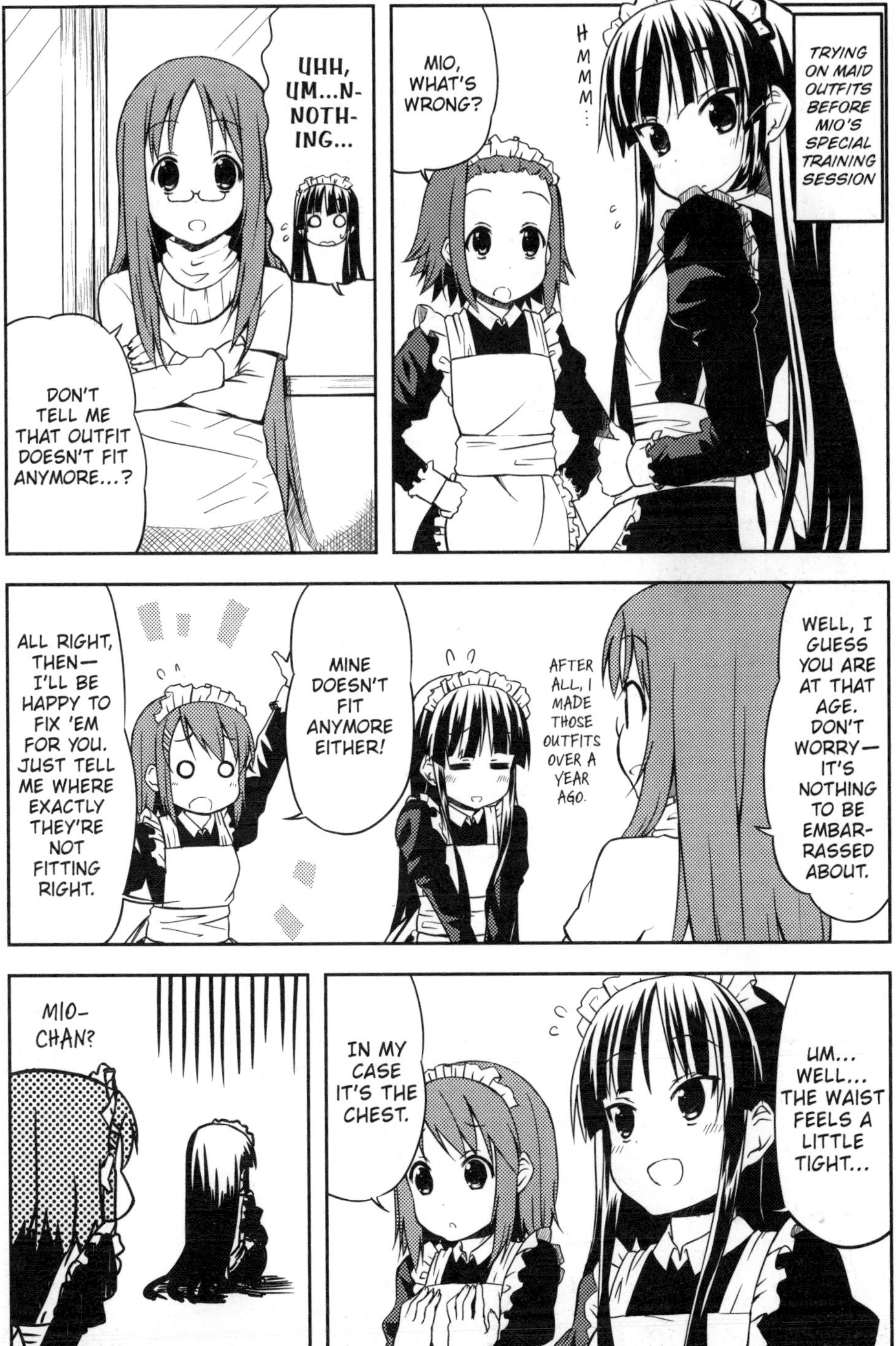
TRYING ON MAID OUTFITS BEFORE MIO'S SPECIAL TRAINING SESSION
HMMM...
MIO, WHAT'S WRONG?
UHH, UM...N-NOTHING...
DON'T TELL ME THAT OUTFIT DOESN'T FIT ANYMORE...?
WELL, I GUESS YOU ARE AT THAT AGE. DON'T WORRY—IT'S NOTHING TO BE EMBARRASSED ABOUT.
AFTER ALL, I MADE THOSE OUTFITS OVER A YEAR AGO.
MINE DOESN'T FIT ANYMORE EITHER!
ALL RIGHT, THEN—I'LL BE HAPPY TO FIX 'EM FOR YOU. JUST TELL ME WHERE EXACTLY THEY'RE NOT FITTING RIGHT.
UM... WELL... THE WAIST FEELS A LITTLE TIGHT...
IN MY CASE IT'S THE CHEST.
MIO-CHAN?

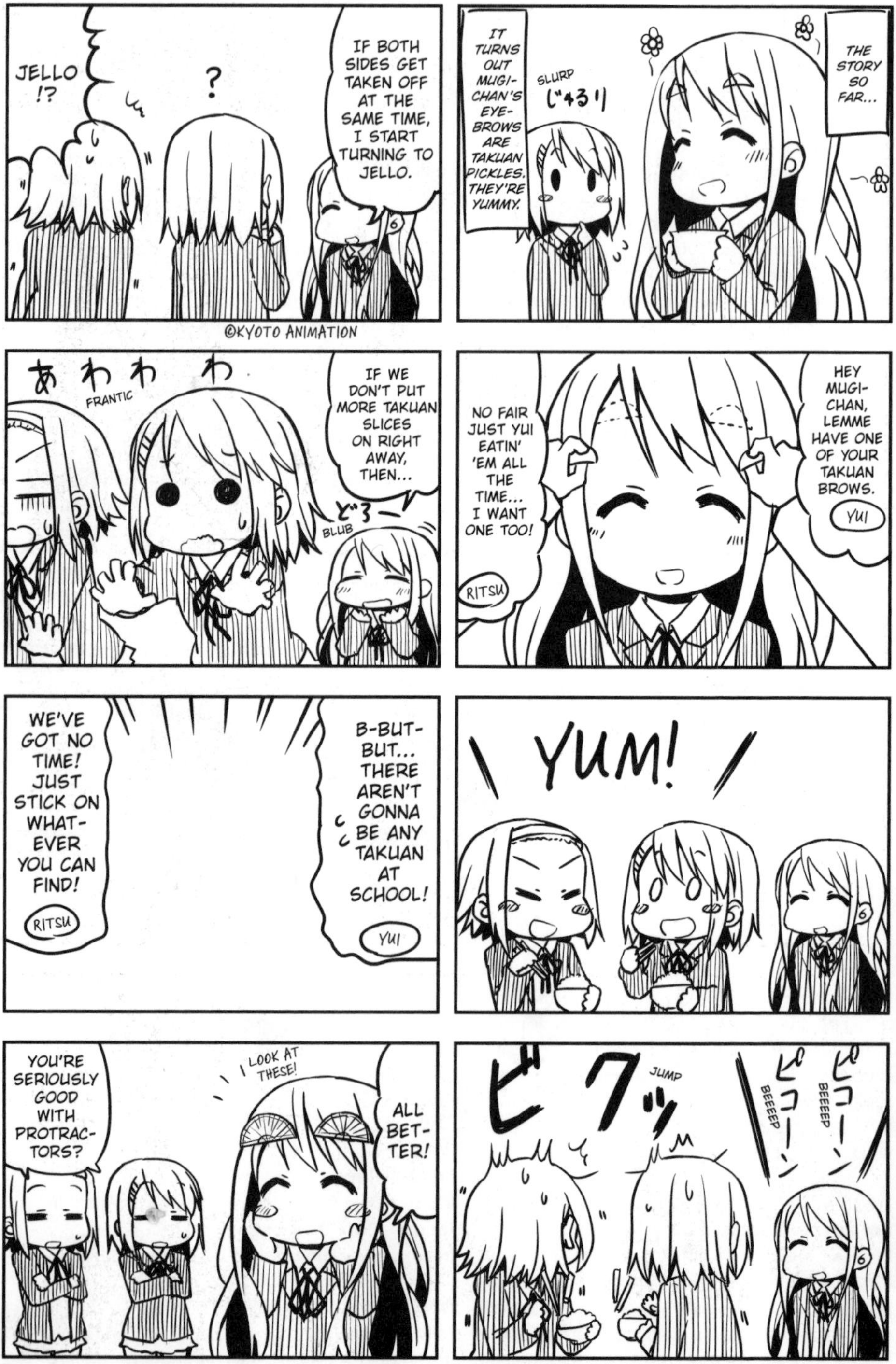
THE STORY SO FAR...
IT TURNS OUT MUGI-CHAN'S EYE-BROWS ARE TAKUAN PICKLES. THEY'RE YUMMY.
じゅるり
SLURP
HEY MUGI-CHAN, LEMME HAVE ONE OF YOUR TAKUAN BROWS.
YUI
NO FAIR JUST YUI EATIN' 'EM ALL THE TIME... I WANT ONE TOO!
RITSU
YUM!
ピコーン
BEEEEP
ピコーン
BEEEEP
ビクッ
JUMP
IF BOTH SIDES GET TAKEN OFF AT THE SAME TIME, I START TURNING TO JELLO.
?
JELLO !?
IF WE DON'T PUT MORE TAKUAN SLICES ON RIGHT AWAY, THEN...
どろー
BLUB
あわわわ
FRANTIC
B-BUT-BUT... THERE AREN'T GONNA BE ANY TAKUAN AT SCHOOL!
YUI
WE'VE GOT NO TIME! JUST STICK ON WHAT-EVER YOU CAN FIND!
RITSU
ALL BET-TER!
LOOK AT THESE!
YOU'RE SERIOUSLY GOOD WITH PROTRAC-TORS?

the term stands in contrast to classical/tradi-tional music and refers to typical pop music.

PAGE 27
Valentine's Chocolate
Valentine's Day in Japan is a big deal for girls. Girls give chocolate to boys they like—even better if it's in the form of homemade fudge—and then any interested boys recip-rocate one month later on White Day (March 14), when they give white-themed presents (like marshmallows or white lingerie) to their pick of the girls who gave them chocolate on Valentine's Day.

PAGE 34
Yui's Collection of Toys
Yui is talking about the UFO Catcher game, where you can pay ¥100 or ¥200 for a chance to grab various toys with a robot claw arm.

PAGE 37
Sawako's Guitar
From the picture on page 35 and the descrip-tion on page 37, the guitar seems to be an early-model Gibson SG Standard, the same model played by the likes of Eric Clapton in the 1960s. An early Gibson SG guitar in prime condition can easily sell for upwards of US$20,000.

PAGE 49
NEET
"NEET" is an acronym for "Not in Educa-tion, Employment, or Training." It's a techni-cal term in both the UK and Japan, referring to the class of relatively young (defined as between the ages of 15 and 34 in Japan) individuals who are unemployed, not in any school or job training, and neither actively seeking work nor engaging in any productive but unpaid economic activity (such as house-work).

PAGE 53
Bo Curry & Otsu Curry
Nodoka's brand of curry is an obvious play on Otsuka Foods' well-known Bon Curry brand of boil-in-the-pouch curries. Yui's brand of curry is based on a pun: o-tsukare ("Good work," an end-of-day farewell greeting in

Japanese offices) vs. otsu-kare ("B curry," an old and well-established joke from online chat rooms).

PAGE 53
Takoyaki
Takoyaki is a kind of fried dumpling filled with octopus bits, ginger, and green onions and served with mayonnaise and a Japanese-style sweet BBQ sauce. It's common to buy them from street vendors, especially in the Kansai region, the area where the dish was invented and is still most strongly associated with.

PAGE 57
Kinkakuji
The Kinkakuji (literally "Temple of the Golden Pavilion") is one of the best-known and most-visited historical sites in Kyoto. The main building is a small Zen Buddhist temple with the top two stories covered in gold leaf. It's surrounded by a moat and gardens.

PAGE 57
Kyoto Dialect
There's no way to translate the differences in dialects of Japanese into English except by exploiting dialect differences in English to give some of the flavor of what's going on. The Kyoto dialect (and the dialect of the Kan-sai region in general) tends to be perceived in Japan as harsher in tone and also more col-orful in expression than standard Japanese, so I've opted for a super-urbanized New York dialect as a fairly close match in feel.

PAGE 58
Arashiyama
Arashiyama is a scenic mountainous area to the west of Kyoto. It's known for its river views and the bands of wild monkeys that live in the area.

PAGE 64
Hair Salon
It's sort of a stock phrase for hairdressers in Japan to ask their customers if they feel any itching while their hair is being worked on.

PAGE 66
Intonation
In musical terms, the intonation (called

TRANSLATION NOTES

COMMON HONORIFICS

no honorific: Indicates familiarity or closeness; if used without permission or reason, addressing someone in this manner would constitute an insult.

-san: The Japanese equivalent of Mr./Mrs./Miss. If a situation calls for politeness, this is the fail-safe honorific.

-sama: Conveys great respect; may also indicate that the social status of the speaker is lower than that of the addressee.

-kun: Used most often when referring to boys, this indicates affection or familiarity. Occasionally used by older men among their peers, but it may also be used by anyone referring to a person of lower standing.

-chan: An affectionate honorific indicating familiarity used mostly in reference to girls; also used in reference to cute persons or animals of either gender.

-senpai: Used to address upperclassmen or more experienced coworkers.

-sensei: A respectful term for teachers, artists, or high-level professionals.

K-ON!

The title *K-ON!* comes from the Japanese word "*kei-ongaku*," meaning "light music" in the sense of casual or easy listening (i.e., not serious or innovative as in serious classical or jazz). In the context of school clubs in Japan, the term "*kei-ongaku-bu*" ("light music club") usually contrasts with "*ongaku-bu*" ("music club") in that it focuses on popular forms of music (pop, rock, folk, etc.) where the latter focuses on symphonic and choral forms.

kakifly

The author's name, "kakifly," comes from the Japanese word "*kaki-furai*," meaning "fried oysters." It seems to be a running joke, as the author comments for this and future volumes reference his feelings toward oysters.

Yen Conversion

A general rule of thumb to use for converting Japanese yen to American dollars is ¥100 to 1 USD.

PAGE 3
New Year's Shrine Visit

A New Year's shine visit (*hatsumode*) refers to the Japanese tradition of visiting one's local neighborhood Shinto shrine immediately after the change of the year.

Heated Table

The "heated table" (*kotatsu*) is a typical piece of furniture in Japanese sitting rooms. It's a small coffee table with a space heater mounted to the underside and quilted material draped around the sides to trap the heat in the space underneath.

PAGE 4
New Year's Cards

In Japan, New Year's cards (*nengajo*) serve the purpose that Christmas cards or other holiday greeting cards do in the U.S. You're expected to send them to all your friends and coworkers, along with any partners or clients you do (or hope to do) business with.

PAGE 7
Fortunes

On a New Year's shrine visit, it's traditional to make a donation to the shrine and get a fortune for the new year in return. The range of possible fortunes at most shrines is as follows:

[GOOD]
"Best" (*dai-kichi*) > "Much Better" (*chu-kichi*) > "Little Better" (*sho-kichi*) > "Good" (*kichi*)
[SO-SO]
"Less Good" (*han-kichi*) > "Marginally Good" (*sue-kichi*) > "Barely Good" (*sue-sho-kichi*)
[BAD]
"Bad" (*kyo*) > "Little Worse" (*sho-kyo*) > "Getting Worse" (*han-kyo*) > "Much Worse" (*sue-kyo*) > "Worst" (*dai-kyo*)

PAGE 8
Clang and Clap

When offering prayers at a Shinto shrine, it's usual to ring the bell (to summon the attention of the spirits) and then clap your hands together twice (for the same reason), holding them together after the second clap as you make your prayer.

Pop Music Club

"Pop Music Club" is literally "Light Music Club" ("*kei-ongaku-bu*," used in the sense discussed in the note above), but in this context

"octave tuning" in Japanese) of an instrument describes the degree to which the notes sound at the correct pitch (i.e., "in tune") independent of how they're played on the instrument.

Half of a Half of a Half-tone Off
In other words, an eighth-tone. Most people aren't sensitive to such microchanges in pitch, but human ears can be trained to perceive differences that small, and some people are even born with the ability to perceive them without any training.

PAGE 67
Mut-*tan*
The suffix *–tan* is a cutesy form of *–chan*, and the first syllable of "Mustang" gets shortened to Mu[.] in Japanese, where the [.] represents a doubling of the consonant that follows (in this case a "t"). But of course Tsumugi's nickname "Mugi" can also be shortened to Mu[.] by the same process, so this sounds like a cutesy form of Mugi-chan.

PAGE 73
Yosakoi
The Yosakoi is a festive and very lively fusion dance unique to Japan, combining traditional costumes and choreographic elements with modern music. It's commonly performed in summer, often in group competitions at festivals or sports meets.

PAGE 75
Entrance Exams
Most high school students in Japan devote their entire senior year to preparation for standardized college entrance exams. Doing well on these exams is a vital component of acceptance to a good school, so schools and parents put a lot of pressure on college-bound students to study intensively and avoid distractions like part-time jobs and boy/girlfriends.

PAGE 81
Drum Mamire
This is a play on Konami's *DrumMania* music video game. The word *mamire* means "filthy with," so the parodied name "covered with/ filthy with drums" is meant to sound similar to "drummania."

PAGE 92
Yakisoba
Yakisoba are pan-fried noodles with meat and vegetables and a sweet-savory sauce. Most outdoor fairs of any sort will have a *yakisoba* booth.

PAGE 95
Wheeen Wheeen
This specifically refers to the sound that cicadas make in the summer.

PAGE 110
Prefecture
A prefecture (*ken*) in Japan is a regional division of government corresponding more or less to a state in the U.S.

PAGE 111
JYAGUCHI T-shirt
Jyaguchi (normally romanized as "*jaguchi*") means "faucet" (and sure enough, sports a picture of a dripping faucet). I believe it's making fun of Mari Yaguchi (of Morning Musume fame) goods, of which there are plenty.

PAGE 117
Dawg
The sentence ending that Ritsu mentions is *da ze*, a sort of macho slangy version of the more generic *da yo* and roughly equivalent to something like "man" (as in "Let's go, man") in English.

PAGE 118
–shan
–shan is just a cutesy variation of *–san* that expresses the intimacy of *–chan* without any of the condescension.

COVER
Ritsu's drumkit is a Yamaha Rick Marotta Signature Hipgig kit in Mellow Yellow finish. (It's a pretty expensive kit, retailing for around US$4000.)

AUTHOR NOTE (opposite)
The left-handed guitar and bass shown at left (kakifly's own) are a Fender Classic Series '65 Mustang (a favorite of Kurt Cobain) and a Fender American Standard Jazz Bass.

kakifly

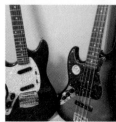

C O M M E N T S

Hi, my name is kakifly. Raw oysters are really delicious, aren't they? Thank you so much for buying my manga.

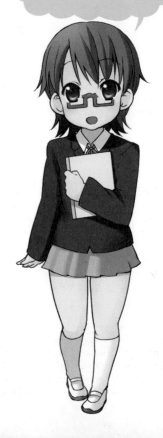

THANK YOU FOR READING.

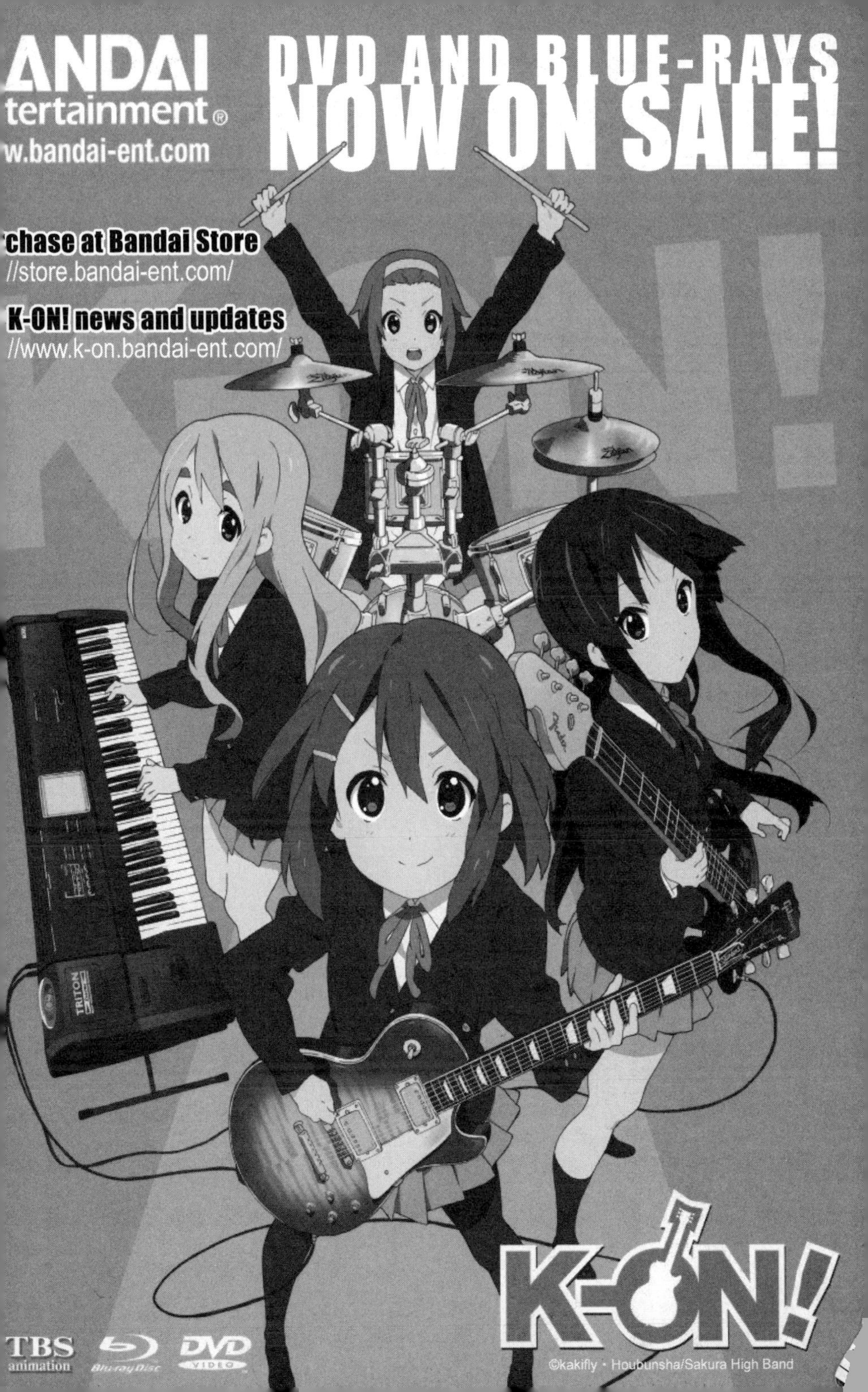

ANDAI
tertainment®
w.bandai-ent.com
DVD AND BLUE-RAYS
NOW ON SALE!
rchase at Bandai Store
//store.bandai-ent.com/
K-ON! news and updates
//www.k-on.bandai-ent.com/
TRITON
K-ON!
TBS animation
Blu-ray Disc
DVD VIDEO
©kakifly · Houbunsha/Sakura High Band

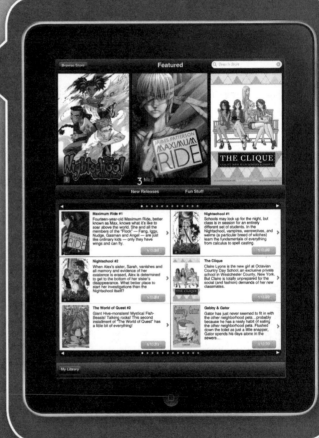
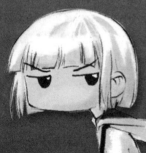

K-ON! ③

Translation: Jack Wiedrick

K-ON! vol. 3 © 2010 Kakifly. All rights reserved. First published in Japan in 2010 by HOUBUNSHA CO., LTD., Tokyo. English translation rights in United States, Canada, and United Kingdom arranged with HOUBUNSHA CO., LTD through Tuttle-Mori Agency, Inc., Tokyo.

Translation © 2011 by Hachette Book Group, Inc.

Yen Press
Hachette Book Group
237 Park Avenue, New York, NY 10017

www.HachetteBookGroup.com
www.YenPress.com

Yen Press is an imprint of Hachette Book Group, Inc. The Yen Press name and logo are trademarks of Hachette Book Group, Inc.

First Yen Press Edition: August 2011

ISBN: 978-0-316-18762-6

10 9 8 7 6 5 4 3

RRD-C

Printed in the United States of America

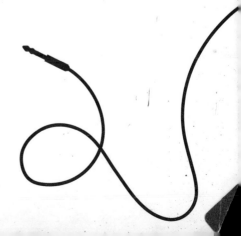